THE TRIBES

Theory, Culture & Society

Theory, Culture & Society caters for the resurgence of interest in culture within contemporary social science and the humanities. Building on the heritage of classical social theory, the book series examines ways in which this tradition has been reshaped by a new generation of theorists. It will also publish theoretically informed analyses of everyday life, popular culture, and new intellectual movements.

EDITOR: Mike Featherstone, *University of Teesside*

Recent volumes include:

The Consuming Body
Pasi Falk

Cultural Identity and Global Process
Jonathan Friedman

The Established and the Outsiders
Norbert Elias and John L. Scotson

The Cinematic Society
The Voyeur's Gaze
Norman K. Denzin

Decentring Leisure
Rethinking Leisure Theory
Chris Rojek

Global Modernities
Mike Featherstone, Scott Lash and Roland Robertson

The Masque of Femininity
The Presentation of Woman in Everyday Life
Efrat Tseëlon

The Arena of Racism
Michel Wieviorka

Undoing Culture
Globalization, Postmodernism and Identity
Mike Featherstone

THE TIME OF
THE TRIBES

*The Decline of Individualism
in Mass Society*

Michel Maffesoli

Translated by Don Smith

SAGE Publications
London • Thousand Oaks • New Delhi

English translation © Sage Publications 1996
Foreword © Rob Shields 1996

First published in English in 1996

Originally published in French as *Le Temps des tribus* by
Méridiens Klincksieck, Paris
© Méridiens Klincksieck 1988

This translation is published with financial support from the
French Ministry of Culture

SAGE Publications Ltd
6 Bonhill Street
London EC2A 4PU

SAGE Publications Inc
2455 Teller Road
Thousand Oaks, California 91320

SAGE Publications India Pvt Ltd
32, M-Block Market
Greater Kailash - I
New Delhi 110 048

Published in association with *Theory, Culture & Society*,
School of Human Studies, University of Teesside

British Library Cataloguing in Publication data
A catalogue record for this book is available from the
British Library.

ISBN 0 8039 8473–1
ISBN 0 8039 8474–X (pbk)

Library of Congress catalog record available

Typeset by Photoprint, Torquay, Devon.
Printed in Great Britain by The Cromwell Press Ltd,
Broughton Gifford, Melksham, Wiltshire

CONTENTS

Foreword: Masses or Tribes?   ix
Rob Shields

By Way of Introduction   1

   1. A few words of warning   1
   2. The quomodo   4
   3. Overture   6

1. The Emotional Community: Research Arguments   9

   1. The aesthetic aura   9
   2. The ethical experience   15
   3. Custom   20

2. The Underground *Puissance*   31

   1. Aspects of vitalism   31
   2. The social divine   38
   3. The aloofness of the people   45

3. Sociality vs. the Social   56

   1. Beyond politics   56
   2. A natural 'familiarism'   64

4. Tribalism   72

   1. The affectual nebula   72
   2. The 'undirected' being-together   79
   3. The 'religious' model   82
   4. Elective sociality   86
   5. The law of secrecy   90
   6. Masses and lifestyles   96

5. Polyculturalism   104

   1. Of triplicity   104
   2. Presence and estrangement   106
   3. The polytheism of the people, or the diversity of God   110
   4. The organic balance   114

6. Of Proxemics   **123**

   1. The community of destiny   123
   2. *Genius loci*   129
   3. Tribes and networks   139
   4. The network of networks   145

Appendix: The Thinking of the Public Square   **152**

   1. The two cultures   152
   2. For the people's happiness   154
   3. The order within   157
   4. Experience, proxemics and organic knowledge   160

Index   166

For Raphaële, Sarah-Marie
and Emmanuelle

FOREWORD: MASSES OR TRIBES?

Earlier in this century, Herman Schmalenbach used Tönnies and Simmel's preoccupation with the forms of social interaction to critique the division of urban and rural or traditional society. Breaking apart the dualism of Gemeinschaft and Gesellschaft, Schmalenbach noted the endurance of networks of acquaintances and circles of friends which stabilized the social worlds of individuals who experienced the trauma of rapid urbanization in nineteenth-century Europe. A similar importance of these 'bunde', Schmalenbach argued, would mark any decline in the reliability and central role of a society dominated by sociality associated with labour contracts and job-based social interaction. These 'elective affinity groups' (Weber) form a transversal structure largely ignored by the class-oriented categories of modernist sociology. While Maffesoli is intensely concerned with 'interaction in public', he transcends Goffman's focus on the interpersonal to consider the sociological implications of the plethora of small groups and of temporary groupings which we are members of at different times during our day. Between the time one might leave one's family or intimates in the morning and the time when one returns, each person enters into a series of group situations each of which has some degree of self-consciousness and stability. While the passengers of a commuter bus are hardly a group, the 'regulars' know and may well salute each other as well as the regular driver. Sports clubs, friends at the office, coffee 'klatches', associations of hobbyists, the crowd of fans at a sports match, the local level of a political party, 'Neighbourhood Watch' community policing, and single-issue pressure groups are all examples of neo-tribes.

Maffesoli develops the concept of neo-tribalism beyond Schmalenbach's 'bund'. The tribus are more than a residual category of social life. They are the central feature and key social fact of our own experience of everyday living. This 'underground centrality' of tribus persists despite the sociological fetish of abstractions, and of more (and often less) realist categories. While the power of class to influence outcomes is not in doubt, it is less significant in everyday social interaction than might appear from the abstractions of sociological statistics. Like other French theorists such as Michel De Certeau and Jean Baudrillard, Maffesoli takes up an engaged position within the flux of social life rather than at a cool distance. The effect is to produce an internal analysis of the 'sociality within' European societies too often known only through the simulacra of statistical demographics. The Weberian perspective of focusing on the meaning of social interaction for participants is foregrounded, but given a new twist in that the affective neutrality of the sociologists – an alienation effected through the abstraction of quantitative data and the reification of social science concepts – is problematized.

Michel Maffesoli is a theorist of the break-up of mass culture. *Le Temps des tribus* – the time of the tribes – can also be translated as 'the time of the masses'. The 'little masses' of Maffesoli's analysis are heterogeneous fragments, the remainders of mass consumption society, groups distinguished by their members' shared lifestyles and tastes. *Tribus* are thus not 'tribes' in the traditional anthropological sense, for they do not have the fixity and longevity of tribes. Nor are they neo-tribes; they are better understood as 'postmodern tribes', or even pseudo-tribes. The 'Time of the Tribes' is a time when the mass is tribalized.

Over a series of works spanning a decade Maffesoli's work moved from Marxist sociological categories to the anomalies of everyday life. As a postmodern sociology, this work proceeds from the premise that the modernist categories and the foundational narratives which 'explain' and thereby buttress the social order of nation states are facing profound challenges. Nonetheless, this work has been seen as ironically reproducing a neo-modernism. Maffesoli refuses to give up the role of the sociologist and the tradition of sociological theory. While he condemns social science dogmatism, these are the jibes and blandishments of a suitor.

Against the theoreticism of lifeless groupings imposed by sociologists, Maffesoli exploits Bergson's vitalism to argue for the power of the basic sociality – the 'being together' – of everyday life. This is married with Durkheim's conceptualization of collective consciousness (*conscience collective*) and the life-affirming, Dionysian quality of the transcendent warmth of the collectivity (*divin social*). This transcendence is, in Maffesoli's word, 'immanent'. In its simplest terms, the Durkheimian insight into idolization and defence of the social group as the most primitive form of religiosity is important because *tribus* become the highest social good for their members. Out of the ethos of these *tribus* emerge ethical orientations and a form of natural law which challenges the legitimacy of traditional morals.

Maffesoli makes a unique contribution by contesting the moral basis of politics in the classic sense. While one might speak of a contingent politics (Finn 1989), or simply ignore the universal and transcendental quality which political principles share with moral dictates, Maffesoli detects the existence of an ethical aesthetics, and art of living which emphasizes 'getting along' and getting by so as to maintain the solidarity of *tribus* and facilitate everyday social interaction. This is not a Fascistic 'aestheticization of politics' but rather aesthetics as the operationalization of situational ethics (Shields 1991). If one wishes to keep close to the etymological meanings of the words, this is an appropriate use of the classical notion of aesthetics (*aesthesis*) which focuses on questions of beauty and correctness as defined by collective experience, not transcendental principles of beauty (a relatively recent corruption of the long history of aesthetic judgement). Rather than questions of universal right or wrong, one deals with questions of appropriateness and 'fit' within situations.

This is far from an abandonment of politics. Instead it indicates the shortcoming of the terms in which politics is normally discussed. Perhaps the most lasting legacy of the 'counterculture' movements of the 1960s was to apply the political to every sphere of life. However, this may obscure as much as it reveals, for the diversity of politico-aesthetical action at the level of personal engagements in everyday life exceeds the merely political. The situationist slogan 'the personal is the political' must be supplemented by an insight that the personal is the ethical and aesthetic centre of social relations.

Typical examples of *tribus* are not only fashion victims, or youth sub-cultures. This term can be extended to interest-based collectivities: hobbyists; sports enthusiasts; and more important – environmental move-ments, user-groups of state services and consumer lobbies. Affinity-based political groups may arise around access to services (for example, Canadian senior citizens lobbying to use national park facilities which normally close in the fall and winter because of a lack of holidaymakers when children are in school). One example of the political mobilization of a *tribus* can be found in the case of the National Riflemen's Association (NRA) in the United States. This group of gun collectors, owners of guns (from sidearms to shotguns and assault rifles), and hunters is a key voice in what is popularly called the 'gun lobby', a group that has successfully campaigned to defeat numerous gun control bills and legislators who are in favour of limiting free access to weapons within the United States and more recently beyond its borders in Canada. Consumer protection and other lobbies may appear unpolitical, but a reflection on the power of the NRA in the United States will quickly dispel this view. Extending the theory of tribalization to such far-flung groups is a bold move which requires more theoretical comment than is possible here. However, the hypothesis that people with the same lifestyle and affinity of habitus may share the same politics of everyday life appears fruitful. One may note, for example, that in the United States the NRA even functions as a surrogate political party which amplifies the voices of poor, disenfranchised white men.

Unlike, for example, Adam Smith's almost metaphysical notion of the invisible hand of the market, Maffesoli's argument that ethical rules emerge from collectivities is strongly buttressed by philosophical analysis and social theory. While they have weak powers of discipline (for example, their only option is to exclude or shun members), they have strong powers of integration and inclusion, of group solidarity. These powers are displayed and actualized in initiatory rituals and stages of membership. As the highest social good, the members of *tribus* are marked by it, wearing particular types of dress, exhibiting group-specific styles of adornment and espousing the shared values and ideals of the collectivity. From the perspective of a sociology of consumption, Maffesoli's work takes on great importance, for *tribus* focus and segment processes of both individual and collective consumption.

Maffesoli is well aware of the potential for this work to be adopted as a new romanticism which eschews the effort to achieve a higher level of communicative rationality and an accessible and open public sphere. He himself calls this a 'new barbarism', but in line with Hegel and Kierkegaard's warnings on the dangers of *sollen* (ought) warns against the hectoring tendencies of social scientists. The power of *tribus* is inscribed within a thoroughgoing relativism. Unlike anthropological tribes, our contemporary social life is marked by membership in a multiplicity of overlapping groups in which the roles one plays become sources of identity which, like masks, provide temporary 'identifications'. Social status thus acquires an ambiguous edge.

What is required is not only a defence of the *tribus* in terms of its realism in contrast with the hopeless idealism of theories such as communicative rationality. An analysis of the implications of tribalization, and in particular its negative and corrosive impact on modernity as a dominant form of social organization, is needed. The focus on the liberatory quality of the *tribus*, the flexibility of identity and the dis-alienating potential of everyday life needs to be expanded to take in the negative tribe-like forms of ethnic nationalism, the Fascistic exploitation of *tribus* and subsequent reification of identity by governments facing simultaneous legitimation and restructuring crises. This text, therefore should be viewed not so much as setting an agenda as opening up an arena of research.

Maffesoli's work undertakes a critique of academicism and dogma within sociology. Here one should note the avoidance of elaborate structuralistic analytical frameworks which stand in for everyday life, such as in the work of Bourdieu. However, Maffesoli's work will still appear to the English reader highly academic because of its essayistic format. Yet the tone of formality and classicism so well preserved by Don Smith in his translation masks the initiatory structure of this work. At first its pretension excludes and intimidates, but this breaks down very quickly into the warmth of a shared vision, for this is truly an intimate sociology.

References

Finn, Geraldine (1989) 'The politics of contingency: the contingency of politics: on the political implications of Merleau-Ponty's ontology of the flesh'. Paper presented at CRCS Symposium, Carleton University, Ottawa, Fall 1990.

Shields, Rob (1991) 'Introduction to "The Ethics of Aesthetics" ', *Theory Culture & Society*, vol. 8, no. 1, 1–5.

BY WAY OF INTRODUCTION

1. A few words of warning

Ambience is a term that will surface again and again in this book, so it might perhaps be useful to describe the ambience surrounding its creation.

I began a previous book by taking Savanarola as my inspiration; this time it is the name of Machiavelli that I would invoke, referring to what he calls 'the thinking of the public square'. The following reflection explores, via such notions as *puissance*,* sociality, the quotidian and the imaginary, the deep foundations of the everyday life of our societies in these closing days of the modern era. With the ground thus cleared, we can forge ahead into the idea of *culture*, to be understood in its strictest sense, now prevailing in the politico-economic procedure. My emphasis on varied rituals, ordinary life, duplicity, the play of appearances, the collective sensibility, destiny – in short, the Dionysian thematic – may raise a few eyebrows; this approach has nevertheless been used in a variety of ways in a number of contemporary analyses. This is only to be expected; the history of thought shows that, along with intellectual mimetism or *a priori* self-justifications, legitimate ideas may develop along the way. Whereas some people possess a capital of knowledge, others, in the etymological sense of the term, invent, that is they extract that which is present but which may be difficult to discern.

There is however no need to cry victory, as this discernment is not easily won. The serious approach reigns in our discipline; but while the application of a degree of prudence is certainly necessary, it can too often be stultifying. Moreover, it is interesting to note that this attitude sometimes goes hand in hand with the most pretentious casualness. Is there such a difference between what Weber called the 'chains' of the techno-cratic approach and the 'damn-it-all' attitude which greatly devalues the ideas he (and others) produced long ago? In fact, they reinforce one another, and their joint praise by an admiring public is worth considering. Must we now revile a shallow and ignorant era, as others do? I will not follow such a facile route. It is only to be expected that some people play

---

* *Transl. note*: The term 'puissance' in French conveys the idea of the inherent energy and vital force of the people, as opposed to the institutions of 'power' ('pouvoir'). Maffesoli makes a clear distinction between these two terms, both of which are usually rendered as 'power' in English. I have chosen to leave the term 'puissance' in the original French, in order to maintain this distinction.

the fool for hard-pressed journalists; after all, that too is part of the social fabric. But others may have different ambitions: to speak to those who wish to think for themselves and who find in such and such a book or analysis a springboard, allowing them to epiphanize their own thoughts. Naive, perhaps? Pretentious? Only time will tell. And only a few informed minds are able – just – to see what the future holds.

Thus, the ambition of this book is to address itself mysteriously, with neither false simplicity nor useless complexity, to the community of minds who, outside of chapels, coteries and systems, can conceive of Montaigne's 'hommerie'* which is also to be their fate. These are certainly open minds as well, for as we shall see, the sinuous journey to come will require a certain mastery of one's thoughts. The *freischwebende intelligentsia*: here is a somewhat insecure prospect, but one with some interest for those willing to give this adventure its due. In short, I have absolutely no wish to write the sort of books that, in the words of Georges Bataille, 'appeal to the facility of their readers . . . [those books which] are enjoyed most often by vague and weak minds seeking to escape and to sleep' (*Oeuvres complètes*, vol. 8, p. 583).

It is not simply a question of frame of mind, but rather of procedure, which would be useful to provide since the discipline's traditional format will not be respected. Of course, this means it will no longer be possible to supply the usual degree of intellectual reassurance. The object of study itself demands this transgression; indeed, it is increasingly an accepted fact that the social existence under study does not easily lend itself to a distillation of concepts. Let us rather leave that job to the academic bean-counters who maintain a scientific air while classifying what by rights should belong to each of us. Whether they make the division by class, socio-professional categories, political views or any other *a priori* determinations, it is no longer of much importance. To use a rather crude term, which I shall continually try to make explicit – to set down for all to see – I shall try to maintain a 'holistic' perspective: a constant reversibility uniting the (social and natural) whole with the various elements (milieux and persons) of which it is constituted. Proceeding from this perspective will amount to grasping both ends of the rope at once: on the one end, an existential ontology; on the other, the simplest of trivialities, the first shining a laser light on the diverse manifestations of the second.[1]

It is clear that from the perspective of 'separation', which still retains a dominant role, this procedure is disquieting, and it would be preferable to take either a monographic or deliberately theoretical approach. However, I will leave aside the intellectual pleasure afforded by each of these attitudes, confident in the fact that certain 'outdated' considerations may be perfectly adequate to their time. I will refer to Lévi-Strauss who showed that the classical division between magic and science should not be exaggerated, and that by its emphasis on 'tangible perceptions', magic

---

* *Transl. note*: the quality of man.

played a considerable role in the progress of science.[2] For my part, I will try to push such a comparison to its logical limits, or at the very least, to apply it to other types of near-polarities. I will explain myself more fully on this point in the final chapter, but it seems to me that herein lies a fertile paradox. It allows us to appreciate fully the social configurations which are increasingly the product of a synergistic relationship formerly seen in its constitutive parts.

The antinomy of serious scholarship and common sense seems to be a given. Naturally, serious scholarship has tended to regard common sense as infirm: when it is not qualified as 'false consciousness', it is at best defective. The scorn heaped on the *anima candida* is the touchstone of the intellectual attitude. I have already written on this phenomenon; I would now like to show how it can account for our failure to understand what, for lack of a better term, we shall call life. To refer to life in general terms carries with it a certain amount of risk. It can lead in particular to vague illusions; but in so far as we can flesh out this consideration of 'tangible perceptions', it will be possible to explore a concrete existence far removed from disembodied ratiocinations. At the same time, it is important to preserve the ability to venture into deeper waters; we will thus be able to 'invent' new lands by applying the general principle. These are the stakes of the synergy in question: to *propose* a vagabond sociology which at the same time is not deprived of its object.

The reversible movement between formism and empathy can also account for the current shift in importance from an essentially *mechanical* social order towards a complex, predominantly *organic* structure. We are witnessing the usurping of linear History by the restorative myth; there is a return to a vitalism whose varied modulations I will attempt to show. The different terms evoked are all linked: organicity refers to Bergson's *élan vital* or life principle. Let us not forget, it was he who proposed the idea of direct intuition in order to account for it. Scheler and Simmel also shared a similar vision of the unicity of life.[3] I will return frequently to such a consideration since, aside from allowing us to understand the Eastern panvitalism at work in many small contemporary groups, it also accounts for the emotional and the 'affectual' dimensions that structure them as such. The reason for the above-mentioned caution becomes clear: the fact that the social dynamic no longer follows the same paths as modernity does not mean that such paths no longer exist. Moreover, following the anthropological path I have indicated puts us in a better position to show that a quasi-animal life is deeply embedded in the various manifestations of sociality. This explains the emphasis on *reliance*,* and on the religiosity which is an essential ingredient in the tribalism we shall be considering.

---

* *Transl. note*: 'reliance' is a term Maffesoli borrows from M. Bolle de Bal. Etymologically speaking, this neologism derives from the verb 'relier': to connect, link or bind together. Maffesoli later relates this term to religion ('religare').

Without in any way attempting to insert some sort of doctrinal content into the present discussion, it is possible to speak of the development of a genuinely holy dimension to social relationships that Durkheim, in his positivist way, called the 'social divine'. This is how for my part I understand sociality's *puissance* which, by abstention, silence and ruse, is the opposite of the politico-economic power. I will finish discussion of this first approach with an insight from the cabbala, for whom these 'forces' (Sefirot)* constitute the divinity. According to Scholem, these powers are the primordial elements 'upon which all reality is founded'; thus 'life flows externally and vitalizes creation while remaining at the same time deeply internal, and the secret rhythm of its movement, of its pulse, is the law of the dynamics of nature'.[4] This small apologia sums up what to me appears to be the role of sociality: above and beyond the instituted forms that still exist and sometimes predominate, there is an informal underground centrality that assures the perdurability of life in society. It is to this reality we should turn: we are not used to it and our analytical tools may be rather rusty. Nevertheless, many clues, which I am attempting to formalize in this book, point us in this direction. These are the stakes for the decades to come. As we know, it is only *post festum* that recognition dawns; even so, we must maintain a certain clarity and dispose of unnecessary intellectual impediments in order to hasten this insight.

2. The quomodo

It is indeed necessary, in so far as is possible, to adjust our ways of thinking to the (re)born objects we are to examine. Must we then speak of a Copernican revolution? Perhaps, however we must add a healthy dose of *relativism*, if only to be more receptive to new developments.[5]

At first, in order to counter an attitude prevalent in modernity, it may perhaps be necessary to accept ourselves as deprived of any purpose, denying any association with the practical, refusing to participate in any instrumental knowledge. With this in mind, it is useful to recall the example, now strangely forgotten, of the founding fathers of sociology who, according to Nisbet – that able historian of the discipline – 'never ceased being artists'. Neither should it be forgotten that the ideas which may later be structured in theory are primarily the product of 'imagination, vision, intuition'.[6] The advice is well taken, for this is how, at the turn of the century, the authors now part of the canon were able to present their pertinent and numerous social analyses. If only by force of circumstance, that is, when confronted with some sort of social renewal – a new society – it becomes important to put into practice a certain theoretical 'laxness',

---

* *Transl. note*: In the Jewish mystical tradition, the ten emanations or powers of God the Creator.

without, of course, as I have indicated, abdicating our obligation to think, or succumbing to laziness or intellectual fatuousness. In the comprehensive tradition, to which I subscribe, one always proceeds by approximate truths. This is all the more important when one's focus is the realm of everyday life. In this aspect, more than any other, we need not concern ourselves with discovering the ultimate truth. Truth is relative, an offshoot of the situation. This is a complex 'Situationism', since the observer is simultaneously, if only partially, implicated in the situation he is describing. Competence and appetence go hand in hand; hermeneutics supposes that we are a part of what we describe; requires a 'certain community of outlook'.[7] Ethnologists and anthropologists have consistently emphasized this phenomenon, so it is time to apply it to the realities at hand.

Just as the newborn is fragile, uncertain, imperfect, our approach must possess the same qualities. This goes far in explaining its apparent slightness; a shifting terrain requires quick movements; there is therefore no shame in 'surfing' over the waves of sociality. It is in fact a judicious and highly efficacious way to proceed. In this respect, the use of metaphor is quite pertinent: aside from its pedigree and the fact that it has played a part in all times of intellectual ferment, the use of metaphor permits those precise crystallizations of approximate and momentary truths. It has been said that Beethoven found inspiration for his most glorious musical phrases among the masses. Why should we not set down our score with the same source in mind?

Just like the person who dons masks in the theatre of everyday life, sociality is structurally deceptive, unknowable – which explains the confusion of the scholars, politicians and journalists who find it turning up *elsewhere*, after believing they had already pinned it down. Backtracking hastily, the most honest among them will surreptitiously change theories to produce a new, systematic and comprehensive explanation of this phenomenon. Would it not be better, as I was saying, to make common cause and practise the same deceptive strategy? Instead of attacking head-on through positivizing or criticizing a fleeting social reality, it would be wiser to approach stealthily, from the side. This is the practice of apophatic theology: we can only know God indirectly. Thus, rather than trying to fool ourselves into thinking we can seize, explain and exhaust an object, we must be content to describe its shape, its movements, hesitations, accomplishments and its various convulsions. But, as they are all of a piece, this strategy could also be applied to the various instruments traditionally used in our disciplines, holding onto those which remain useful, but also overcoming their rigidity. In this way, it would be desirable to do the same as that other outsider, Erving Goffman, who invented concepts, although he preferred 'old words used in new ways or in new intriguing combinations over clumsy neologisms'.[8] Favouring 'mini-concepts' or ideas over established certainties may be surprising; however, I believe that it is the proof of an intellectual outlook which most closely follows the bumpy route taken by all social life.

3. Overture

These are the wide brushstrokes filling the canvas of the various sociological considerations to follow. The ambience of an era, and perforce the ambience of scholarship, covers a period of years. Interim results were tested on various colleagues and young researchers in France, as well as in many foreign universities. The ambience is built on a fundamental paradox: the constant interplay between the growing massification and the development of micro-groups, which I shall call 'tribes'.

This appears to me the founding tension characterizing sociality at the end of the twentieth century. The masses, or the people – not to be confused with the proletariat or other classes – are not posited on a logic of identity; without any precise goals, they are not the subjects of historical movement. As for the metaphor of the tribe, it allows us to account for the process of disindividuation, the saturation of the inherent *function* of the individual and the emphasis on the *role* that each person (*persona*) is called upon to play within the tribe. It is of course understood that, just as the masses are in a state of perpetual swarm, the tribes that crystallize from these masses are unstable, since the persons of which these tribes are constituted are free to move from one to the other.

The following list explains the shift under way and its resultant tension:

Social		*Sociality*
Mechanical structure		**Complex or organic structure**
(Modernity)		(Post-modernity)
Political-economic organization		Masses
↕		↕
Individuals	*versus*	Persons
(function)		(role)
↕		↕
Contractual groups		Affectual tribes

←→

(Cultural, productive, religious, sexual, ideological domains)

It is as a function of this double hypothesis (shift and tension) that, true to form, I will incorporate various theoretical readings and empirical research which seem to me to contribute to the present discussion.* As I have indicated, there is no reason to discriminate, and apart from sociological, philosophical and anthropological works, the novel, poetry or anecdotes also play their part. The essential task will be to highlight several *forms*, which are perhaps 'unreal', but which help in the comprehension, in

---

* There is an exoteric as well as an esoteric aspect to any inquiry, expressed by the critical apparatus. In order to avoid overloading the body of the text, the apparatus describing my views has been put at the back of the book. Aside from their illustrative role, these references may also encourage the reader's own research.

the strictest sense of the word, of the multiplicity of situations, experiences, logical and non-logical actions that constitute sociality.

Among the forms to be analysed, there is of course the *tribalism* which lies at the heart of this work. Around this central theme, I shall be discussing forms such as the emotional community, *puissance* and the sociality from which tribalism springs. Following on from the question of tribalism, I will touch on such forms as polyculturalism and proxemics, which are its consequences. I am proposing, *in fine*, a theoretical 'method' to serve as a guide through the confusion surrounding tribalism.

There is, to be sure, a certain monotony to the subjects under consideration, as well as redundancy. This is an apt description of the 'obsessive images' to be found in any literary, poetic or cinematographic endeavour. Each era hauntingly repeats multiple variations on a few familiar themes. Thus, the same preoccupations can be seen in every form we examine; only the angle of approach is changed. I hope in this way to be able to account for the polychromatic aspect of the social entity. In a remarkable attack on the causal machinery, Gilbert Durand mentions the 'theory of the recital' which is advanced as the most adequate way of translating the redundancy of the mythical narrative, its doublets and variants.[9] This theory meshes nicely with the everyday knowledge I am attempting to explain. It is limited to seeking out and re-citing the efflorescence and the recurring hodge-podge of a vitalism that is battling with the anguish of death in a cyclical, self-perpetuating way.

However, this rather aesthetic theory of the recital is not designed for those who think it is possible to shed light on men's actions, much less is it for those who, confusing knowledge and politics, believe action is possible. It is rather a kind of quietism which is limited to recognizing that which is, which occurs, in a sort of revaluing of the *primum vivere*. As I have said before, these pages are directed at the 'happy few'. Acknowledging the nobility of the masses and the tribes is limited to a certain aristocracy of the mind; nevertheless, it is not the prerogative of a certain social class or profession, much less a band of privileged specialists. Through speeches, colloquia and discussions, I have discovered that such a cast of mind is evenly distributed among a good number of students, social workers, decision-makers and journalists, not forgetting of course those who can simply be deemed cultured. It is to these people that I address this book, which is but a mere introduction to what are further explorations.

If this is a work of fiction, that is one which pushes a certain logic to its limits, this book 'invents' only that which already exists, preventing it, of course, from proposing any solutions for the future. On the other hand, by attempting to ask key questions, this book is attempting to spark open, unwavering, honest debate.

In times of constant effervescence, certain stimulating impertinences are required: I hope I have made my fair share. Utopias become commonplace; revived dreams bubble up to the surface. Who was it who said such moments dreamed the next? Perhaps less in terms of projections than in terms of fictions pieced together from scattered fragments, incomplete constructions, variously successful attempts. It is undoubtedly worthwhile fashioning a new interpretation of these everyday dreams. Dream on, sociology!

Notes

1. We can see here an approach that was shared by thinkers such as A. Schutz, G.H. Mead and E. Goffmann. On this matter, I refer to U. Hannerz, *Exploring the City: Inquiries toward an Urban Anthropology*, New York, Columbia University Press, 1980, ch. 6, particularly p. 221 for the question of this coming and going movement. One can also cite P. Berger and T. Luckmann, *The Social Construction of Reality*, New York, Anchor Books, 1967.

2. C. Lévi-Strauss, *The Savage Mind*, London, Weidenfeld and Nicolson, 1968, p. 11 *et seq.*

3. M. Scheler, *The Nature of Sympathy*, London, Routledge and Kegan Paul, 1970, p. 74.

4. G. Scholem, *La Mystique juive*, French transl. Paris, Cerf, 1985, p. 59 *et seq.*

5. I have devoted a book to this question: M. Maffesoli, *La Connaissance ordinaire. Précis de sociologie compréhensive*, Méridiens Klincksieck, 1985.

6. R. Nisbet, *The Sociological Tradition*, London, Heinemann Educational, 1970, p. 18.

7. Cf. 'a certain community of outlook' in W. Outhwaite, *Understanding Social Life: the Method Called Verstehen*, London, Allen and Unwin, 1975.

8. Hannerz, *Exploring the City*, p. 209.

9. G. Durand, 'La Beauté comme présence paraclétique: essai sur les résurgences d'un bassin sémantique' in *Eranos*, 1984, vol. 53, Frankfurt am Main, Insel Verlag, 1986, p. 128. On the question of 'obsessive images' mentioned above, cf. C. Mauron, *Des Métaphores obsédantes au mythe personnel*, Paris, J. Corti, 1962.

1
THE EMOTIONAL COMMUNITY: RESEARCH ARGUMENTS

1. The aesthetic aura

At the risk of sounding dogmatic, it will be necessary to return regularly to the problem of individualism, if only because it obscures, in a more or less pertinent way, the whole of contemporary thinking. Individualism, either properly speaking or in its derivative form of narcissism, is central to many books, articles and theses which, naturally enough, take a psychological, as well as historical, sociological or political perspective. This is a kind of obligatory rite of passage for those wishing to build a knowledge of modernity. While certainly not without its uses, this approach becomes increasingly questionable when used in countless newspaper articles, political speeches or moral posturings as a kind of magical key to understanding. So-called experts, untroubled by caution or scholarly nuance, disseminate a body of conventional, and somewhat disastrous, wisdom about the withdrawal into the self, the end of collective ideals or, taken in its widest sense, the public sphere. We then find ourselves face to face with a kind of *doxa*, which may perhaps not endure but which is nevertheless widely received, and at the very least, has the potential to mask or deny the developing social forms of today. While some of these new forms are quite obvious, others remain underground; moreover, the spectacular aspect of the former leads one to dismiss them as irrelevant, a criticism that seems to flourish during times of crisis. This of course paves the way for the lazy tendency inherent in any *doxa*.

I don't intend to confront the question of individualism head-on; however I will be regularly addressing it *a contrario*. The main thrust of my arguments will be to show, to describe and to analyse the social configurations that seem to go beyond individualism, in other words, the undefined mass, the faceless crowd and the tribalism consisting of a patchwork of small local entities. These are of course metaphors that aim above all to accentuate the untidy aspect of sociality. Here once again we may turn to the emblematic figure of Dionysus. In the guise of fiction, I intend to assume that the category that has served us well over two centuries of social analysis is completely exhausted. It is often said that truth is stranger than fiction; let us therefore try to measure up to the truth. Perhaps we ought to show, as certain novelists have, that the individual is no longer as central as the great philosophers since the age of the

Enlightenment have maintained. This naturally represents a bias, but one that I will adopt in any case, clarifying it along the way with notations, remarks or anecdotes which, while impertinent, will not be unfounded.

Beckett's plays shatter our illusions of the individual in control of himself and his destiny. In a paroxysmal* and premonitory way, he shows the contingent and ephemeral nature of all individualism and underlines the factitiousness inherent in the process of individuation which can only lead to a prison. Individualism is an outdated bunker and as such deserves abandonment, according to the playwright. This attitude is not without its stimulating originality in an era where the consensus likes its thinking ready-made. Of course, this view must have escaped many of his sycophants; but it is nevertheless in perfect congruence with the ancient wisdom that sees every individual as the single link [*punctum*] in an uninterrupted chain, multifaceted and microcosmic, the *crystallization* and *expression* of the general macrocosm. Here we can recognize the idea of the *persona*, the changeable mask which blends into a variety of scenes and situations whose only value resides in the fact that they are played out by the many.

The multiplicity of the self and the communal ambience it induces will serve as a backcloth to these reflections. I have proposed calling this the 'aesthetic paradigm', in the sense of fellow-feeling. Indeed, whereas the individualist logic is founded on a separate and self-contained identity, the person (persona) can only find fulfilment in his relations with others. Gilbert Durand, in looking at several modern authors (Thomas Mann, William Faulkner) speaks from a sociological perspective in which we exist only in the 'minds of others'.[1] Such a point of view obliges us to go beyond the classical subject/object dichotomy that is fundamental to the entire bourgeois philosophy. The accent is then on that which unites, rather than that which separates. No longer is my personal history based on a contractual arrangement with other rational individuals; rather it is a myth in which I am an active participant. Heroes, saints or emblematic figures may be real, however they exist more or less as ideal types, empty 'forms' , matrices in which we may all recognize ourselves and commune with others. Dionysus, Don Juan, the Christian saint or Greek hero – we could go on and on listing the mythical figures and social types that enable a common 'aesthetic' to serve as a repository of our collective self-expression. The multiplicity inherent in a given symbol inevitably favours the emergence of a strong collective feeling. Peter Brown put his finger on the question when he analysed the cult of the saint of late Antiquity.[2] By creating a chain of intermediaries, this cult allowed one to reach God. The fragmented persona and the specific links represented by the saints are thus the main elements forming the deity and the ecclesiastical collective that serves as its vector.

We may apply this analysis to our research: there are times when the social 'divine' is embodied in a collective emotion that recognizes itself in

---

* *Transl. note*: Maffesoli uses this term throughout to mean 'extreme' or 'acute'.

one or another typification. In this scenario, the proletariat and the bourgeoisie could be 'historical subjects' with a task to accomplish. A certain scientific, artistic or political genius could deliver a message indicating the path to follow; however, they could remain abstract and inaccessible entities, setting a goal to be achieved. In contrast, the mythical type has the simple role of collector, a pure 'container'. Its sole purpose is to express, for a precise moment in time, the collective spirit. This is the main distinction to be drawn between abstract, rational periods and 'empathetic' periods of history. The rational era is built on the principle of individuation and of separation, whereas the empathetic period is marked by the lack of differentiation, the 'loss' in a collective subject: in other words, what I shall call neo-tribalism.

There are many examples in our everyday life to illustrate the emotional ambience exuded by tribal development. Moreover, it is noteworthy that such examples are no longer shocking to us: they are a part of the urban landscape. The many punk or 'paninari'* looks, which are the expressions of group uniformity and conformity, are like so many punctuations in the permanent spectacle offered to us by the contemporary megalopolis. With respect to the tendency to examine the *orientation* of existence evident in the cities of the West, one may be reminded of Augustine Berque's analysis of the 'sympathetic' relationship between the self and the other in Japan. Such a weak demarcation – to the point of indistinguishability, even – between the self and the other, the subject and the object, gives pause for reflection. The idea of the extensibility of the self ('a relative and extensible ego') may be a pertinent methodological tool for understanding the contemporary scene.[3] It is almost not worth mentioning the fascination that Japan holds for us today; nor is it necessary to refer to its economic or technological supremacy in order to underscore the fact that, although *distinction* is perhaps applicable to modernity, it is by contrast totally inadequate in explaining the varied forms of social groupings that are today at the forefront. Their outlines are ill-defined: sex, appearance, lifestyles – even ideology – are increasingly qualified in terms ('trans', 'meta') that go beyond the logic of identity and/or binary logic. Briefly, and taking the terms in their most accepted sense, we can say that we are witnessing the tendency for a rationalized 'social' to be replaced by an empathetic 'sociality', which is expressed by a succession of ambiences, feelings and emotions.

For example, it is interesting to note that the German Romantic idea of *Stimmung* (atmosphere) is more and more often used on the one hand to describe relations between social micro-groups, and on the other to show the way these groups are situated in spatial terms (ecology, habitat, neighbourhood). The same holds true for the constant use of the term 'feeling'** to describe interpersonal relationships. It will be a useful

---

* *Transl. note*: A kind of Italian preppy, or as the French would say, 'bon chic, bon genre'.
** *Transl. note*: This word appears in English in the text.

criterion for measuring the quality of the exchanges, for deciding on how far and how deep they go. If we are referring to a rational organizational model, the most unstable notion we can employ is sentiment. In fact, it seems necessary to make a change in the way we consider social groupings; in this respect, Max Weber's socio-historical analysis of the 'emotional community' (*Gemeinde*) can be put to good use. He specifies that this emotional community is in fact a 'category', that is, something that has never existed in its own right but that can shed light on present situations. The major characteristics attributed to these emotional communities are their ephemeral aspect; 'changeable composition'; 'ill-defined nature'; local flavour; their 'lack of organization' and routinization (*Veralltäglichung*). Weber also points out that we find these groupings under many different names, in all religions and in general, alongside the rigidity of institutions.[4] In the eternal riddle of the chicken and the egg, it is difficult to determine which comes first; however, his analysis makes clear that the link between shared emotion and open communal relationships leads to this multiplicity of groups which manage, at the end of the day, to form a rather solid social arrangement. This adjustment, like a common thread through the social fabric, is no less permanent for all that. Permanency and instability are the two poles around which the emotional will navigate.

It should be pointed out right away that the emotion in question is not to be confused with any common or garden pathos. It seems to me a mistake to interpret the Dionysian values, to which this thematic refers, as the ultimate manifestation of a collective bourgeois activism. According to this interpretation, the common march towards the Enlightenment came first, followed by the attempt to master nature and technology, and culminating in the coordinated orchestration of social affects. But this perspective is far too closed or dialectical; of course, certain examples, such as the paradigm represented by 'Club Med', may lead to this conclusion. Nevertheless, this analysis must be careful to consider the fact that the key characteristics of the group attitude are its expenditure, the notion of chance and disindividuation.

This does not allow us to regard the emotional community as yet another stop along the pathetic and linear march of the history of humanity. I was much drawn to this point through conversations I had with the Italian philosopher Mario Perniola.[5] To extend his work from a sociological point of view, I would say that the aesthetic of the 'we' is a mixture of indifference and periodic bursts of energy. In a paradoxical way, we exhibit singular disdain for any projectivist attitude, and experience an undeniable intensity in whatever action we take. Thus can be characterized the impersonal nature of proxemics.

Durkheim underlined this fact also, and although he retains his wonted caution, he still speaks of the 'social nature of sentiments' and shows its effectiveness. 'We are indignant together,' he writes, referring to the proximity of the neighbourhood and its mysterious, formative 'force of attraction'. It is within this framework that passion is expressed, common beliefs are developed and the search for 'those who *feel and think as we do*' takes place.[6] These remarks, ordinary as they may appear, are applicable to many objects, and reinforce the insurmountable nature of the everyday substrate. This is the matrix from which all representations are crystallized: the exchange of feelings, conversation in the restaurant or shop, popular beliefs, world views and other insubstantial chit-chat which constitute the solidarity of the community's existence. Contrary to what has been previously considered good form, we can agree on the fact that reason plays only a small part in the formation and expression of opinions. Their expression, whether by the early Christians or the socialist workers of the nineteenth century, owes considerably more to the mechanisms responsible for the spread of commonly held feelings or emotions. Whether in the context of the network of tiny convivial cells or at a favourite local pub, the collective emotion becomes concrete, playing on the multiple facets of what Montaigne called the 'hommerie': that blend of greatness and turpitude, generous ideas and venal thoughts, of idealism and convinced worldliness – in a word: man.

Nevertheless, it is precisely this mixture that assures a form of solidarity, of continuity across the various histories of humanity. I have previously mentioned the community of destiny that sometimes may find expression within the framework of a rational and/or political project but that at others takes the more hazy and ill-defined path of the collective sensibility. In this latter case, the emphasis is placed on the disordered aspect of the small group which, in interaction with other forms of organisation, guarantees the perdurability of the species. The first case produces what Halbwachs calls the 'view from without', which is History, and the second, the 'view from within', or collective memory.[7]

To stretch this paradox even further, the collective memory is on the one hand tied to the immediate surroundings and, on the other, transcends the group itself, which is located in a long 'line' that we can take either *stricto sensu* or from an imaginary perspective. In any case, whatever we call it (emotion, sentiment, mythology, ideology) the collective sensibility, by superseding the atomization of the individual, creates the conditions necessary for a sort of aura that characterizes a certain period: the theological aura of the Middle Ages, the political aura of the eighteenth century or the progressive aura of the nineteenth. We might possibly be witnessing the development of an *aesthetic* aura containing varying proportions of elements related to the communal drive, mystical propensity or an ecological perspective. However it should appear, there is a strong link between these various terms; each in its own way takes into account the organicity of things, the *glutinum mundi* from which, despite (or because of) such diversity, a whole emerges. This organic sense of solidarity expresses itself in a multitude of ways, and it is surely from this angle that we must interpret the resurgence of the occult, syncretism and, more commonly, a heightened appreciation of the spiritual or astrological. This latter phenomenon especially is no longer the exclusive preserve of the credulous or naive. Researchers are now finding a double layer of meaning attached to astrology, both cultural and natural. Gilbert Durand has shown how individually centred astrology is of relatively recent origin, for classical astrology 'concerned itself above all with the *destiny of the group*, of the earthly domain'.[8] Astrology can be placed in an ecological perspective, represented by the 'houses' which predispose all of us to live in a natural and social environment. Without going too deeply into the matter, we may note that it has something of the aesthetic aura (*aisthétikos*) which is found in the union, however tenuous, of the macrocosm and the microcosms, and the union between these microcosms. What should be remembered from this and related examples is that they serve to reveal the holistic climate underlying the resurgence of solidarity and the organicity of all things. Thus, despite the connotation all too often attributed to them, emotion or sensibility must in some way be treated as a blend of objectivity and subjectivity. In my examination of the question of proxemics (cf. Chapter 6), I propose calling this a material spirituality, a somewhat Gothic expression that refers to what Berque termed, in referring to the effectiveness of the milieu, the 'transubjective' (subjective and objective) relationship. It is indeed time to note that the *binary logic of separation* that once predominated in all domains is no longer applicable as such. The soul and the body, mind and matter, the imagination and economics, ideology and production – the list could go on – are no longer seen as complete opposites. In fact, these entities, and the minuscule concrete situations they represent, come together to produce a day-to-day life that more and more resists the simplistic taxonomy to which we had been accustomed by a certain reductionist positivism. Their synergy produces the complex society that is deserving of its own complex analysis. The 'multidimensional and the inseparable', to borrow Morin's phrase,[9] take us into a 'continuous loop' which will render out of date the tranquil and terribly boring practices of the accountants of knowledge.

With the necessary precautions and clarifications out of the way, it becomes possible to attribute to the metaphor of sensibility or collective emotion a function of knowledge. This methodological tool allows us to travel to the heart of the organicity that so characterizes the contemporary urban scene. Thus, the following apologia becomes possible: 'Imagine for a moment that the Lord wishes to call up to heaven a typical house from Naples. Before his amazed eyes would amass a column of all the houses of Naples, one behind the other, trailing their laundry, complete with singing women and noisy children.'[10] This is the emotion that cements the whole. This whole may be made up of a plurality of elements, but there is always a specific ambience uniting them all.

At first, experience is lived in its own right and the scholarly observer should realize this. To summarize, it may be said that the aesthetics of sentiment are in no way characterized by an individual or 'interior' experience, but on the contrary, by something essentially open to others, to the Other. This overture connotes the space, the locale, the proxemics of the common destiny. It is this which allows us to establish a close link between the aesthetic matrix or aura and the ethical experience.

2. The ethical experience

As I have already indicated, particularly when referring to ethical immoralism, this term has nothing to do with the nondescript sort of moralism held in such high regard these days. I will return to this question; however, in a few words, let me say that I would contrast an abstract and overshadowing morality with an ethic that wells up from a specific group; it is fundamentally empathetic and proxemical. History may promote a moral (political) attitude, but space will favour an aesthetics and exude an ethics.

As we have seen, the emotional community is unstable, open, which may render it in many ways anomic with respect to the established moral order. At the same time, it does not fail to elicit a strict conformity among its members. There is a 'law of the milieu' that is difficult to escape. The more paroxysmal elements of this are well known: the Mafia, the underworld; but what is often forgotten is that a similar conformity reigns in the business world, the intellectual realm, and many others. Of course, since in these different milieux the degree of belonging varies, fidelity to the often unstated rules of the group shows just as many signs of variability. However, it is difficult to ignore this conformity altogether. Whatever the case, it is important, in a non-normative way, to appreciate its effects, its richness and perhaps its prospective dimension. Indeed, from the point of view of the individualist *doxa* mentioned earlier, the persistence of a group ethos is very often considered a fading anachronism. It would seem that an evolution is under way today. Thus, from the small productive groups best symbolized by Silicon Valley, up to what we call the 'groupism' operating within Japanese industry, it becomes clear that the communal tendency can go hand-in-hand with advanced technological or economic performance. Drawing on various studies that confirm this, Berque notes that 'groupism differs from the herd instinct in that each member of the group, consciously or otherwise, attempts above all to serve the interests of the group, instead of simply seeking refuge there'.[11] The term 'groupism' may not be particularly sonorous, but it does have the merit of underlining the strength of this process of identification which allows for the attachments that reinforce our common bonds.

It is perhaps premature to extrapolate on the basis of a few isolated examples or from a particular situation such as that of Japan; however, these examples are at least as relevant as those that give greater importance to the current narcissism. What is more, they are related to the economic sphere, which remains, for the moment in any case, the main fetish of the dominant ideology. I see this as one more illustration of the holism taking shape before our eyes: throwing wide the doors of privacy, sentiment takes over, and in certain countries its presence is reinforced in the public sphere, thus producing a form of solidarity that can no longer be denied. Of course, we must note that this solidarity reinvigorates, quite apart from technological developments, the communal form that seemed to have been left behind.

We may wonder about the community and the nostalgia underlying it or about the political uses to which it is put. For my part, and I reiterate it, this is a 'form' in the sense that I have defined this term.[12] Whether or not it exists independently is of little importance; it is enough that it serves as a backcloth, allowing us to highlight a particular social phenomenon. No matter that it is imperfect or even *ad hoc*, it is no less the expression of a particular crystallization of shared feelings. From this 'formist' perspective, the community is characterized less by a project (*pro-jectum*) oriented towards the future than by the execution *in actu* of the 'being-together'. In everyday language, the communal ethic has the simplest of foundations: warmth, companionship – physical contact with one another. Psychologists have pointed out that there is a *glischomorphic* tendency in all human relationships. Without wishing to judge in any way, it seems to me that it is this viscosity which is expressed in the communal being-together. Thus, and I must stress this rigorously in order to avoid any moralizing digression, it is by force of circumstance; because of proximity (promiscuity); because there is a sharing of the same *territory* (real or symbolic) that the communal idea and its ethical corollary are born.

It is worth remembering that this communal ideal can be seen in the populist and later anarchist ideology whose basis is to be found in the proxemic crowds. For these people, especially Bakunin and Herzen, the village community (*obschina* or *mir*) is at the very heart of working socialism. Supplemented with the artisans' associations (*artels*), it paves the way for a civilization built on solidarity.[13] The interest of such a romantic vision goes well beyond the habitual dichotomy of the latest bourgeois ideal, as much in its capitalist version as its Marxist version. Indeed, human destiny is seen as a whole, giving the *obschina* its prospective aspect. I should reiterate that this social form has, with good reason, been closely identified with Fourierism and the phalanstery. Franco Venturi, in his now classic book on Russian populism of the nineteenth century, points out this connection; moreover, and more to the point in our reflections, he notes the link between these social forms and the search for 'a different system of morality'. He does this with some reticence; for him, especially with regard to the phalanstery, this search lies somewhat in the realm of 'eccentricity'.[14] What the esteemed Italian philosopher failed to notice was that, beyond their apparent functionalism, all social groups include a strong component of shared feeling. It is these feelings that give rise to this 'different morality' which I prefer to call here an ethical experience.

To pick up again on the classic opposition, we might say that society is concerned with history in the making, whereas the community expends its energy in its own creation (or possibly recreation). This allows us to establish a link between the communal ethic and solidarity. One of the most striking aspects of this relationship is the development of the ritual. As we know, this is not strictly speaking finalized, that is, goal-oriented; it is, on the other hand, repetitive and therefore comforting. Its sole function is to confirm a group's view of itself; Durkheim's example of the 'corroboree' festivities is very helpful in this respect. The ritual perpetuates itself, and through the variety of routine or everyday gestures the community is reminded that it is a whole. Although it does not need putting into words, it serves as an anamnesis of solidarity and, as L.-V. Thomas remarks, 'implies the mobilization of the community'. As I have just stated, the community 'exhausts' its energy in creating itself. In its very repetitiveness, the ritual is the strongest proof of this expenditure and by so doing it guarantees the continued existence of the group. In the anthropological view of death, it is this paradox with regard to the funeral ritual that reintroduces 'the community ideal which attempts to reconcile man to death as well as to life'.[15] As I will explain more fully, there are times when the community of destiny is felt more acutely, and it is through gradual condensation that more attention is focused on uniting factors. This union is a pure one in some ways, with undefined contents; a union for confronting together, in an almost animal way, the presence of death, the presence at death. History, politics and morality *overtake death* in the drama (*dramein*) that evolves as problems arise and are resolved or at least confronted. Destiny, aesthetics and ethics, however, *exhaust death in a tragedy* that is based on the eternal moment and therefore exudes a solidarity all its own.

Experiencing death matter-of-factly may be the outcome of a collective sentiment that occupies a privileged place in social life. This communal sensibility favours a proximity-centred ethos; that is, simply put, a way of being that offers an alternative to both the production and distribution of goods (economic or symbolic). In his occasionally perfunctory but usually rich analysis of crowds, Gustave Le Bon notes that 'it is not with rules based on theories of pure equity' that the crowd is to be led and that, generally speaking, impressions play a considerable role.[16] What can we assume from this other than that justice itself is subordinate to the experience of closeness; that abstract and eternal justice is relativized by the feeling (whether hate or love) experienced in a given territory? Many everyday occurrences, whether examples of carnage or generosity, illustrate this general point. The doctrinally racist shopkeeper will protect the neighbourhood Arab; the contented bourgeois will fail to denounce the petty thief, and all in the most natural way. The code of silence is not confined to the Mafia; police officers who have had occasion to make inquiries in such and such a village or neighbourhood can testify to that. The common denominator of these attitudes (which are deserving of further elaboration) is the solidarity derived from a shared sentiment.

If we were to expand the field somewhat, with help from the media, we would find similar reactions throughout the 'global village'. It is not an abstract sense of justice that gives rise to soup kitchens, leads us to help the unemployed or other charitable endeavours. We could even say that, from a linear and rational view of justice, these activities appear somewhat anachronistic or even reactionary. In a very *ad hoc* and haphazard way, without attacking a given problem head-on, they risk serving as an excuse and being nothing more than a Band-Aid solution. While no doubt true, such activities nevertheless accomplish their aim, as well as mobilize the collective emotions. We may wonder about the significance or the political repercussions of these actions; we may also note – and this is the point of these remarks – how we no longer expect the all-pervasive state to remedy by itself the problems whose effects we see around us, as well as how the synergy of these activities brought home to us through the medium of television can exert its own influence. In both cases, that which I see around me, or which is brought closer to me through an image, strikes a chord in all of us, thus constituting a collective emotion. The mechanism in question is far from being of minor importance, which brings us back to the holistic principle underlying these reflections: the common sensibility at the heart of the examples cited is derived from the fact that we *participate in* or *correspond to*, in the strictest and possibly most mystical sense of these words, a common ethos. In formulating a sociological 'law', I will state as a leitmotif that less weight shall be given to what each individual will *voluntarily adhere to* (contractually or mechanically) than to that which is *emotionally common to all* (sentimentally and organically).

This is the ethical experience that had been abandoned by the rationalization of existence; it is also what the renewed moral order falsely portrays, since it tries to rationalize and universalize *ad hoc* reactions or situations and present them as new *a priori*, whereas their strength is derived from the fact that they are grounded in a local sensibility: it is only *a posteriori* that they can be linked in an overall structure. The community ideal of the neighbourhood or the village acts more by permeating the collective imagination than by persuading the social reason. To employ a term Walter Benjamin used in his reflections on art, I would say that we are in the presence of a specific aura, which in a process of feedback comes out of the social body and determines it in return. I will summarize this process in the following way: *the collective sensibility which issues from the aesthetic form results in an ethical connection.*

It would be useful to insist on that fact, if only to relativize the positivist ukases which insist that the collective imagination is superfluous and can be dispensed with in times of crisis. In fact, it can be shown that it assumes the most varied guises: at times it is manifested on the macroscopic level, spurring on great mass movements, varied crusades, occasional revolts or political or economic revolutions. At other times, the collective imagination is crystallized in a microscopic way, providing deep nourishment to social groups. Finally, there is on occasion a continuum between this latter process (esoteric) and the just-mentioned general manifestations (exoteric). Whatever the case, there is a wide-ranging aura which serves as a matrix to the always and freshly astonishing reality that is sociality.

It is from this perspective that the community ethos must be considered. What I here call *aura* spares us from deciding on its existence or non-existence; it so happens that it functions 'as if' it existed. It is in this way that we can understand the ideal type of the 'emotional community' (Max Weber), the 'orgiastic-ecstatic' (Karl Mannheim), or that which I have termed the dionysiac form. Each of these examples caricatures, in the simplest sense of the term, this exit from the self, ex-stasis, which is part of the social logic.[17] This 'ecstasy' is much more effective in smaller groups, when it becomes more perceptible to the social observer. In order to account for this complex entity, I propose to use, in the metaphorical sense, the terms 'tribe' and 'tribalism'. While refraining from overuse of quotation marks, I will insist on the 'cohesive' aspect of the social sharing of values, places or ideals which are entirely circumscribed (localism) and which can be found, in varied forms, at the heart of numerous social experiences. It is this constant interplay of the static (spatial) and the dynamic (becoming), the anecdotal and the ontological, the ordinary and the anthropological, that makes the analysis of the collective sensibility such a potent tool. To illustrate this epistemological remark, I will give but one example: the Jewish people.

Without wishing, nor indeed being able, to make a specific analysis, and confining ourselves to indicating a course of research, we can show that the Jewish people are particularly representative of the antinomy I mentioned. On the one hand, they have an intense experience of the tribe's collective sentiment which, on the other hand, has not prevented them throughout the centuries from assuring the existence of general and (without any pejorative connotations) cosmopolitan values. This sentiment includes a tribal religion that has enabled them to resist assimilation; tribal customs, which are the very basis of the community of destiny; and of course, tribal sexuality which assured the survival of the race through the carnage and vicissitudes of the ages. The flow of words, goods and sex: these are the three anthropological pivots around which social life generally turns. In essence, they have a strong tribal component. Many historians and sociologists have highlighted the vitality, the ambience and strong cohesiveness, in many countries, of the 'ghetto', the shtetl, the synagogue. And like a reserve of energy, these places were the source of a good portion of what was to become the medieval city, the modern metropolis and, perhaps, the megalopolis of today. Thus, the ethos of the Gemeinschaft, of the tribe, regularly permeates the evolution of Western civilization.[18] As I have said, this is but a course of inquiry; indeed, many domains, whether intellectual, economic or spiritual, have been influenced, in a prospective way, by what came out of the stockpot of the Jewish emotional culture.

There is no better way of expressing this 'concrete universal', which was one of the principal tenets of nineteenth-century philosophy. By extrapolating, in a heuristic manner, the aforementioned example, it is possible to state that, paradoxically, it is the tribal values which on occasion characterize an epoch. Indeed, a significant portion of those characteristics

which will later be diffracted throughout the social body may be crystallized in these values. The tribal moment may be compared to a period of
gestation: something that is perfected, tested and tried out, before taking
flight into the great beyond. In this way, everyday life could be, to use the
words of Benjamin, 'the most extreme concrete'. This short description
lets us see the shared lives and experiences as the purifying fires of the
alchemical process in which the transmutation takes place. The nothing or
near-nothing becomes a totality. The minuscule rituals are inverted until
they become the basis of sociality – *multum in parvo*. Of course, it is
difficult to predict what will be transformed from minuscule to macroscopic, as long as there are so many extraneous elements. However, this is
not the essential factor; it is enough, as I have said, to indicate the 'form' in
which the growth of social values is born. We may then say that the ethic is
in some way the glue that holds together the diverse elements of a given
whole.

Nevertheless, if one is to understand what I have just said, it is necessary
to lend this term 'ethic' its simplest meaning: not an indifferent *a priori*
theorizing but one which on a daily basis serves as a vessel for the
collectivity's emotions and feelings. In this manner, with varying degrees of
success and in a given territory, we all adjust to one another and to the
natural environment. This accommodation is of course relative; carried out
in happiness and sadness, the product of often conflictual relationships, it
exhibits a certain necessary flexibility, but nevertheless is astonishingly
long-lived. This is certainly the most characteristic expression of the social
'will to live'. It is therefore necessary to take the time to consider, if only
for an instant, several manifestations of this ethic of the everyday, since as
an expression of the collective sensibility it gives us wide access to the life
of these tribes that, *en masse*, constitute contemporary society.

3.   Custom

From Aristotle to Mauss, by way of Thomas Aquinas, many have
examined the importance of the *habitus* (*exis*), a term which has since
passed into the sociological *doxa*.[19] This is all to the good, for this thematic
is of primary importance. It is related to the common aspects of everyday
life, in a word the customs, which are, according to Simmel, 'one of the
most typical forms of everyday life'. Since we know the importance and
effectiveness he attached to 'form', it becomes possible to imagine that we
are dealing with more than the empty word. Further on, he is more
specific: 'custom determines the social life as would an ideal power'.[20] We
are led back to a persistent action that instills in beings and things their way
of seeing the world; it is practically a matter of genetic coding, limiting and
delineating, in a much more profound manner than the economic or
political situation, their way of being with others. Thus, together with the
aesthetic (the shared sentiment) and the *ethic* (the collective bond), *custom*

is surely a good way of characterizing the everyday life of contemporary groups.

I will adopt the following concern of Mallarmé: 'to give a purer sense to the words of the tribe'. And like all other 'mini-concepts' used previously, I will use the term 'custom' in its most widely held sense, one that is also closest to its etymological roots (*consuetudo*): the collection of common usages that allow a social entity to recognize itself for what it is. This link is a mysterious one, only rarely and indirectly put into so many words (for example in the treatises on manners and customs). Nevertheless, it is at work in the deepest layers of any society. Custom, in this way, is the unspoken, the 'residue' underlying the 'being-together'. I have proposed calling it the *underground centrality* or the social *puissance* (as opposed to power), an idea found in Goffman (*The Underlife*) and later on in Halbwachs (*La Société silencieuse*).[21] These expressions emphasize the fact that a large part of social existence cannot be accounted for by instrumental rationality; nor does it let itself be finalized or reduced to a simple logic of domination. Duplicity, subterfuge and the will to live are all expressed through a multitude of rituals, situations, gestures and experiences that delineate an area of liberty. A tendency to see life as alienation or to hope for a perfect or authentic existence makes us forget that daily routine is stubbornly founded on a series of interstitial and relative freedoms. As has been seen in economics, it is possible to demonstrate the existence of a *black-market sociality*, which is easily tracked through its diverse and minuscule manifestations.

I am adopting the perspective of Durkheim and his followers, who always placed the greatest weight on the sacredness of social relationships. As I have often said: I consider that any given entity, from the micro-group to the structure of the state, is an expression of the social divine, of a specific, even immanent, transcendence. But as we know, and many religious historians have shown, the sacred is mysterious, frightening, disturbing; it needs to be coaxed and cajoled, and customs fulfil this function. They are to everyday life what the ritual is to religious life, strictly speaking.[22] Moreover, it is striking that in popular religion especially it is very difficult, as the ecclesiastical hierarchy was obliged to do, to draw the distinction between customs and canonical rituals. Thus, just as the liturgical ritual renders the Church visible, custom makes a community exist as such. Furthermore, at a time when the division was not yet firmly established, according to Peter Brown, it was by ritually exchanging relics that the various local churches were constituted as a network. These relics are the bond that held a small community together, allowing them to unite and, in so doing, to transmute 'the distance from the holy into the deep joy of proximity'.[23]

Any organization *in statu nascendi* is fascinating to the sociologist; relations between individuals are not yet fixed and social structures retain the suppleness of youth. At the same time, it is useful to find points of comparison in order to formalize our observations. In this respect, the analysis carried out by the scholars of Christianity is very apposite. It is certainly possible, if only as a working hypothesis, to apply the double process of social *reliance* and of negotiation with the holy characteristic of the early Christian communities to the various tribes that are made and unmade *in praesenti*. In more than one respect, the comparison is illuminating: the organization, grouping around an eponymous hero; the role of the image; the common sensibility, and so on. But it is fundamentally the local membership, the spatial emphasis and the mechanisms of solidarity which are their corollaries that creates the whole. This, moreover, characterizes what I previously termed the increased sacredness of social relationships: the complex mechanism of give and take that develops between various persons, on the one hand, and between the entity thus created and the milieu on the other. Whether these are real or symbolic exchanges is of little importance; indeed, communication, in its widest sense, takes the most varied routes.

The term 'proxemics' proposed by the Palo Alto School appears to me a good way of accounting for both the cultural and natural elements of the communication under consideration. For his part, Berque emphasizes the 'transubjective' (subjective *and* objective) aspect of such a relationship. Perhaps we should just resort to the old spatial notion of the neighbourhood and its affective connotation. It is an old-fashioned term, but one that is making a reappearance today in the writings of many observers of the social scene – a sure sign that it is at the forefront of many minds.[24] This 'neighbourhood' can be manifested in many diverse ways: it can be delineated by a collection of streets, it may be invested with a libidinal dimension (a 'red-light district', for example), refer to a commercial entity or a public transit hub. The detail is unimportant; what matters is that it represents the overlapping of a certain functionality with an undeniable symbolic weight. An integral part of the collective imagination, the neighbourhood is nevertheless only constituted by the intersection of ordinary situations, moments, spaces and individuals; moreover, it is most often expressed by the most common stereotypes. The town square, the street, the corner tobacconist, the bar at the PMU,* the newsagent, centres of interest or necessity – just so many trivial examples of sociality. Nevertheless, it is precisely these instances that give rise to the specific aura of a given neighbourhood. I use this term deliberately, as it translates beautifully the complex movement of an atmosphere emitted by places and activities, giving them in return a unique colouring and odour. And so it may be for spiritual materialism. Morin speaks poetically of a certain New York neighbourhood that shines with brilliance while at the same it is founded on the 'lack of brilliance of the individual'. In widening his scope, the whole city becomes a *chef-d'oeuvre* whereas its 'lives remain pitiful'. However, he continues, 'if you allow yourself to be possessed by the city, if you really get into its sense of energy, if the forces of death which exist only

---

* *Transl. note*: PMU = *parimutuel urbain* (race-track betting).

to crush you instead awaken in you an intense will to live, then New York will dazzle you'.[25]

This metaphor is an effective expression of the constant interplay of the customary stereotype and the founding archetype. It is this process of constant reversibility which seems to me to constitute what Durand calls the 'anthropological course'; in essence, the close connection that exists between the great works of culture and this 'culture' experienced on an everyday level constitutes the critical bond in any society's life. This 'culture', to the amazement of many, is made up of the varied 'nothings' which, through sedimentation, form a meaningful system. It is impossible to give a complete list, although such a project would have much merit for us today. It would range from the culinary fact to the fantasy world of home appliances, without forgetting advertising, mass tourism and the resurgence and multiplication of festive occasions: in other words, all those things that describe a collective sensibility which no longer has much connection with the politico-economic domination characteristic of modernity.[26] This sensibility is no longer part and parcel of a finalized, directed rationality (Weber's *Zweckrationalität*), but is rather experienced in the present tense, inscribed in a defined space – *hic et nunc*. Thus we have everyday 'culture'; it permits the emergence of true values, surprising or shocking as they may be, expressive of an irrefutable dynamic (perhaps closely paralleling what Weber calls the *Wertrationalität*).

In understanding custom as a cultural fact we may appreciate the vitality of the metropolitan tribes. They are responsible for that aura (informal culture) which surrounds, *volens nolens*, each of us. There are many instances one could cite as an example; however they all possess the common trait of being derived from proxemics. Thus, it is possible to explain all those friendship networks which have no other goal than of congregating, with no fixed purpose, and which more and more cut across the everyday lives of all collectivities. Some studies have shown that these networks are rendering associative structures obsolete.[27] These structures are supposedly flexible, easily accessible to the users, giving them a direct line on their problems; however, they are too finalized, organized, founded for the most part on a political or religious ideology, in the abstract (remote) sense of the term. In the friendship networks, *reliance* (the link) is experienced *for its own sake*, without any projection; moreover, it may be *ad hoc* in nature. With the help of technology, as in the groups fostered by the 'Minitel', an ephemeral framework for a specific occasion is provided, so that a certain number of individuals can (re)connect. Such an occasion may lead to continuing relationships or it may not. In any case, it is certain to create friendship 'chains' which, following the formal model of networks studied by American sociology, give rise to multiple relationships based solely on the device of proxemics: so-and-so introduces me to so-and-so who knows someone else, and so on.

Such a proxemical concatenation, without a project, is bound to produce offspring: mutual aid, for example. This is a product of ancient wisdom, a wisdom it is no longer considered trendy to heed and which holds that 'life is hardest on the poor . . . money is difficult to come by and therefore we have an obligation to pull together and help one another'.[28] Poulat thus sums up the popular substrate of the 'democratic-Christian' ideology. In many respects, this is a model that merits a further look, for beyond the Christian democracies *stricto sensu*, there is an echo of what for years was the Thomist social doctrine and which was a significant factor in the development of a common symbolism. Therefore, alongside a socio-political analysis, we can also underline the socio-anthropological dimension and emphasize the close links between proxemics and solidarity. In some ways, such mutual aid exists by force of circumstance, not out of purely disinterested motives: the help given can always be redeemed whenever I need it. However, in so doing, we are all part of a larger process of correspondence and participation that favours the collective body.

This close connection is also discreet; indeed, we give veiled accounts of our personal, family and professional successes and failures and this orality works as a rumour with an essentially intrinsic function: it delineates the territory where the partaking takes place. There is no place here for the stranger, and if necessary, we may remind the press, the public authorities or the merely curious that 'dirty laundry does not get washed in public'. This survival mechanism works just as well for happy news as for unsavoury information. Indeed, in various ways, the customary word or the shared secret are the primordial glue of all sociality. Simmel showed the example of secret societies, but it can also be found in studies on traditional medicine which show that the individual body can be healed only with the help of the collective body.[29] This is an interesting metaphor since we know that this approach to medicine considers each body as a whole that must be treated as such. But we must also note that this overall vision is often augmented by the fact that the individual body is but an offshoot of the community. This observation allows us to give full weight to the term 'mutual aid' as it refers not only to the mechanical actions that constitute neighbourly relations; indeed, mutual aid as we understand it here is part of an organic perspective in which all the elements through their synergy reinforce life as a whole. Mutual aid could thus be said to be the 'unconscious' animal response of the social 'will to live'; a sort of vitalism that 'knows' implicitly that '*unicity*' is the best response to the onslaught of death – a challenge laid down, in a sense. Let us leave such thoughts to the poet:

> To be one with all living things! On hearing these words . . . Virtue abdicates, death leaves the realm of creatures and the world, relieved of separation and old age, shines with new light. (Hölderlin, *Hyperion*)

This collective feeling of shared *puissance*, this mystical sensibility that assures continuity, is expressed through rather trivial vectors. Without being able to go into detail here, these are found in all the places where chit-chat and conviviality are present. Nightclubs, cafés and other public spheres are 'open areas', in other words those places where it is possible to speak to others and, in so doing, address alterity in general. I took as a point of departure the idea of the sacredness of social relationships. This can best be seen in the transmission of the word that in general accompanies the flow of food and drink. Let us not forget that the Christian eucharist which underlies the union of the faithful is just one of the developed commensal forms found in all word religions. Thus, in a stylized way, when I am sitting in the café, eating a meal or addressing the other, I am really addressing the deity. This leads back to the confirmation, expressed countless times, of the link between the divine, the social whole and proximity.[30] Commensality, in its various forms, is only the most visible evidence of this complex relationship. However, it is worth remembering that the divine issues forth from daily realities and develops gradually through the sharing of simple and routine gestures. The *habitus* or custom thus serves to concretize or *actualize* the ethical dimension of any sociality.

One need only remember that custom, as an expression of the collective sensibility, permits, strictly speaking, an ex-stasis within everyday life. Having a few drinks; chatting with friends; the anodyne conversations punctuating everyday life enable an exteriorization of the self and thus create the specific aura which binds us together within tribalism. As we can see, it is important not to reduce this ecstasy to a few highly stereotyped and extreme situations. The dionysiac refers of course to sexual promiscuity, as well as to other affectual or festive outbursts; but it also allows us to understand the development of shared opinions, collective beliefs or common *doxas*: briefly, those 'collective frameworks of memory', to borrow Halbwachs' expression, which allow one to emphasize what is lived, the 'tides of experience'.[31]

Alongside a purely intellectual knowledge, there is a knowledge [*connaissance*] which encompasses the feeling dimension, an awareness that, taken to its etymological origins, we are 'born with' [*'co-naissance'*].* This embodied knowledge is rooted in a corpus of customs deserving of analysis in its own right. We would then be able to appreciate the contemporary formulation of the 'palaver' whose varied rituals played an important role in the social equilibrium of the traditional village or community. It is not impossible to imagine that, correlatively with technological developments, the growth in urban tribes has encouraged a 'computerized palaver' that assumes the rituals of the ancient agora. We would no longer face the dangers, as was first believed, of the macroscopic computer disconnected from reality, but on the contrary, thanks to the personal computer and cable TV, we are confronted with the infinite diffraction of an orality disseminated by degrees; the success in France of

---

* *Transl. note*: This etymological observation is not really translatable, The French for knowledge is 'connaissance' and birth 'naissance', hence 'co-naissance' = 'born with'.

the Minitel should be interpreted in this light. In a number of domains –
education, leisure time, job-sharing and culture – the close communication
engendered by this process forms a network with all the attendant social
effects imaginable.[32]

At first, the growth and multiplication of the mass media led to the
disintegration of the bourgeois culture founded on the universality and the
valuing of a few privileged objects and attitudes. We may well ask
ourselves whether this pursuit of growth and the generalization to which it
leads may bring the mass media closer to everyday life. In this way, they
could be said to reinvest a certain traditional culture whose orality is an
essential vector. In so doing, the contemporary media, by presenting
images of everyday life rather than visualizing the great works of culture,
would be playing the role that used to fall to the various forms of public
discourse: to ensure by means of myth the cohesion of a given social entity.
This myth, as we know, may be of several types; for my part, I believe that
there is a mythic function which runs transversely through the whole of
social life. A political event or harmless, trivial fact, the life of a star or a
local guru, can all take on mythic proportions. In his study of these mass
media, Fernant Dumont subtly underlines that these myths, whatever their
precise contents, serve mainly to 'nourish, as in days gone by, gossip and
normal conversation . . . what we used to say about the parish priest or the
notary, we now say about such and such a film star or politician'.[33] It is
impossible not to be struck by the appropriateness of this remark, at least
to those of us who have had the experience of overhearing office, factory or
playground conversations; even the notorious café conversations can be
instructive for the observer of the social scene. I would go even further and
say that it is within the logic of the media to set themselves up as a *simple
pretext* to communication, as may have been the case with the ancient
philosophical diatribe, the medieval religious sermon or the political
speech of the modern era.

In some cases, the content of these varied forms is not inconsiderable.
But it is because they reaffirm the feeling of belonging to a larger group, of
getting out of oneself, that they apply to the greatest number. Thus, we pay
more attention to the form that serves as a backcloth; which creates an
ambience and therefore unites. In any case, it is a question, above all, of
allowing for the expression of a common emotion, which causes us to
recognize ourselves in communion with others. It would be worth examining whether the expansion of local television or radio has had any effect in
this regard. This is at least a possible hypothesis, one which does not
completely deprive custom of its important role. By revealing our near
neighbours, custom secretes a 'glue' holding a given community together.
Neighbourhoods or even buildings with access to cable TV will perhaps
experience values not so far removed from those which guided the clans or
tribes of traditional societies.

Consequently, and taking the term 'communication' in its narrowest
sense – that which structures social reality and which is not an offshoot – we

can see custom in the light of one of its particular manifestations, a manifestation that takes on increased importance when, as a consequence of the saturation* of organizations and overarching social representations, proxemic values (re)surface. One might even say that at this stage of the game, the scale tilts more towards the communications mode, since it is experienced for its own sake, without any sort of finalization as a pretext. There is a direct link between this emphasis on communication for its own sake and the surpassing of the critical attitude that is tied to a more instrumental, mechanical and operational approach to society. With the communications mode predominant, the world is accepted as it is. I have already proposed calling this 'the social given', to explain the link that can be made between custom and communication. The world accepted for what it is lies of course within the realm of the natural 'given', part of a two-way flow common to the ecological perspective. But it is also part of the social 'given', in whose structure each of us fits and which leads to an organic sense of commitment between individuals, in other words, tribalism. This is certainly where the theme of custom leads us; the *individual* counts for less than the *person* who is called upon to play his or her role on the global scene, according to some very precise rules. Can we thus speak of regression? Perhaps, if we consider individual autonomy as the base-line of any existence in society. But, aside from the fact that anthropology has shown us that this is a value which is immutable neither in time nor in space, then we may grant that the *principium individuationis* has become increasingly contested in the very heart of Western civilization. The poet's or novelist's sensibility can serve as a barometer (cf. Beckett's plays, for example) of this tendency or, more empirically, we can see evidence of it in the various group attitudes that colour the life of our societies.

Finally, it is worth noting that certain countries which have not developed from a tradition of individualism nevertheless are currently exhibiting signs of an undeniable *vitality* that, moreover, seems to exert a lasting fascination for us. Japan is just such a country and so, paradoxically, is Brazil. We must take both these countries to be prototypes whose auras are essentially ritualistic, whose inner structures are the 'tribe' (or the organic grouping, to be less blunt), and which are, for at least one if not both, poles of attraction for the collective imagination, whether from the existential, economic, cultural or religious point of view.

Of course, it is not a matter of presenting them as finished models, but rather of demonstrating that, as an alternative to the *principle of autonomy*, or however we wish to call it (self-direction, autopoeïsis, etc.), we can posit a principle of allonomy** which is based on adjustment, accommodation, on the organic union with social and natural alterity.[34] This principle goes against the activist model built by modernity. Under the present hypothesis,

---

* *Transl. note*: here and elsewhere, Maffesoli uses the term 'saturation' to describe the worn-out nature of institutional power, just as a sponge saturated with water can absorb no more.
** The law as an external force.

this principle is a customary one, and it reinvests, in a prospective way, the traditional values long since thought to be surpassed. In fact, after the period of 'disenchantment with the world' (Weber's *Entzauberung*), I am suggesting that we are witnessing a veritable re-enchantment with the world, whose logic I will try to make clear. For the sake of brevity, let us say that, in the case of the masses which are diffracted into tribes, and the tribes which coalesce into masses, the common ingredient is a shared sensibility or emotion. I think back to the beginning of this discussion and the prophetic meditations of Hölderlin on the peaceful banks of the Neckar, where he made the connection between the 'nationel',* the shared sentiment which holds a community together, and the 'shades of the Greek gods [who] are returning to earth just as they were'. Upon revisiting this oasis of calm, he found it imbued in these gods. It is also in the solitude of that footpath in Eze that the other 'madman' Nietzsche experienced the dionysian irruption. His vision was no less premonitory:

> Now solitary, living in isolation from one another, some day you will be one people. Those who have chosen themselves will one day form a chosen people from whom will emerge an existence which surpasses man.

Our own *Philosophenweg* passes over beaches crammed with holiday-makers, department stores thronged with howling consumers, riotous sporting events and the anodyne crowds milling about with no apparent purpose. In many respects, it would seem that Dionysus has overwhelmed them all. The tribes he inspires demonstrate a troublesome ambiguity: although not disdaining the most sophisticated technology, they remain nonetheless somewhat barbaric. Perhaps this is a sign of postmodernity. Be that as it may, the principle of reality, on the one hand, forces us to accept these hordes, since they are there, and on the other, urges us to remember that time and again throughout history it was barbarity that brought many moribund civilizations back to life.

Notes

1. Cf. G. Durand, 'Le Retour des immortels' in *Le Temps de la réflexion*, Paris, Gallimard, pp. 207, 219. On the 'aesthetic paradigm', cf. my article in *G. Simmel*, Paris, Méridiens Klincksieck, 1986. Cf. also T. Adorno, *Notes to Literature*, trans. Sherry, Weber and Nicholson, New York, Columbia University Press, 1992, p. 249, on the question of the 'outdated bunker' of individualism.

2. P. Brown, *The Cult of the Saints: Its Rise and Function in Latin Christianity*, Chicago, University of Chicago Press, 1981, p. 51.

3. A. Berque, *Vivre l'espace au Japon*, Paris, PUF, 1982, p. 54. For an example of the uniform, cf. F. Valente, 'Les Paninari' in *Sociétés*, Paris, Masson, no. 10 (Sept. 1986).

4. M. Weber, *Economy and Society*, Berkeley, University of California Press, 1978, for example vol. 2, pp. 452–456.

5. M. Perniola, *Transiti*, Bologna, Cappeli, 1985; or in French, *L'Instant éternel*, Paris, Librairie des Méridiens, 1982.

---

* Referring to the popular substrate.

6. E. Durkheim, *The Division of Labour in Society*, New York, Free Press, 1964, p. 102 (my emphasis).

7. M. Halbwachs, *La Mémoire collective*, Paris, PUF, 1968, p.78, on the trans-individualist ideology; cf. also J. Freund, *Sociologie du conflit*, Paris, PUF, 1983, p. 204.

8. G. Durand, *La Foi du cordonnier*, Paris, Denoël, 1983, p. 222; cf. also the theses under way on astrology by B. Glowczewski and S. Joubert (Paris V – Centre d'études sur l'actuel et le quotidien). It would also have been possible to speak of the 'transmigration' of souls in the cabbala, which fits in with the present holistic perspective. Cf. G. Scholem, *La Mystique juive*, Paris, Cerf, 1985, pp. 215, 253, *et seq.*

9. A. Berque, 'Expressing Korean mediance', from the colloquium The Conditions and Visions of Korea's Becoming an Advanced Country, Seoul, Sept. 1986. We must also refer here to the remarkable analysis by E. Morin which should be a cause for worry among the more honest of his detractors: *La Méthode*,vol. 3, *La Connaissance de la connaissance/1*, Paris, Seuil, 1986. On the 'notion of milieu', cf. J. F. Bernard-Bécharies, in *Revue Française du marketing*, vol. 1, no. 80 (1980), pp. 9–48.

10. Cited by A. Médam, *Arcanes de Naples*, Paris, Editions des Autres, 1979, p. 202.

11. Berque, *Vivre l'espace*, pp. 167, 169.

12. At the moment of writing, a pointed and rather caustic analysis has just come out: J.L. Nancy, *La Communauté désoeuvrée*, Paris, C. Bourgeois, 1986. On the question of 'formism', cf. my book, M. Maffesoli, *La Connaissance ordinaire. Précis de sociologie compréhensive*, Paris, Librairie des Méridiens, 1985.

13. See the remarkable and erudite analysis of this by B. Souvarine, *Stalin, A Critical History*, London, Secker and Warburg, 1940, p. 22.

14. F. Venturi, *Les intellectuels, le peuple et la révolution. Histoire du populisme russe au XIXe siècle*, Paris, Gallimard, 1972, p. 230.

15. L.-V. Thomas, *Rites de mort*, Paris, Fayard, 1985, pp. 16 and 277. It might also be pointed out that J. L. Nancy, p. 42 *et seq.* makes the link between community and death. On the cyclical and tragic aspect of the ritual, I refer to my book, M. Maffesoli, *La Conquête du présent. Pour une sociologie de la vie quotidienne*, Paris, PUF, 1979.

16. G. Le Bon, *The Crowd*, New York, Viking, 1960, p. 20.

17. However it may appear to hurried minds, the orgiastic-ecstatic thematic is a constant of the sociological tradition, e.g. Weber, *Economy and Society*, p. 554; K. Mannheim, *Ideology and Utopia*, New York, Harcourt Brace, 1954, p. 192. One must also refer to E. Durkheim, *The Elementary Forms of the Religious Life*, New York, Collier, 1961. I would also refer to my own short synthesis, *L'Ombre de Dionysus, contribution à une sociologie de l'orgie*, Paris, Librairie des Méridiens, 2nd edition, 1985.

18. I must refer of course to the classic book by L. Wirth, *The Ghetto*, Chicago, University of Chicago Press, 1966. On the metropolis in the Austro-Hungarian Empire, cf. W.M. Johnston, *L'Esprit viennois*, transl. Paris, PUF., 1985, pp. 25–28. On the work of the Chicago School, see U. Hannerz, *Exploring the City: Inquiries toward an Urban Anthropology*, New York, Columbia University Press, 1980, pp. 40–44 and 65.

19. Cf. for example the article by G. Rist, 'La Notion médiévale d'*habitus* dans la sociologie de Pierre Bourdieu', *Revue européenne des sciences sociales*, vol. 22 (1984), no. 67, pp. 201–212 and Maffesoli, *La Connaissance ordinaire*, p. 224 and notes 60, 61.

20. G. Simmel, 'Problèmes de la sociologie des religions', *Archives des sciences sociales des religions*, Paris, CNRS, no. 17 (1974), pp. 17 and 20.

21. I have developed this theory of 'underground centrality' in my previously cited works; Halbwachs, *La Mémoire collective*, pp. 130–138; on Goffman's analysis of this question, cf. Hannerz, *Exploring the City*, p. 216, *et seq.*

22. On the *tremendum* [fear], cf. R. Otto, *Le Sacré*, Paris, Payot, 1921; on popular religion, M. Meslin, 'Le phénomène religieux populaire' in *Les Religions populaires*, Presses de l'Université Laval, Québec, 1972.

23. P. Brown, *The Cult of the Saints: Its Rise and Function in Latin Christianity*, Chicago, University of Chicago Press, 1981, p. 90. On contemporary 'reliance', without sharing many of his pessimistic nor indeed his hopeful analyses, I would refer to the informed book by M.

Bolle de Bal, *La Tentation communautaire, les paradoxes de la reliance et de la contre culture*, Bruxelles, Université de Bruxelles, 1985.

24. The Palo Alto School is now well known in France; the works of Bateson and Watzlawick are generally found in translation published by Seuil, cf. the 'digest' offered by Y. Winkin, *La Nouvelle communication*, Paris, Seuil, 1982; the term 'transubjective' is used by A. Berque in his article 'Expressing Korean Mediance'. On the neighbourhood, cf. K. Noschis, *La Signification affective du quartier*, Paris, Librairie des Méridiens, 1983 and F. Pelletier, 'Lecture anthropologique du quartier' in *Espace et Société*, Paris, Anthropos, 1975, no. 15.

25. E. Morin, and K. Appel, *New York*, Paris, Galilée, 1984, p. 64; On the 'anthropological course', I would refer naturally to the classic work by G. Durand, *Les structures anthropologiques de l'imaginaire*, Paris, Bordas, 1969.

26. This type of research is a speciality of the Sorbonne's Centre d'Etudes sur l'Actuel et le Quotidien [CEAQ] (Paris V). As an example, I would refer to *Sociétés* issues 8 (tourism), and 7 (cooking), as well as the article by L. Strohl, 'L'électroménager' [household appliances], in *Sociétés*, 9.

27. See J.C. Kaufmann, *Le Repli domestique*, Paris, Méridiens Klincksieck, 1988. On the networks and their formalization cf. Hannerz, *Exploring the City*, pp. 210–252.

28. E. Poulat, *Catholicisme, démocratique et socialisme* (the Catholic movement and Mgr Benigni, from the birth of socialism to the victory of Fascism), Paris, Casterman, 1977, p. 58.

29. Cf. the African example in E. Rosny, *Les Yeux de ma chèvre*, Paris, Plon, 1981, pp. 81 and 111. On rumour and its uses, cf. the research by F. Reumaux, *La Rumeur* (thesis in progress at the time of writing), Université Paris V. Also, cf. Simmel's article 'Les Sociétés secrètes' in *Nouvelle Revue de Psychanalyse*, Paris, Gallimard, 1977.

30. A study on public spheres remains largely to be undertaken. Research on cafés is under way at the CEAQ. One can however refer to C. Bouglé, *Essays on the Caste System*, Cambridge, Cambridge University Press, 1971, p. 45; cf. also Hannerz, *Exploring the City*, p. 198, *et seq*.; and J.M. Lacrosse et al. 'Normes spatiales et interactions', *Recherches sociologiques*, Louvain, vol. 6, no. 3 (1975), p. 336, especially with regard to the café as 'open area'.

31. Halbwachs, *La Mémoire collective*, p. 51, *et seq*.

32. Readers are referred to a report by M. de Certeau and L. Giard, *L'Ordinaire de la communication*, Paris, 1984 (Report of the Ministry of Culture) also cf. a more specific area detailed in the thesis by P. Delmas, 'L'Elève terminal, enjeux sociaux et finalité des nouvelles technologies éducatives', Université Paris VIII, 1986 and a work in progress, C. Moricot, 'La Télévision câblée', CEAQ – Paris V.

33. F. Dumont, on the origins of the notion of popular culture in *Cultures populaires et sociétés contemporaines*, Presses de l'Université du Québec, Québec, 1982, p. 39. It is also worth consulting Dumont's *L'Anthropologie en l'absence de l'homme*, Paris, PUF, 1981.

34. Berque analysed this principle of allonomy in Japan, in *Vivre l'espace au Japon*, p. 52. On the significance of ritual custom in Brazil, cf. R. Da Matta, *Carnaval, bandit et héros*, Paris, Seuil, 1983.

2

THE UNDERGROUND *PUISSANCE*

1. Aspects of vitalism

It was Emile Durkheim who remarked that 'if existence endures, then it is because, generally speaking, men prefer it to death' – a sensible statement, for all its surface banality.[1]

There is no point in going over the difficulty some intellectuals have in understanding this 'will to live' (*puissance*) which, despite or perhaps because of its many impositions, continues to nourish the social body. Without knowing all the reasons for it, it is interesting to speculate on why this question can no longer be ignored. Let us remain within the limits of banality, if only to enrage the university 'bean-counters' who hide behind a scientific aura in order to disguise the triviality of their thinking. Some art historians distinguish between periods in which the 'tactile arts' predominate and others in which 'visual arts' prevail, or in other words, between art which must be 'seen close up' and art which requires a certain 'distance' in order to be fully appreciated. It is by relying on such a dichotomy that Worringer develops his famous opposition between abstraction and empathy (*Einfühlung*). Briefly, empathy is intuitive in terms of its representation and organic in terms of structure. Or, we may base ourselves on the idea of *Kunstwollen*, which refers to the masses and to the collective force which drives them – in short, to this remarkable vitalism.[2]

Obviously, this classification must be considered from an archetypal point of view, that is, it does not exist in a pure form. It can be seen as an 'unreality' whose sole function is to reveal current situations which are themselves very 'real'. Thus, in order to answer the previously stated question, it is possible that, following a period in which distance prevailed – an 'optical' period which we might refer to etymologically as theoretical (*theorein*: to see), we are now entering a 'tactile' period in which proxemics predominates. To put it in terms more in keeping with sociology, this trend can be seen as the transition from the global to the local, the passage from the proletariat as an active historical subject to the masses freed of responsibility for the future. We are thus obliged to contemplate the saturation of the question of power (i.e. of politics) in its projective function, and the emergence of the question of the *puissance* at the heart of the many sparse, splintered, communities. These communities are still linked in a sort of differentiated architectonic, expressing themselves in what I have called 'conflictual harmony'.[3] It is within this schematic framework that vitalism's emergence should be considered: that is, that life exists in opposition to nothing. Usually seen as fodder for 'separation', alienation and the critical attitude which is its expression, it is important to analyse the 'affirmative' quality of life, the societal 'will to live', which, even from a relativist perspective, nourishes everyday life 'seen close up'.

Returning once again to my outline of the emblematic figure of Dionysus, it seems to me that the role of *puissance* is continually at work. However, its action may be either secret, discreet or displayed. When it is not expressing itself in one of its effervescent forms such as revolts, festivals, uprisings and other heated moments of human history, it is hyperconcentrated in the secretive world of sects and the avant-garde, in whatever form these may take, or hypoconcentrated in communities, networks and tribes – in short, in the smallest details of everyday life which are lived for their own sake and not as a function of any sort of finality.[4] I am referring to the mystic or gnostic tradition, as opposed to the critical or rationalist approach; but from the ancient gnoses to the gnosis of Princeton, by way of the mysticism of Böhme and Loisy,[5] from the unleashing of the senses and mores to 'New Age' medicines and contemporary astrological explorations, there is a common thread running through: that of *puissance*. We might call the spiritual attitude 'dionysian' and the more sensual perspective 'dionysiac'; however, they are both founded on the primacy of experience, on a deep vitalism and a more or less explicit vision of the organicity of the various elements of the cosmos. A number of issues surrounding political saturation – changes in values; the failure of the myth of progress; the resurgence of the qualitative; the increased devotion to hedonism; the continued preoccupation with the religious; the significance of the image – which we had thought drained of all meaning but which increasingly intrudes on our everyday life (advertising, television) – all of these questions are drawn against a backcloth of what one might call an irrepressible *puissance*. This energy is very difficult to explain; however, its effects may be observed in the various manifestations of sociality: cunning, aloofness, scepticism, irony and the tragic amusements which persist in the midst of a world supposedly in crisis. In fact, the real crisis exists for the powers in their overarching and abstract nature. It is this opposition between *extrinsic power* and *intrinsic puissance* which must rigorously guide our thinking and which is the translation into sociological terms of the previously mentioned aesthetic dichotomy (optical versus tactile). In considering this movement of the pendulum, by which issues (re)appear and fade away in a circular movement of return, one should refer to the canonical author Célestin Bouglé. While of his time (the turn of this rationalist century) and place (the French Positivist School), Bouglé nevertheless suggested inherent qualities which were not strictly derived from Western tradition. Thus, in his highly nuanced appraisal of the caste system – to which we will return – he remarks that 'the land of castes' could well be the cradle of the myth of Dionysus (p. 146), and goes on to show us how there is a shift between the 'life of the Greeks' (and we might also say their descendants), which was 'full of reality' and the fact that for the Hindu it was a 'deceptive illusion' (p. 144). This sceptical view is nevertheless expressed in a 'breath of sensuality', even 'brutality' (p. 145). Thus, by going beyond accepted truths, he cannot help noting that non-activism (as opposed to passivity) can be dynamic. It is not possible to go into great detail in these pages; however, we can recognize along with Bouglé that the 'ordering intellect' can be set against an 'amplifying imagination' (p. 178), and that each of these may represent fertile ground in its own right.[6]

It is of course possible to extrapolate from his idea, and to go beyond the constricting framework of 'race', in order to add the socio-anthropological dimension which interests us here. It is possible that the *puissance* at work today may not be separate from the fascination which Eastern thought and customs currently have for us. Of course, these do not hold a monopoly as the European model once did or the 'American way of life'* still does for the time being. Rather, according to differentiated modalities, they may (and do already) fit into an intercultural composition which will reanimate the tradition versus modernity debate. In this respect, the place occupied by Japan in the contemporary imagination is a clear indicator; in my opinion, its industrial performance and its conquering dynamism are incomprehensible unless we bear in mind the heavy dose of tradition and the ritual dimension which permeate the various manifestations of its collective life, the importance of which has been widely acknowledged. The three-piece suit has its place alongside the kimono in the wardrobe of the efficient manager. Here again, one might say that we are in the presence of a 'dynamic rootedness'.[7]

Thus, at a time when it has become fashionable to lament (or to celebrate, which is much the same thing) the end of the social, we must, with common sense and lucidity, remember that the end of a certain form of the social order, and the obvious saturation of the political order, can more than anything leave an opening for the emergence of a *vital instinct*, which is itself far from exhausted. The disastrous scenarios around us are in fact very dialectical (Hegelian); too linear (positivist); and still too Christian (parousia**) to account for the multiple explosions of vitalism which are coming from those groups or 'tribes' in constant fermentation. They are taking personal responsibility for multiple aspects of *their* collective existence: this can truly be called polytheism. As is often the case, the intellectuals, and more precisely the sociologists, will only comprehend this *post festum*!

Let us venture a few metaphors: just like the phoenix of Antiquity, the death of an old form inevitably gives rise to a new one. The 'expansive imagination' mentioned earlier allows us to understand that the death of the historical or of political monovalence can represent an opportunity for reinvesting the natural matrix. I have already explained this process: the

---

* This appears in English in the text.
** *Transl. note*: referring to the Second Coming of Christ.

transition from an all-pervasive economy to a generalized ecology, or in the words of the Frankfurt School, the passage from nature as object (*Gegenstand*) to nature as partner (*Gegenspieler*). Moreover, the ecological movements (whether in the form of political parties or not), the fads of natural foods, macrobiotics and other natural movements are instructive in this regard. This is not a useless detour in my reflections, but rather a parameter whose importance escapes only too often the nay-sayers, except when reduced to its political component. One may think of Jünger and his fascination with minerals, or refer to the poet Lacarrière who described forcefully and beautifully the resurgence of the great Goddess Earth:

> I have always found a certain resemblance between myths and coral: they both exist on a common living branch which . . . becomes transformed into minerals over the centuries . . . the burgeoning, living flowers, the tentacle-like branching . . . in short, the verbal and ephemeral arteries which continually nourish the abyssal vigour of the phylum.[8]

The whole of this beautiful book, which is comparable to Henry Miller's *Colossus of Marousia*, continues in the same vein; it describes the re-enchantment with the world by showing the close connection which exists between the arborescence – even mineral – of nature and the explosion of life to which the myth testifies. The phylum in question reminds us, advisedly, that although civilizations are mortal or even ephemeral, the substrate in which they implant themselves is invariable, at least in the eyes of the sociologist. It would be wise to remember this truism, which in our self-absorption we tend to forget.

That being said, it is now possible to understand what I have termed 'social perdurability', a rather uncivilized term which describes the ability of the masses to resist. This ability is not necessarily conscious, it is incorporated; like a mineral in some ways, it outlasts political change. I would hazard to say that there exists within the masses a 'sure knowledge', an 'assured direction', after Heidegger, which makes them a *natural entity* far exceeding their various historical or social manifestations. This may seem a somewhat mystic vision; but it is the only one that allows us to explain how across carnage and war, migration and death, splendour and decadence, the human animal has continued to prosper. Now that we need no longer fear invective and accusations; now that theoretical terrorism no longer paralyses the adventure of thought (or even adventurous thought), it is fitting that sociologists examine rigorously this global, holistic perspective which was affirmed by the very founding of our discipline. The recognition of an irrepressible vitalism may go hand in glove with this. There is no question of making an exhaustive survey of this research;[9] it is enough to show that, according to Goethe's theme of the *Natur-Gott*, the Nature-God, this vitalism has formed an integral part of the depth psychology so central to the twentieth century.

It was patently obvious in the work of Carl Jung, whose fecundity is only now being (re)-examined, but also on the fringes of the Freudian movement: the 'organizing principle of life' is at the heart of Groddeck's work. Thus, according to one of his critics, the latter always displayed a 'great interest in the *phusis*, that is, the spontaneous growth; the accomplishment of a destiny, in nature as in human beings'.[10] If in the psychoanalytic tradition I quote Groddeck, it is because, on the one hand, he was inspired by Nietzsche, whose topicality has still not been fully explored, but also because the adage he took as his own – *Natur sanat, medicus curat* – is at the heart of the alternative movements which the world over are in the process of overturning the social configuration. Furthermore, we will have to be careful to gauge the relevance of what I call *puissance*. It is possible to imagine that this 'fulfilment' in the natural order – the arborescence or ever-continuing growth – will have its effect on the social order. It is in rediscovering the virtues of Mother Nature that a feeling of wholeness is restored. There is a reversibility at play, rather than unilateral domination, which allows us to claim that all those groups for whom nature is seen as a partner are alternative forces. These groups signal at once a decline in a certain type of society as well as an irresistible renaissance.

Of course, this process which we see *in statu nascendi* is completely chaotic, disordered, effervescent. But we have known since Durkheim that this effervescence is the surest sign of the prospective, of that which is called upon to last, to be institutionalized even. Bachelard calls this frenzy of activity a 'primal image', reminding us that in the seventeenth century, 'the word "chaos" was spelled "cahot" '.* This parallel is elucidating, especially when one is aware that chaos is the foundation upon which the cosmos is constructed, as well as the micro-cosmos which is the social order. The throng is a sign of animalization but also of animation,[11] a fact clearly illustrated by Durand. This throng, with its strong natural connotation, can be seen as an expression of the *puissance* or the 'will to live', which are the cause and effect of the vital phylum. In the words of the German psychoanalyst: 'Kot ist nicht Tot, es ist angfang von allem'.

Let us be even more precise: although there is a decline in the great institutional and activist structures – from political parties, as required mediator, to the proletariat as historical subject – there is on the other hand the development of what might be termed very generally the basic communities. These are built on a *proxemic* reality whose finished form is nature. With great insight, Simmel showed that 'the sentimental attachment to nature' and the 'fascination with power' must surely be transformed into religion. There is, in the strictest sense of the term, *communion* with beauty and nature.[12] Here, religion binds; it binds precisely because of the close co-existence, because of physical proximity. Thus, contrary to historical 'ex-tension', which is built upon vast and increasingly impersonal structures, nature favours 'in-tension' (*in-tendere*), with all the commitment, enthusiasm and warmth that it supposes. The

---

* *Transl. note*: This etymological observation is not really translatable. The word 'chaos' in French has the same meaning as in English; the word 'cahot' can be translated as 'jolt'.

rather cavalier reference to nature and the 'religion' which flows from it is only made in order to show that beyond the arbitrary division between the physical and the psychical, and hence between nature and the sciences of the mind – divisions imposed by the nineteenth century – we are in the midst of rediscovering a global perspective that is nothing short of prospective.

There are a number of scientists (physicists, astrophysicists, biologists) who are actively working towards just such a revision. Some, such as Nobel laureate Fritz Capra or biologist R. Sheldrake, even refer to the Tao or to Hindu thought in order to express their hypotheses. In his case, physicist J.E. Charron tries to show that 'in physics, the spirit is inseparable from research'. Since I am not competent in this area, I will refrain from entering into the fray. I can, however, use his analyses metaphorically in order to illustrate the path taken by this vitalism or the *puissance* at work in the social given, in particular with respect to 'black holes', those stars which through a breathtaking process of increasing density die in our space-time in order to be reborn 'in a new space-time', which he calls a 'complex space-time'.[13] In answer to those who question the decline of the classic modes of social structuring, let me create a clearer image by suggesting that it is the density of sociality, what I have just called its 'in-tension' (*in-tendere*), which helps it reach another space-time where it moves about easily. Such a density has always existed; it is experience in its various dimensions, the lived life in all its concreteness, the feeling or passion which, contrary to conventional wisdom, constitutes the essential ingredient of all social aggregations. In general, this density is expressed through the delegations and representations that occur throughout human history (general assemblies, councils, direct democracies, nascent par-liaments, etc.). However, over time, and because of the inevitably increased rigidity of institutions, we see an increasing separation which may lead to divorce. When this happens, this 'density' will be exiled to another space-time while waiting for new forms in which to express itself, since, to borrow the term from Bloch who applied it to other phenomena, there is quite often 'non-contemporaneity' between an institution and its popular foundations. Thus, in our democratic countries, what some pundits refer to as the development of anti-parliamentarianism is perhaps nothing but a strain in the *libido dominandi* which sustains public life, or even a saturation of the political game whose abiding interest remains its theatrical gestures.

However, leaving aside those who make their living at questioning this decline to their puerile games, it is still necessary to question the 'importance of the "black holes" of sociality'. This has the merit at least of forcing us to turn our attention to the too often ignored basis of our discipline. Let us leave behind celestial architecture for the bricks and mortar of our cities. Reflecting on the spaces contained therein, Dorflès, inspired by the aesthetic movement, stated that there can be no architec-ture 'without an interior space'. Moreover, he widens the debate by showing that this interior spatiality has important anthropological roots (grotto, niche, shelter) as well as psychological (maternal breast, uterus, digestive tract). The reflection on the 'labyrinth', which was particularly well exploited by the Surrealists and the Situationists, or the 'empty spaces' mentioned by Durand, highlights the fact that any construction requires an interior space on which to rest.[14] What has been applied to architecture can be extrapolated to the architectonics of sociality. This has been the central hypothesis of my work for many years: the necessity of an *underground centrality*. The fact that contemporary architects or urban designers are rediscovering the desire for lost space, the agora, the underground passage, porticos, patios and so on is just the constructivist transliteration of the pressing need for the 'empty space'. I have already said that, before becoming the world we know, the *mundus* was the 'hole' into which were thrown sacrificial victims to the gods, infants rejected by their fathers as well as refuse,[15] in short, all those things that give meaning to the city.

One fact (pointless to the urbanists of the time but which was to be felt later on) which has enlivened many discussions with friends from Grenoble, such as C. Verdillon, is worth singling out. When the City of Grenoble decided to construct 'Villeneuve', a living laboratory for a new way of experiencing city living, it asked urban planners to design long 'passageways' linking the apartments to the elevators, and 'galleries' which would provide a place for people to congregate. These became a place of draughts, of joggers – even panic. They also planned for, in conformity with regulations, a 'social square footage'. Thus, on top of socio-educational provisions, one room was left empty at the end of each passageway. It was to be the place for meetings, groups, workshops. In fact, these rooms were quickly occupied in an informal way for activities which could be classed as anodyne or against the traditional morality. In any case, they were places where it was thought – through projections or fantasizing – that something extraordinary was occurring which was necessary to group life: *mundus est immundus*. The 'social square footage' was the place for the squalid, permitting communication, diatribes or vicarious living. Of course, it was not to last and locks were put on these places of freedom which were then ingloriously handed over to social directors!

But beyond this anecdote, what I am trying to emphasize is that there is always, to borrow an expression from Simmel, 'a secret behaviour of the group hidden from the outside'.[16] It is this behaviour which, following the more or less established eras, is the basis of social perdurability and which, apart from occasional declines, guarantees the continued existence of the phylum. If it should be necessary to clarify further, I am talking about an ideal type which does not exist in pure form, which is rarely presented as such by the protagonists themselves, naturally enough; however, it is certainly this 'secrecy' which allows us to measure the vitality of a social group. Indeed, it is in protecting the stages of a revolution, the reasons for a conspiracy or more simply through passive resistance or 'aloofness' with regard to a particular (political, state, symbolic) power that a community is forged. Whether explosive or silent, there is a violence whose founding functions we have only begun to explore. And *puissance* also has a role to play here.

To sum up these few remarks, this surprising 'vitalism', which is the condition for understanding the *puissance* of the life without qualities, can be understood only by abandoning the judgemental (or normative) attitude which generally belongs to the keepers of knowledge and power. Julien Freund, in speaking of the fickleness of the crowd, proposes classifying it 'under the category of the privative', that is, neither positive nor negative, 'at the same time both socialist and nationalist'.[17] I will put it in my own terms by saying that the crowd is hollow, vacuity itself, and it is in this that its *puissance* resides. Refusing the logic of identity, which transforms the masses into the proletariat (into the 'subject' of history), the crowd may be, either sequentially or concurrently, the everyday crowd or the crowd in revolt, the racist crowd or the generous crowd, the naive crowd or the cunning crowd. Philosophically speaking, this is an incomplete chapter, and as such it holds great promise. Imperfection is a sign of life; perfection a synonym for death. It is only in its hodge-podge, its effervescence, its disordered and stochastic aspects, its touching naivety, that the vitalism of the people is of interest to us. It is because it is in this *nothingness* which gives shape to everything that, relatively speaking, we can see an alternative to decline; but at the same time it tolls a bell for modernity.

2. The social divine

We may ask ourselves about another aspect of the *puissance* of the masses, that is the 'social divine', a term coined by Durkheim to describe that aggregate force which is the basis of any society or association. We could also use the word 'religion', if it is used to describe that which unites us as a community; it is less a content, which is the realm of faith, than a container, that is, a common matrix, a foundation of the 'being-together'. In this regard, I will refer to Simmel's definition: 'the religious world sinks its roots into the spiritual complexity of the relationship between the individual and his peers or a group of his peers . . . these relationships constitute the purest of religious phenomena in the accepted sense of the term'.[18]

There is no question of doing a sociology of religion here; besides, the specialists in our field become reticent as soon as reference is made to the resurgence of the religious. I will take care not to tread on any toes and will limit myself to the fluid, nebulous world of religious sentiment. Moreover, I will do so purposefully, paying careful attention to religious developments strictly speaking (especially their non-institutional manifestations), as well as to the importance accorded to the imaginary and the symbolic, all things which encourage preoccupied or predisposed minds to speak of the return of irrationalism.

First, there is a definite link between the restoration of the natural (naturalism) and the re-enchantment with the world which we are witnessing today. Beyond the demystifications and the 'demythologizing', which have found their supporters even in the midst of theological reflections, the social 'sleuth' that is the sociologist is sure to consider all those various elements which lend importance to fate, destiny, the stars, magic, tarot, horoscopes, nature, cults, etc. Certainly, the development of games of chance as we know them in France, of casino-type popular games (lotto, tacotac, tiercé, national lottery), is part of this process. These are topics which merit separate treatment; there is no need here to ring the alarm bells. Indeed, let us recall Durkheim's 'essential postulate of sociology': 'that a human institution cannot rest upon an error and a lie without which it could not exist. If it were not founded in the nature of things, it would have encountered in the facts a resistance over which it could never have triumphed.'[19] The wisdom of this remark can be applied to the subject at hand. Common sense, empirical observation, newspaper articles – they all agree on the multiplication of religious phenomena. It is therefore appropriate to deal with them, without unduly exaggerating their impact, nor discounting them *a priori*.

First, let us consider a phenomenon which is widespread at all levels of society. As far as the 'crowd' is concerned, it is not surprising to find interest in horoscopes; they are also the topic of conversation (albeit discreet) among the intelligentsia, who can be seen wearing various charms or amulets around their necks or wrists. As for the other layers of society, studies under way will show the same phenomena occurring. Let me recount the following anecdote: recently, at a dinner which brought together top civil servants (plus a few 'stand-ins' such as a bishop, a university professor and an astrologer), I was able, on the one hand, to have a long conversation with a certain well-known astrologer who named all the politicians, of various political stripes, who were clients of hers and on the other, to listen to a certain regional politician, a rational man if ever there was one, explain to me in confidence the magical thrill – like a weekly fix – he felt when the winning lottery numbers were drawn. Naturally, in order to avoid total indiscretion, it was his driver who was charged with the task of purchasing the fateful ticket. Of course, this is all anecdotal, but it is these facts, however minuscule they may be, which by successive layers constitute the substrate of both individual and collective existence. They underline in the strongest terms another way of relating to the natural or cosmic environment than the one to which we had become accustomed by purely rationalist thinking. Naturally, this different way of relating is not without consequence for our relationships with others (family, office, factory, neighbourhood), since it is true that it is the way in which the 'human being thrown into the world' is experienced and represented that determines his or her performance. What I mean by this is the handling of all those situations which bit by bit constitute the existential concatenation. If we can thus speak of the re-enchantment with the world, then it is because this 'is a given'. This naturalism and connivance are worth highlighting; they are what make it possible to talk of the social 'order' or, to use Schutz's expression the 'taken for granted'.[20] We join in as best we can; we are part of this miserable world, so imperfect and yet so much better than 'nothingness'. Such a tragic vision, to be sure, which is based less on change (reform, revolution), than on an acceptance of things as they are: the status quo. Some would cry fatalism, and they would be partially correct; however, opposing this (Anglo-Saxon) activism which pits individuals against one another, is a certain (Mediterranean?) fatalism, which by integrating the individual into the matrix, reinforces the collective spirit. Let me specify that although the human or social 'divine' (from Feuerbach, by way of Comte and Durkheim) is a preoccupation of social thinking, we can nonetheless draw a parallel with a certain mystical tradition which has as its goal to lose oneself in the 'greater whole'. Such an attitude, on the one hand, refers to the naturalism mentioned earlier, as well as functions as the basis for the formation of small groups (communion, erotic or sublimated identification, sects, congregations, etc.) which are not unrelated to things we can observe today.[21] It must not be forgotten that the theological expression which best describes this process – 'the communion of saints' – is based primarily on the idea of participation, correspondence and analogy, notions which seem perfectly appropriate for analysing social movements that cannot be reduced to their rationalist or functional dimensions. The great sociologist Roger Bastide, the importance of whose analyses will one day be acknowledged, spoke of religion in terms of an 'arborescent development'.[22] There again, apart from the naturalist image it conjures up, we are encouraged to see elements in an organic structure (branches forming a tree), of rings and of concatenation, of communities interwoven on a larger canvas. There is the old biblical image of mythical Jerusalem 'where all are as one', prefiguring the conviviality of the paradise to come. Based on these few remarks, can we extrapolate and make a link with the *puissance* of the masses? I believe it is legitimate to do so, especially since the essential characteristic of religion, in its different manifestations, remains nevertheless intangible: its transcendence. Whether it can be situated in a great beyond or whether it is an 'immanent transcendence' (the group, the community transcending individuals) does not alter the truth of the matter. My hypothesis, as distinct from those who lament the end of great collective values and the withdrawal into the self – which they falsely parallel with the growing importance of everyday life – is that a new (and evolving) trend can be found in the growth of small groups and existential networks. This represents a sort of tribalism which is based at the same time on the spirit of religion (*re-ligare*) and on localism (proxemics, nature). Perhaps, since the era of individualism inaugurated by the French Revolution is coming to a close, we will be confronted with what was an abortive experiment (Robespierre): that is, the 'civil religion' advocated by Rousseau. This hypothesis is not without foundation, all the more so since, as Poulat notes, it continued to interest, throughout the nineteenth and up until the turn of the century, thinkers such as Pierre Leroux, Comte of course, Loisy and Ballanche who thought that 'humanity would be called on to form a fourth heavenly being'.[23] Inspired by a term applied to Lammenais, we can say that this 'demotheistic'* perspective allows us to understand the strength of tribalism, or the strength of a sociality which remains impervious to economic-political analyses.

As we know, Durkheim remained preoccupied with the religious connection: 'how a society which nothing transcends but which transcends its members can hold together'. This happy formula of Poulat's[24] clearly sums up the theme of immanent transcendence. Causality or utilitarianism alone are insufficient to explain the propensity for association. Despite the various egos and interests involved, there remains a glue which guarantees perdurability. Perhaps its source can be found in the shared sentiment. Depending on the era, this sentiment may be based on lofty ideals or on more powerful objectives nearer to home. In the latter case, it cannot be unified, rationalized *a fortiori*; and its scattered nature will only serve to highlight its religious dimension. Thus, the 'civil religion', which is difficult to apply to an entire nation, can be quite easily experienced at the local level by a multiplicity of towns (the Greek example) and special groupings. At this stage, the solidarity it leads to becomes concrete. In this way, a certain consecutive uniformity, flowing from the globalization and homogenization of customs and even thoughts, can occur simultaneously with a growing emphasis on individual values which are granted an intense new meaning by some. Thus, we are witness to an ever-increasing penetration of the mass media, uniformity in our dress, the victory of the fast food outlet; and at the same time we can also see the development of local communication (private radio, cable TV), the rise of individual fashions, local produce and cuisine, so that it would sometimes seem that we are in the process of reappropriating our existence. One is drawn to this conclusion by the fact that, far from erasing the strength of our ties (religion), technological advances sometimes even bolster them.

It is because there is a saturation of abstract phenomena, of overarching values, of great economic or ideological structures that we can notice, without in any way contesting these structures (which would only be to accord them too much weight), a reorientation towards goals near to hand, genuinely shared feelings; in short, all those things which constitute a world: customs and rituals which are 'taken for granted'.**

It is precisely this proximity that gives much of its meaning to what we call the 'social divine'. It has nothing to do with any kind of dogmatism or institutional formula; it strengthens the pagan fibre which, whether historians like it or not, has never entirely disappeared from the masses.

---

* The people as god, or the 'social divine'.
** *Transl. note*: 'taken for granted' appears in English in the text.

Like the Lares, the cause and effect of the family group, the divine of which we speak allows us to recreate the cenacles that keep us warm and provide social spaces in the heart of the cold, inhuman metropolis. The dizzying growth of metropolises (megalopolises, rather) as demographers inform us, can only foster the development of 'villages within the city', to paraphrase a well-known title. Alphonse Allais' vision has come to pass. Great cities have supplanted the countryside; their neighbourhoods, ghettos, parishes, terrain and various tribes which inhabit them have replaced the villages, hamlets, communes and cantons of yesteryear.* But since it is necessary to gather round a protective figure, the patron saint of our worship will be replaced by the guru, the local celebrity, the football team or the much more modest sect.

The idea of 'keeping warm together' is a way of acclimatizing to or domesticating an environment without it becoming in any way threatening. Empirical research in urban settings has clearly demonstrated these phenomena. In analysing social changes flowing from urban migration in a Zambian city, Bennetta Jules-Rosette noted that 'there are residents who have always played an active part' in the reorganization and the growth of the community. And she continues: 'The most distinctive characteristic shared by many of these residents is their membership in indigenous African churches.'** It is moreover this participation which creates the most visible of the sub-groups of the community.[25] Thus, urban change can perhaps be correlated to a rapid de-Christianization; however, it is bound to favour a religious syncretism with yet unknown results.

In one of his writings on 'the social aspects of religion', which remains surprisingly up to date, Durkheim, for whom 'religion was the most primitive of social phenomena', notes the end of the old ideals and divinities. Nevertheless, he goes on to underline that one must dig 'below the moral chill which reigns at the surface of our collective life to feel the sources of warmth that our societies carry within'. These sources of warmth he situates 'within the popular classes'.[26] This appraisal is well within the bounds of my reflections here (and is increasingly shared by a number of researchers): the obvious dehumanization of urban life is giving birth to specific groupings for the exchange of passion and feelings. Let us not forget: the dionysiac values, which seem very topical, concern sex, but also religious feelings; they are both signs of passion.

It is only because the 'social divine' functions in a minor key of adaptation, or even a sort of preservation, that we notice its presence, in a major key, in revolutionary explosion. I have already touched on this

---

* *Transl. note*: Alphonse Allais (1854–1905) was a popular French humourist who wrote for the cabaret journal *Le Chat noir*. His writings focussed on the absurdity of modern life. 'La Forêt enchantée' (The Enchanted Forest) (*Le Chat noir*, 27 October 1888) tells the story of an entire Parisian neighbourhood, newstands and cafés included, arising out of the forest before the astonished gaze of the narrator.

** *Transl. note*: This quotation appears in English in the text.

theme in the notion of 'ouroborus revolution',[27]* by showing that there has always been a heavy religious dimension to revolutionary phenomena which were later classified as purely political. This is obvious in the case of the French Revolution. It was also the case for the 1848 revolutions in Europe; Henri de Man has shown that the Bolshevik Revolution was not immune either. The Peasants' Revolt can be seen as a paradigm of this phenomenon; Bloch's beautiful book makes an undeniable case for this dimension. Moreover, it is on this topic that Mannheim spoke of 'orgiastic-ecstatic energies' which had their 'roots in deeper-lying vital and elemental levels of the psyche'.[28] It is important to refer to these effervescent moments, if only to demonstrate that there is a constant to and fro between explosion and release and that this process is cause and effect of the religious link, i.e. the sharing of passion. In fact, religion in this sense is the matrix of all social life.[29]

It is the crucible in which all the various manifestations of the 'being-together' are created. Ideals can of course age, collective values become saturated, however, religious feeling continually secretes that 'immanent transcendence' which explains the perdurability of societies across human history. It is in this sense that we are concerned with an element of this mysterious *puissance*.

I have mentioned the ex-static attitude which should be understood here in its narrowest sense as an exteriorization of the self. Indeed, the above-mentioned perdurability is based primarily on the existence of a mass, a people. Le Bon even talks of 'the moralization of the individual by the crowd', and he cites several examples.[30] This is what was understood by the Catholic theologians for whom faith was of secondary importance to its actual expression in a church setting. To use the language of the moralist, the religious authority (or ecclesiastical conscience), is for them more important than the 'inner conscience'. To use terms which are more familiar to me, developed previously when referring to what I called 'the ethical immoralism': whatever the situation and the moral qualification, which are, as we know, ephemeral and localized, the shared sentiment is the true social bond. It can lead to political upheaval, occasional revolts, bread riots, strikes for solidarity; or instead it can lead to festivities and everyday banalities. In each of these cases, there is an ethos at work by which, come hell or high water, carnage and genocide, a mass holds together as such and survives the vagaries of politics. This 'demotheism' has been exaggerated here for our purposes (even caricatured), but, in my opinion, this is necessary in order to understand the extraordinary resistance to the multiform impositions which constitute societal living. If we were to extend this hypothesis still further, based on the afore-mentioned, we might propose a minute change to the classic adage and substitute *populo* for *deo*. Thus, for the sociologist trying to understand the vitalism of sociality, the magic words could be *Omnis potesas a populo*.

---

* *Transl. note*: 'ouroborus': the Greek symbol of a snake (or dragon) devouring its own tail.

Indeed, and this is where the socio-anthropologist can bring a prospective not to mention prophetic dimension to his or her work: it is possible that the structuring of society into many smaller groups in combination will make it possible to escape or at least relativize the institutions of power. This is the great lesson to be learned from the polytheism which has already been the subject of numerous analyses; it also suggests that there remains fertile ground for research. More specifically, it is possible to imagine a power in the process of globalization, two- or three-headed, disputing and sharing economic-symbolic zones of influence, playing the game of nuclear intimidation. And beyond this trend, or alongside it, there would be a proliferation of groupings with varied interests, the creation of individual fiefdoms, the multiplication of theories and ideologies which are in opposition to one another. On the one hand we would find homogeneity, on the other, heterogeneity; in other words, to dust off an old image: the dichotomy on a universal scale of the country as a series of borders and the 'real' country. This perspective is being rejected by the majority of political or social observers, in particular because such a vision contradicts their frameworks of analysis which are derived from the positivist and dialectical traditions of the last century. However, if we are capable of seeing the indications before us (*index*: the pointing finger) such as massive political and union disengagement; the greater attraction of the here and now; the view of politics and what it really represents – theatrics or spectacles of varying degrees of interest; the investment in new economic, intellectual, spiritual or existential adventures – all of this should cause us to consider that the sociality which is being born owes nothing to the old socio-political world (which is our heritage).

In this regard, science fiction is a useful example: dressed in techno-Gothic trappings, it represents heterogeneity and insolence with respect to the above-mentioned conformist behaviours.[31]

It is through this growing autonomy with respect to the overarching powers that the social divine can find its expression. Indeed, leaving aside the question as to what the society of the future 'ought to be', we sacrifice to local 'gods' (love, commerce, violence, territory, festivities, work activities, food, beauty, etc.) whose names may have changed since Graeco-Roman times but whose emblematic influence remains the same. Thus, we can witness the reappropriation of our 'real' existence, which lies at the heart of what I call the *puissance* of the masses. With assurance and stubbornness, in a perhaps animalistic way – that is, more as an expression of a vital instinct than a critical faculty – groups, small communities, affinity networks and neighbourhoods are preoccupied with close social relationships. This is also the case with respect to our relationship with the natural environment. *Thus, even if one feels alienated from the distant economic-political order, one can assert sovereignty over one's near existence.* This is the goal of the 'social divine', and is also the secret of its perdurability. It is in the secret, the near, the insignificant (which escapes macroscopic finality) that sociality is mastered. One might even go so far as to say that the powers can only be exercised if they are not too distanced from this sovereignty. This 'sovereign' state can be understood within the contractual perspective of Rousseau, which confers upon it a unanimist and rather idyllic dimension.[32]

This state can also be seen as that 'conflictual harmony' in which, by a process of action–reaction, a group manages more or less to adjust its natural, social and biological components and thereby assure its stability. The theory of systems, as well as the writings of Morin, show with precision how up to date and pertinent such a perspective is. Thus, even if it seems a figure of speech to many, the link that can be made between the masses and their sovereignty is perfectly well founded. Moreover, whether through uprisings, violent actions or democratic means; by silence or withdrawal; by scornful disdain, humour or irony, there are multiple ways the masses have of asserting their sovereign *puissance*. The whole art of politics consists of ensuring that these expressions do not take over.

Abstract power can occasionally triumph. We might ask La Boétie's question: 'What is the basis of voluntary servitude?'* Certainly, the response can be found in that inbred assurance of the social body which knows that in the long term, the Prince, in whatever form he takes (aristocrat, tyrant, democrat, etc.) is always subject to the popular verdict. If power is the issue of individuals or a succession of individuals, then *puissance* is an attribute of the phylum and takes its place in the continuum. In this way, *puissance* is a characteristic of what can be termed the 'social divine'. It all comes down to a question of precedence. To speak of *puissance*, sovereignty and the divine in connection with the masses is to recognize, to borrow Durkheim's expression, 'that law derives from custom, that is, life itself'[33] and that it is 'customs which form the real basis for states'. This vitalist priority, penned by that most positivist of hands, is worth underlining; it is surely this reflection that allows him to highlight the importance of the religious link in the social structure. Of course, it is a general idea which needs to be brought up to date; however, the recognition that the close link between vitalism (naturalism) and the religious constitutes a veritable force propelling the masses and assuring their continuity and *puissance* is significant at a time when communications, leisure, art and the everyday life of the masses are forcing a new social deal.

3. The aloofness of the people

When we look at human history, we can say that politics, in the form of the adjustments of individuals and groups between themselves, is an unsurpassable structure. On this matter, one can only agree with Julien Freund who spoke of 'the political essence'. Nevertheless, although this essence

---

* *Transl. note*: Étienne de la Boétie (1530–63), author of *Discours de la servitude volontaire* (1576).

may be permanent, it is no less full of movement. There are modulations in the world of politics; depending on the situations and the values which predominate at a given moment, the political order will exercise more or less influence on the social structure. Naturally, this relative importance depends for a large part on the attitude of those who govern. To return to an expression applied to the sociological writings of Pareto, as long as there is a 'physiological link' between those who govern and the masses, a certain reversibility will continue to be at work. There will be, if not consensus, then exchange and legitimation.[34] This phenomenon is far from an exception: from the leaders of Antiquity to a certain business paternalism, through the equanimity of the Antonines and a certain ecclesiastical populism, there exists a type of power which is based above all on the real obligations of the leaders.[35] They are responsible for their authority and they must respond as much to famine and natural catastrophe as to economic or social disaster. The symbolic function they hold ceases or is fractured as soon as the equilibrium of which they are the guarantors no longer works.

Here it is not possible to develop this line of inquiry further. I only point to it in order to shed light on that form of the *puissance* of the masses which is 'aloofness'. Indeed, it is when the order of reversibility no longer exists (and the analysis of this breakdown can surely not be reduced to moralistic considerations) that one can see the development of attitudes of withdrawal.

In order to understand this development, let us refer once again to the metaphor of the 'black holes' which a certain number of us (Baudrillard, Hillman, Maffesoli) have borrowed from astrophysics. In a book intended not so much to popularize as to reveal, the physicist J.E. Charron showed how a black hole is a star whose increasing density gives birth to another space – a 'new universe', he said.[36] Proceeding by analogy (a practice that many refuse, although it retains some interest for our discipline) we can formulate a hypothesis that at certain periods of history, when the masses are no longer interacting with those in government, or *puissance* is completely dissociated from power, the political universe dies and sociality takes over. Furthermore, I believe that this movement is a swing of the pendulum, proceeding by saturation: on the one hand, direct or indirect participation predominates; on the other hand, there is an increased emphasis on everyday values. In the latter case, one can say that sociality preserves energies which in the political reign tend to take place in public.

Moreover, it is interesting to note that, in general, this refraining from public expression goes hand in hand with an 'expenditure' in the existential sphere (physical pleasure, hedonism, *carpe diem*, the body, sun-worship). In the bourgeois reign, the opposite effects predominate: coldness, an economy of (and in) existence and an expenditure of energy in the public realm (the economy, public service, grand inspiring ideologies . . .).

Be that as it may, it is against this backcloth that one must understand a whole series of events that underline a growing detachment from the abstract and general public sphere. The 'silent majority', which in fact is no more than a conglomeration of juxtaposed or intersecting groups and networks, can no longer be defined in terms of an abstract, common front decided in isolation. It can no longer be characterized on the basis of a goal to be realized, that is as the proletariat, an agent of social change, or as the object of a structural and congenital mark: the feeble and/or childish populace which must be led by the hand or protected. Between these two opposites lie a number of ideologies and actions in which politicians (conservatives, revolutionaries, reformers), public officials, social workers and economic forecasters are still engaged. In fact, the debate has already moved elsewhere. Indeed, by pursuing the hypothesis of the saturation of the political order, one can explain the attitude of the masses – the cause of so much worry to political commentators and analysts – by virtue of the fact of a latent anthropological reticence with regard to those powers which continue to assert themselves from time to time and with varying degrees of effectiveness according to time and place. As an example, in order to understand this phenomenon one may refer to those countries – like the Sicily portrayed in Lampedusa's *Guépard** – which were able to preserve their originality owing in whole or in part to the many invasions they suffered. Because they knew enough to keep their heads down and rely on their cunning, the inhabitants were able to maintain their particular customs intact. In Bouglé's analysis of India, he states: 'All sorts of authorities have tried to rule over these immense masses: the people have seen empires succeed each other and principalities multiply without equal. The truth remains that all governments of whatever kind, have only rested on the surface of the Hindu world. They never reach . . . its deepest sense.' These remarks seem most up to date where the sociologist explains the impossibility of mastering the 'real' country, owing to the caste system. He makes the following delicious remark: the Hindus, because of this fact, 'seem made for subjugation by the entire world, without being assimilated or unified by anyone'.[37] At the risk of causing Bouglé to turn in his grave, we can extrapolate this remark heuristically in order to state that the 'non-domestication' of the masses, which constitutes their most solid defence against the various dominations, is based above all on *pluralism*. In the Indian example, it may be the caste system; in Sicily, we may talk of the *puissance* of localism, the many 'countries' and 'families' that make up this island. In our societies, it could be the various networks, affinity and interest groups or neighbourhood ties that structure our megalopolises. Whatever the case, *puissance* is set against power, even if *puissance* can only advance in disguise, to avoid being crushed by power. If the many examples of history are any guide, however, it is possible to show that the sketchy details of today, whose birth we can observe, will become much

---

* *Transl. note*: *Le Guépard* (1958), a novel by the Italian writer Guiseppe Tomasini, Prince of Lampedusa (1896–1957), presents a chronicle of Sicilian life between 1860 and the turn of this century.

clearer in the decades to come. With every resurgence of this 'polytheism of values' as used by Weber, and which, apart from a few researchers brave enough to weather the ambient conformity,[38] seems to worry right-thinking people, a relativization of the unifying structures and institutions is under way. There is no reason to get upset about it; on the contrary, since the effervescence flowing from this polytheism is on the whole the surest sign of a renewed dynamism in all aspects of social life, whether the economy, spiritual or intellectual life or, of course, the new forms of sociality. It is striking to note that, as a rule, the withdrawal from the political sphere seems to shed light on the aforementioned dynamism. This withdrawal is in fact the reactivation of the vital instinct of preservation, of conservation in oneself. It is the demonic figure found in all myths and religions, the biblical Satan who refuses to be subjugated. Although it is occasionally destructive, the satanic figure continues to exert a basic function. In this manner, it ties in with the *puissance* of the masses. I have stated elsewhere that there has always been a 'demonic wisdom' at work in the social body to which we can surely attribute, at least in part, this faculty of retreat, of refusal to be part of a structure. It is notable that, even in the nineteenth century, a time when the workers' movement was just getting organized, the movement found its expression in many tendencies: communist, anarchist, cooperative, utopian, all with their own infinite subdivisions. What can this mean, other than that no political institution can claim a monopoly? As Poulat notes correctly: 'the popular masses retain a certain degree of independence . . . by which they are only paying back the upper classes'.[39] I would add: even when certain members of the upper classes claim to speak in the name of the masses, or to lead them, which amounts to much the same thing. Those who are 'not one of us' can never be completely trusted since, from time immemorial one knows that those who, inspired by the *libido dominandi*, rely on the masses to attain power are bound, for whatever valid-sounding reason, to practise a realpolitik which has but faint origins in the popular will.

It would be easy to digress *ad infinitum* on this theme; however, one need only show that this 'aloofness' is much more stubborn than the temporary or superficial loyalties to such and such a party or political creed. For my part, I see it as an anthropological structure which, by way of silence, ruse, battle, passivity, humour or derision, is well able to stand up to the ideologies, teachings and claims of those who wish either to dominate or be the salvation of the masses, which in this case are not so very different. Such aloofness does not mean that one pays no attention at all to the game of politics/politicians, but rather the contrary, precisely because it is seen as a game. I have proposed calling it the 'politics of the Bel Canto': the content matters little, as long as the song is beautifully sung. We know that political parties are increasingly concerned with getting their message across, rather than explaining the fine print. It is impossible to go into this trend in any depth, but it seems as if it is the product of popular relativism: in order to reply to disengagement and retreat, image is carefully cultivated. Passion is addressed more than reason and the variety show aspect of political rallies is much more important than the politician who increasingly finds him- or herself reduced to the role of a Hollywood star.

It is with this in mind that one can understand how it is possible to 'pretend', while still caring about the actions and the sincerity of the political salesman. In my book on everyday life, I showed the importance of the category of duplicity: this trivial game of deception which plays such a strong part in all our lives.[40] It is within this framework that one can appreciate the attitudes of 'pretending' as manifestations of *puissance*. Duplicity is what allows us to live. Let us remember the following aphorism of Nietzsche's: 'Everything that is profound loves the mask . . . I would say that, around every profound spirit there continually grows a mask.'*

This remark is not just applicable to the solitary genius, it is also a fact of the collective genius. To be aware of this is to introduce into sociology an ontological vitalism. It is within this context that we can understand the peasant's cunning, the mockery of the worker; more generally the sense of resourcefulness which, although we cannot put it into words, manifests a structural distrust of all that is instituted, while at the same time affirming the irrepressible aspects of life. However, since it is not possible to express openly this distrust and this will to live, one uses the 'perverse' (*per via* = detour) procedure of simulated acquiescence.

This is the old anthropological structure of magic, which can yet be found in persistent rituals and superstitious practices. One participates and then withdraws; this is why these rituals sum up the ambivalence of man, at once *sapiens* and *demens*. With a different application in mind, Morin describes this double-dealing as 'aesthetic participation'.[41] It may be believed that the popular devotion to such television series as *Dallas* is the expression of this deeply engrained sense of play. Although this 'aesthetic' attitude is at work with respect to the symbolic powers of television, art and school, there is no reason why it should not also apply to the realm of politics, if only as a function of what we have called its spectacular or theatrical manifestations. A vote cast for such and such a deputy or party may go hand in hand with a deep conviction that nothing will change with respect to the 'recession', which is what we now call insecurity or increased unemployment.

But by 'pretending', we are participating magically in a collective game which reminds us that something like the 'community' has existed, does exist or will exist. It is a question of aestheticism, derision, participation and reticence all at once. It is above all the mythical affirmation that the masses are a source of power. This aesthetic game or sentiment is collectively produced just as much for oneself as for the power which orchestrates it. At the same time, it allows one to remind this power that it is only a game, and that there are limits which must not be breached. What

---

* *Transl. note*: F. Nietzsche, *Beyond Good and Evil : Prelude to a Philosophy of the Future*.

is called the versatility of the masses (one vote for the Left, one vote for the Right) can be interpreted in this way, occasionally even expressing itself paroxysmally. All political minds have pondered this phenomenon; this versatility, a veritable sword of Damocles, is in control of the game, since it haunts the politicians who will decide on their strategy or tactic as a function of it; it is one of the manifestations of *puissance* which, strictly speaking, determines power. A singular remark of Montesquieu sums it up best: 'The people has always either too much action or too little. At times, with the strength of one hundred thousand arms, it topples all; at other times, one thousand feet march as insects'.[42] Thus, passivity and activity are all rolled into one, in a way that escapes logic or reason. From a purely rationalistic perspective, we cannot trust the masses. Basing himself on a few historical examples, Julien Freund showed this ambivalence which is all the more remarkable during paroxysmal situations: wars, riots, factional fighting, revolutions.[43] In fact, from this perspective, what can be called the stochastic strategy of the masses is in fact the expression of a true vital instinct. In the manner of warriors on the field of battle, its zigzags help it to duck the bullets of the authorities.

Referring to a particularly resonant emblematic figure from Italy, one may compare the versatility of the masses to la Pulcinella in whom the contradictory is united: 'My destiny is to be a weathervane: servile and rebellious, moron and genius, courageous and cowardly.' In some versions of this myth, Punch is a hermaphrodite or a child of noble birth and/or the offspring of peasants. What is certain is that he is the incarnation of that absolute duplicity (double, *duple*) which permits one to escape the various political upheavals and restorations. It is not without coincidence that this figure has its origins in teeming, lively Naples.[44]

Furthermore, it so happens that its perpetual ambiguity is expressed in the form of derision for the powers that be and all forms of institution, whether of political or even familial, economic or social nature. By extrapolating, one may say that in this attitude there is no question of attacking head-on the overarching powers, which is the job of political organizations, but rather of cheating and sidestepping. To restate a situationist expression, rather than 'fighting alienation with alienated methods' (bureaucracy, political parties, militancy, deferment of pleasure), one uses derision, irony, laughter – all underground strategies which undermine the process of normalization and domestication which are the goals of the guarantors of the external and hence abstract order. As far as our society is concerned, this domestication of mores leads to what I have termed 'social asepsis'.[45] This has as a consequence the ethical crisis and the social dismantling we are currently witnessing.

Nevertheless, irony inhibits this domestication from being total. From the dionysiac laughter of the bacchanal, at the expense of the astute administrator Pentheus, to the sad smile of the good soldier Schweik, updated for modern Czechoslovakia, the list of mind-sets that betray nonconformity is a long one. This is particularly annoying for those in power, who obviously try to master the masses but who know only too well that in order for this mastery to be long-lasting it must be accompanied by the control of men's minds. The aloof quality of irony, albeit in a minor way, introduces a rift into the logic of domination. Jests, fabrications, pamphlets, songs and other popular word-play and even the whim of 'public opinion' allow us to measure its development.

And there has never been an era nor a country where this defence mechanism has not produced positive results. We can see it at work in recent years in France or the US, for example. It may be as a consequence of an outbreak of scandal with inevitable political reverberations or the progressive discrediting which gradually eats away at the legitimacy of those in power. I would only point out quickly that, like late eighteenth-century France or early twentieth-century Russia, this climate of subversive irony generally precedes great revolutionary upheavals.

In his remarkable book on the formation of Brazilian society, Gilberto Freyre gives many examples of what he calls the 'people's malice'. Thus, in a country where the colour of one's skin is of great significance, one can hear nicknames and puns which play on the 'negroid traces in illustrious families', as well as a whole series of traits which highlight their alcoholism, their avarice or erotomania.[46] It is not at all certain that these are moralistic reactions, but rather a manner, if only symbolic, of relativizing power. This can be seen in particular in the example above as underlining all that which, against their will and despite their stated ideologies, the dominant classes owe to the turpitude and weaknesses of human nature.

This points to one of the hypotheses underlying previous reflections on the *puissance* of the masses: that of vitalism, or a natural evolution which translates to the social plane the whole dynamic of the *phusis*.* Laughter and irony are an explosion of life, even and especially if this life is exploited and dominated. Derision underlines that, even in the most difficult conditions imaginable, one is able, together with or against those responsible, to reappropriate one's existence and, in relative terms, to enjoy it. This is a thoroughly tragic perspective, which is aimed less at changing the world than getting used to and tinkering with it. While it is true that we cannot change death (the paroxysmal form of alienation), we can get used to it, play with it and soften it.

It is thus quite natural that irony and humour lead us to the festive dimension, in which the tragic, as we are too often liable to forget, plays an important role. Borrowing the terminology of Georges Bataille, one can say that the 'expenditure' sums up both the natural vitalism of the masses and the derisory aspect of power (cf. the mechanisms of inversion, the fools' festivals, etc.). This 'expenditure' is but a paroxysmal way of expressing irony, laughter or humour and in an almost institutional manner. It is at the same time both cause and effect of this social *puissance* which is left unexhausted by the games and arcana of power. Plato was

---

* *Transl. note*: 'phusis' = 'growth'.

interested only in the elite and was unconcerned with the ordinary man. He even thought that, in order to avoid being exposed to the temptations of power, the masses needed to be ruled by an 'intelligent hedonism' which was 'the best practicable guide to a satisfactory life'.[47] This lesson was heeded by many tyrants and various powers who were unstinting in providing their populace with its quantum of games in order to keep the peace. Some have pointed out, not unjustly, that this role is still played by various shows, sports and other soothing television programmes. In the familiar context of a soft totalitarianism, a programme such as *Les Chiffres et les lettres** has replaced bloody circus games. This thematic is not untrue, but it does not take into account the structural ambivalence of human existence. The black and white absolutism that has prevailed in criticism, offspring of the Enlightenment, and which continues to prevail in our discipline, is incapable of comprehending the conflict of values that underpins all social existence. One may however be convinced that the fecundity of sociology lies in this acknowledgement. In this respect, it is interesting to note a very fine analysis by the sociologist Henri Lefebvre, representative emeritus of this critical approach, in which he cannot help but underline the 'double dimension of everyday life: trite and profound'. In somewhat dated terms and while playing down his remarks, he is obliged to recognize that 'in the daily rituals, the alienation, fetishism and reification . . . they all produce an effect. At the same time, needs, becoming (to a certain extent) desire, encounter objects and appropriate them'.[48] In making this reference, I am trying above all to emphasize the impossibility of reducing the polysemy of social existence. Its strength resides precisely in the fact that each of its acts is at once an expression of a certain alienation and of a certain resistance. It is a mixture of the ordinary and the exceptional, the morose and the exciting, the effervescent and the relaxing. This is particularly keenly felt in the area of play, which can be commercialized as well as being the realm of a real collective desire to reappropriate existence. I have explained this phenomenon in all of my previous books; it seems to me one of the essential characteristics of the masses. This characteristic is more or less self-evident; but it translates far beyond the Judaeo-Christian notion of separation (good–evil, God–Satan, true–false) the fact that there is an organicity to things and that, in a differential manner, everything converges in their unicity. Along with traditional cultural festivals, the multiplication of village feasts, folk gatherings or better yet festive meetings grouped around the agricultural produce of a given country are very instructive. Indeed, the celebration of wine, honey, nuts, olives etc., during the tourist season is highly commercial, but also reinforces collective ties, at the same time as it shows how these derive from nature and its bounty. In Francophone Québec, the

---

* *Transl. note*: a popular quiz show in France based on forming the longest word possible from randomly drawn letters, as well as devising a mathematical problem to arrive at a randomly chosen number.

Society of Popular Festivals has thus been able to punctuate the calendar with a whole series of gatherings around the theme of ducks, pheasant, blueberries, apples and so on. These replay the cycle of nature at the same time as they reinforce the collective feeling Québec has of itself.

This then is how an 'expenditure', whether commercial or recycled, as some cynics would put it, is an indication of resistance and *puissance*. To seek everyday pleasure, to live for the present and enjoy its fruits, to take pleasure in the good things in life – any analyst not yet detached from everyday life is able to observe such behaviour in every situation and instance which occur throughout the life of societies. 'The members of the working class have always been epicureans of everyday life.' In his book, R. Hoggart makes this pertinent remark and gives many examples. He underlines that this epicureanism is directly tied to the masses' distrust of politicians who supposedly have their interests at heart. Since we are aware of the illusory nature of their promises, their actions are generally greeted with scepticism and irony. 'One may die from one day to the next'; therefore, it is important to counter those who are always thinking of tomorrow or the day after by reaffirming the perhaps precarious rights of the present. This relativist philosophy is born of the harsh realities of life and underlies the aloofness and hedonism of the masses.[49]

Notes

1. E. Durkheim, *The Elementary Forms of the Religious Life*, New York, Collier, 1961.

2. Cf. the evolution of the history of art in W. Worringer, *Abstraction and Empathy: A Contribution to the Psychology of Style*, transl. M. Bullock, New York, International Universities, 1967. See preface to the French edition by Dora Vallier: Klincksieck, Paris, 1978, pp. 13–14.

3. Cf. M. Maffesoli, *Essais sur la violence banale et fondatrice*, Paris, Librairie des Méridiens, 2nd edition, 1984.

4. I have borrowed this scale of 'hyper' and 'hypo' from the endocrinology of Brown Sequart for my book *L'Ombre de Dionysos. Contribution à une sociologie de l'orgie*, Paris, Librairie des Méridiens, 1982; I am also indebted to G. Durand. Cf. especially his article 'La Notion de limite' in *Eranos*, 1980, Frankfurt am Main, Jahrbuch ed Insel, 1981, pp. 35–79.

5. Cf. for example A. Faivre, *Eckarthausen et la théosophie chrétienne*, Paris, Klincksieck, 1969, p. 14 or the study on Loisy by E. Poulat, *Critique et mystique*, Paris, Le Centurion, 1984.

6. Cf. C. Bouglé, *Essays on the Caste System*, Cambridge, Cambridge University Press, 1971; I would also refer to A. Daniélou, *Shiva et Dionysos, la réligion de la nature*, Paris, Fayard, 1979.

7. The title of my doctoral thesis, Grenoble, 1973, pursued in M. Maffesoli, *Logique de la domination*, Paris, PUF, 1976.

8. J. Lacarrière, *L'Été grec*, Plon, Paris, 1976, p. 148.

9. The *Thèse d'État* under way at the time of writing by Tufan Orel (Université de Compiègne) on vitalism will undoubtedly provide notable insight.

10. Cf. M. Lalive d'Epinay, *Groddeck*, Paris, Editions Universitaires, 1984, p. 24. Cf. pp. 125–134 for the fine bibliography.

11. Cf. the analysis by G. Durand, *Les Structures anthropologiques de l'imaginaire*, Paris, Bordas, 1969, p. 76, *et seq.* and his citation of G. Bachelard, *La Terre et les rêveries du repos*, Paris, Corti, 1948, pp. 56, 60, 270.

12. Cf. G. Simmel, *Problèmes de la sociologie des religions*, Paris, CNRS, no 17, 1964, p. 15.

13. Cf. J.E. Charron, *L'Esprit cet inconnu*, Paris, Albin Michel, 1977, pp. 83, 65–78.

14. Cf. G. Dorflès, *L'Intervalle perdu*, French transl., Paris, Librairie des Méridiens, 1984, p. 71, *et seq*; Cf. also G. Durand, *Les Structures anthropologiques*, p. 55. On Situationism and the labyrinth: *Internationale situationisme*, Amsterdam, Van Gennep, 1972. I have also written a short monograph on the labyrinth in Genoa, Doctoral notes, Urban Studies Research Unit, Université de Grenoble, 1973. Also on the importance of grottoes to Naples' vitality, cf. A. Médam, *Arcanes de Naples*, Editions des Autres, Paris, 1979, p. 46 and J.F. Matteudi, *La Cité des cataphiles*, Librairie des Méridiens, Paris, 1983.

15. Cf. M. Maffesoli, *La Conquête du présent. Pour une sociologie de la vie quotidienne*, Paris, PUF, 1979, Chapter 3, 'Sociality's space', pp. 61–74.

16. G. Simmel, 'La Société secrète', *Nouvelle revue de psychanalyse*, Gallimard, no. 14 (1976), p. 281.

17. J. Freund, *Sociologie du conflit*, Paris, PUF, 1983, p. 214.

18. Simmel, *Problèmes de la sociologie des religions*, p. 24.

19. Durkheim, *Elementary Forms*, p. 14.

20. On the social 'given', see M. Maffesoli, *La Violence totalitaire*, Paris, PUF, 1979. Cf. the work of A. Schutz, *Collected Papers*, Vols 1, 2 & 3, Amsterdam, Martinus Nijhoff Amsterdam, 1962–1966.

21. On this subject cf. the work of J. Zylberberg and J.P. Montminy, 'L'Esprit, le pouvoir et les femmes . . .' in *Recherches sociographiques*, Québec, vol. 222, no. 1, January-April, 1981.

22. R. Bastide, *Éléments de sociologie religieuse*, p. 197, cited by C. Lalive d'Epinay, 'R. Bastide et la sociologie des confins', *L'Année sociologique*, vol. 25 (1974), p. 19.

23. Poulat, *Critique et mystique*, pp. 219, 230 and the references to Ballanche: *Essais de Palingénésie sociale*, and to Lammenais: *Paroles d'un croyant*, note 26.

24. Poulat, *Critique et mystique*, p. 241.

25. B. Jules-Rosette, *Symbols of Change: Urban Transition in a Zambian Community*, Norwood, NJ, Ablex Publishing, 1981, p. 2. Regarding the importance of syncretist religions in large urban agglomerations such as Recife, cf. R. Da Matta, *Cidade e devoçao*, Recife, 1980.

26. E. Durkheim, *La Conception sociale de la religion, dans le sentiment religieux à l'heure actuelle*, Paris, Virin, 1919, p. 104 *et seq*, cited by Poulat, *Critique et mystique*, p. 240. Studies under way at the Centre d'études sur l'actuel et le quotidien (C.E.A.Q.) are attempting to highlight this conviviality ('keeping warm') among urban sects. Cf. as well the following definition: 'We call religious elements those emotional elements that form the internal and external aspects of social relations', Simmel, *Problèmes de la sociologie des religions*, p. 22.

27. If we wish to be more precise in the gradation of relationships, of any social life, of any sociability, of any sociality. M. Maffesoli, *La Violence totalitaire*, Chapter 2, pp. 70–115.

28. K. Mannheim, *Ideology and Utopia*, New York, Harcourt Brace, 1954, p. 192, *et seq.*; E. Bloch, *Thomas Münzer, théologien de la révolution*, Paris, Julliard, 1964.

29. Regarding the theme of explosion-relaxation, cf. Durkheim, *Elementary Forms*.

30. G. Le Bon, *The Crowd*, New York, Viking, 1960, p. 58.

31. Cf. on this subject the excellent work by L.-V. Thomas, *Fantasmes au quotidien*, Paris, Méridiens, 1984 and the work under way at the C.E.A.Q. (Paris V), as well as V. Gaudin-Cagnac. Also Maffesoli, *La Conquête du présent*, 'Le fantastique au jour le jour', pp. 85–91.

32. E. Durkheim, *Montesquieu et Rousseau, précurseurs de la sociologie*, Paris, Librairie Marcel Rivière, 1966, pp. 40, 108.

33. Cf. for example Freund's presentation of the subject: Freund, *Sociologie du conflit*, p. 31.

34. On the relationship between the elites and the masses, cf. the analysis by E.A. Albertoni, *Mosca and the Theory of Eliticism*, transl. P. Goodrick, London, Blackwell, 1987.

35. On this theme, cf. for example the analysis done by E. Poulat on the church, *Catholicisme, démocratie et socialisme*, Paris, Casterman, 1977, p. 121, or the one by

E. Rénan, *Marc-Aurèle ou la fin du monde antique*, Paris, Livre de Poche, 1984, Chapter 2, p. 40.

36. Charon, *L'Esprit, cet inconnu*, p. 216.

37. Bouglé, *Essays on the Caste System*, p. 131. On Sicily, refer to my analysis: Maffesoli, *Logique de la domination*.

38. Cf. for example M. Augé, *Le Génie du paganisme*, Paris, Gallimard, 1983.

39. E. Poulat, *Église contre bourgeoisie*, Paris, Casterman, 1977, p. 131. On this aloofness, cf. Maffesoli, *Essais sur la violence*, Ch. 3, p. 139. With respect to the 'demonic wisdom', cf. my article 'L'Errance et la conquête du monde', ibid., p. 157.

40. Maffesoli, *La Conquête du présent*, pp. 138–148.

41. E. Morin, *L'Esprit du temps*, Paris, Livre de Poche, 1984, p. 87. On television, cf. D. Wolton, *La Folle du logis*, Paris, Gallimard, 1983.

42. Montesquieu, *De l'esprit des lois*, Part I, Book II, Chapter 2.

43. Freund, *Sociologie du conflit*, p. 212, *et seq.*

44. Cf. remarks and references to Pulcinella in A. Médam, *Arcanes de Naples*, Paris, Editions des Autres, 1979, p. 84 and 118, *et seq.*

45. Maffesoli, *La Violence totalitaire*, pp. 146–147.

46. Cf. G. Freyre, *The Masters and the Slaves: A Study in the Development of Brazilian Civilization*, New York, Alfred E. Knopf, 1963, e.g. p. 268. On subversive laughter, cf. Maffesoli, *Essais sur la violence*, p. 78.

47. Cf. the analysis done by E. R. Dodds, *The Greeks and the Irrational*, Berkeley, University of California at Berkeley, 1956, Chapter 7: 'Plato, the irrational soul', p. 216 and the quotation of Plato, note 11, p. 211. For an analysis of contemporary 'free time', cf. J. Dumazédier, *Toward a Society of Leisure*, transl. E. McClure, New York, Free Press, 1967.

48. H. Lefebvre, *Critique de la vie quotidienne*, Vol. II, Paris, l'Arche éditeur, 1961, pp. 70–71. These passages are symptomatic of the difficulty an author faces when reality does not conform to his *a priori*.

49. R. Hoggart, *La Culture du pauvre*, French transl., Paris, Editions de Minuit, 1970, p. 183. This book's interest cannot be overestimated; it is the fruit of an author who comes out of the milieu he describes.

3
SOCIALITY VS. THE SOCIAL

1. Beyond politics

As a general rule, the intellectual will approach a subject *in absentia*, investigate and then present his diagnosis. Thus, our discipline shows a certain inborn mistrust of the common sense of the masses ('the worst of metaphysics,' stated Engels). This mistrust is lacking somewhat in originality; but it is deeply rooted in the collective memory of the scholar, undoubtedly for two principal reasons: on the one hand, the masses* are shamelessly preoccupied, i.e. without hypocrisy or desire for legitimation, with the materiality of life; with the near-to-hand, one might say, in contrast with an ideal or a deferment of pleasure. On the other hand, the masses have escaped the great numbers game, the quantifying, a concept which has always belonged to theoretical procedure. We can sum up this concern with a saying of Tacitus: 'Nihil in vulgus modicum' ('the multitudes have no measure': *Annals I*, 29) or with Cicero's powerful expression 'immanius belua' ('the most monstrous animal': *Republic* II, 45). It would be easy to multiply remarks of this type concerning the masses; such comments reproach them, in varying degrees of euphemism, for their monstrosity: the fact that they do not easily lend themselves to being labelled.

It is in this Ciceronian tendency that we can place Durkheim's fear of a 'spontaneous sociology' or even the scorn heaped by Pierre Bourdieu on the cultural jargon and the bric-à-brac of notions constituting popular know-how.[1] Anything heterogeneous or complex is repugnant to the administrators of knowledge, just as it worries the bureaucrats of power. By referring to Plato and his desire to advise the Prince, we may then understand that the close ties between knowledge and power go back very far indeed.

Something very specific is inaugurated however with the advent of modernity. The French Revolution brought about a radical transformation of political life, as well as of the role the intellectual was called upon to play within it. One can refer to an analysis by Nisbet, who stated that 'politics now became an intellectual and moral way of life'. It is possible to discourse at length on this fact; however, one can say that it is the very foundation of the whole of nineteenth- and twentieth-century political and

---

* I mean, of course, the people as 'myth' (cf. note 1).

social thought. But it also explains the near-impossibility of our understanding anything which strays from the realm of the political. For the protagonist of the social sciences, the people or the mass are the object and field which remain his private territory. This gives him a rationale and justification, but at the same time it is rather difficult to speak of with any degree of serenity. The dogmatic *a priori* and preconceptions proliferate, which, according to a logic of 'ought', will try to mould the masses into a 'subject of history' or some such commendable and civilized entity. It is but a short step from scorn to abstract idealization, given that this movement is not irreversible: if the subject turns out not to be a 'good' one, then one returns to the initial evaluation. This is a sociology which 'can only recognize a social entity that is always restored to the order of the state'.[2]

In fact, the masses as such, in all their ambiguity and monstrosity, can only be perceived in a pejorative sense by the political intellectual, who measures everything by the yardstick of the project (*pro-jectum*). At best, the people's (thought, religion, way of life) is considered as proof of its inability to be *something else*, an inability which must thus be corrected.[3] As a matter of fact, we could try applying this criterion to ourselves and see whether that which characterizes us is not in fact this inability to understand the something else which is the people! It is a shapeless mass, at once mob-like and idealistic, generous and wicked, in short, a contradictory mixture which, like any other living thing, is based on a paradoxical tension. Can we not see such ambiguity for what it is?: the rather chaotic, indeterminate mass which in a quasi-intentional way has as its sole 'project' its perdurability in existence. Taking into account the natural and social impediments which abound, this is no mean feat.

Let us take a step or two back. To paraphrase Machiavelli, we could consider the thinking of the public square rather than that of the palace. This concern never disappears: from the cynic of Antiquity to the populist of the nineteenth century, several philosophers and historians have pursued this course. At various times, the primacy of the 'village point of view' over the intelligentsia is even proclaimed;[4] but it is becoming crucial at a time when 'villages' are burgeoning within our megalopolises. This is not just any state of mind, pious vow or shallow proposal, but rather a necessity which corresponds to the spirit of the times. This can be summarized as follows: it is the 'local', the territorial and proxemic that determines the life of our societies and anything which appeals to local knowledge and no longer to a projective and universal truth. Undoubtedly, this requires the intellectual to be able to make himself a part of the very thing he is describing; to experience himself, and why not, as a kind of 'modern *narodnik*',[5*] the protagonist and observer of an everyday knowledge. But there is another, equally important consequence, which is to be able to highlight the permanency of the popular thread running through all political and social life.

---

* *Transl. note*: referring to the Russian populist movement of the nineteenth century.

This means that History and significant political events are above all the creation of the masses. In his writings on the philosophy of history, Walter Benjamin drew our attention to this point; in his own particular style, Gustave Le Bon remarked that the kings were not the cause of the Saint Barthelomew's Day massacre or the religious wars, any more than Robespierre or Saint-Just were responsible for the Terror.[6] There may be processes of acceleration or personalities who may be considered as necessary vectors; there are undoubtedly objective causes which act, but none of these is sufficient. They are simply ingredients which need, in order to be combined, a specific *puissance*. This *puissance* may take different names, like 'effervescence' (Durkheim) or *virtu* (Machiavelli); it is completely undecidable. Nevertheless, it is this 'je ne sais quoi' which acts as a glue. It is only after the fact that we are able to dissect objective reason from such and such an action, which will from then on seem frigid, too predictable, completely unavoidable; whereas we know that it is dependent above all, in both the literal and figurative senses, on a mass in heat. Witness Canetti's splendid description of the fire at the Vienna Courthouse in which the police were acquitted of murdering workers. 'That was forty-six years ago, and the excitement of that day still lies in my bones . . . . Since then, I have known very precisely that I need not read a single word about what happened during the storming of the Bastille. I became a part of the crowd, I dissolved into it fully; I did not feel the least resistance to what it did.'[7] One can clearly see how out of the fire of common emotion a compact and solid block is forged; how every single person is melded into a whole with its own autonomy and specific dynamic.

We could give many examples of these, examples which may be either paroxysmal or rather anodyne; nevertheless they all underline the existence, in the narrowest sense of the term, of an 'ex-static' experience at the core of this being-together in motion which is a revolutionary or political mass. This experience in fact owes very little to the logic of the project. Thus, appearances to the contrary, the above-mentioned *puissance*, which is both cause and effect of the societal symbolism, can be termed a sort of *underground centrality* which we find constantly in individual histories and communal life.

In *Ideology and Utopia*, Karl Mannheim was able to sum up this view: 'There is thought to be an intuitive and inspired source of history which actual history only imperfectly reflects.'[8] This is a mystical, even mythical perspective, but one which sheds light on a number of aspects of the concrete life of our societies. Moreover, the mystical is a more popular derivation than one might suspect, at least as far as its rootedness is concerned. In its etymological sense, it refers to a logic of union: that which unites the initiates among themselves – a paroxysmal form of religion (*re-ligare*).

One will remember that Karl Marx defined politics as the secular form of religion. Thus, in the context of these remarks, and forcing the connection somewhat, it would be utterly inept to say that in weighing human histories, the emphasis placed on the mystico-religious perspective relativizes the political investment. The former favours above all being-together, whereas the latter grants primacy to action and the finalization of that action. In order to illustrate this hypothesis with an up-to-date example (and everything has its use for understanding the spirit of the times), we may recall that Zen thought (Ch'an) and mystic Taoism, which are deeply rooted in the Chinese masses, are regularly resurgent and always in opposition to the instituted forms of the ideology and official policy of the Chinese state. The fragmentation of the concept and the spontaneity and proximity they induce allows them to favour a half-hearted resistance or an active revolt by the masses.[9] That is to say, the mysticism as I just described it is a popular repository where, beyond individualism and its projective activism, experience and imagination reinforce one another; their synergy forming these *symbolic wholes* which are the basis, in the strongest sense of the word, of any societal life.[10] This has nothing whatever to do with the spasmodic relationship uniting the subjective aspect of a close intimism and the objectivism inherent in the economic-political conquest. Rather, these symbolic wholes must be understood as matrices, or in an organic manner; the various elements of the worldly context intertwine and cross-fertilize, giving rise to an irrepressible vitalism which ought to be explored in detail.

Naturally, it must be pointed out that the religious space in question here has nothing to do with the usual manner of understanding religion in the official Christian tradition. This is particularly so on two essential points: on the one hand, with respect to the equivalence of religion and *interiority*, and on the other, with respect to the relationship generally seen between religion and *salvation*. Moreover, these two points could be summarized by the individualist ideology which draws a privileged relationship between the individual and the deity. Indeed, in the image of Greek polytheism, one can conceive of an idea of religion which above all insists on the being-together, on what I called 'immanent transcendence' – another way of describing the *puissance* which binds together small groups and communities.[11] Of course, this is a metaphorical perspective which allows us to understand how the diminished presence of the political goes hand in hand with the development of these small 'oracles' (P. Brown) which are both cause and effect of the multiplication of numerous contemporary tribes.

Let us also state, if only by allusion, that, although the Christian religion was officially and doctrinally soteriological and individualist, its practice by the masses was otherwise convivial. It is not possible to broach this subject in this limited space; however, we may point out that, before becoming dogmatized in faith, popular religiosity – pilgrimages, the cult of saints and other various forms of superstition – was above all an expression of sociality. More important than the purity of doctrine, it is the communal life or survival which preoccupies the basic communities. The Catholic Church did not fall into this trap, since, in an almost intentional way, it has avoided restricting itself to being a Church of the pure. First, it fought against heresies which sought to circumscribe it in such a logic (such as Donatism); second, it reserved the 'withdrawn' aspect of the priesthood, monachism and *a fortiori* hermitism to those who wished to heed and live the 'words of the gospel'. For the rest, the Church firmly maintained a multitudinous dimension which at times flirted with moral or doctrinal laxity. Such a perspective can be seen in the practice of indulgences which led, as we know, to Luther's revolt, or the benevolence of the court Jesuits which so displeased Pascal. This 'multitudinousness' can be linked to the notion of the repository mentioned earlier. It makes a group responsible for the sacred trust which is the collective life.[12] Thus, popular religion is truly a symbolic whole which permits and reinforces the proper functioning of the social bond.

As a form of amusement, I will propose a first sociological 'law': The various forms of social structuring are only worthwhile in so far as they remain adequate for the popular base which has acted as a support.

This law is applicable to the Church, just as to its worldly manifestation: politics. Renan said 'A Church cannot last without its people'[13] and the various decadent periods that are scattered throughout human history could be seen in the light of such a remark. The disconnection from the base causes institutions to become hollow and empty of meaning. However, against this, the perspective this book has adopted indicates and underlines forcefully that although sociality can periodically structure itself in institutions or specific political movements, it transcends them all. To reuse a mineralogical image, they are but pseudo-metamorphoses, taking part in a matrix which outlives them. This perdurability is what interests us and which also explains how the massive political disengagement we can see around us today is in no way a correlative of an accelerated dismantling, but rather a sign of renewed vitality. This perdurability is a mark of the divine, which is not an overarching and external entity, but rather is located at the heart of the reality of the world, at once both its essence and its destiny. One may refer in this regard to the classic terminology of German sociology, for instance Tönnies' Gemeinschaft–Gesellschaft opposition or Weber's 'communal relationships' (*Vergemein-schaftunge*) and 'associative relationships' (*Vergesellschaftunge*).

The community ethos identified by the first group of expressions refers to a common subjectivity, a shared passion, whereas anything which has to do with society is essentially rational in nature: it is a case of value rationality (*Wert*) or instrumental rationality (*Zweck*). One of Weber's writings elucidates this point: he notes that all associative relationships which 'spill over the framework of goal-oriented association . . . may give rise to sentimental values which surpass the objective established through free will'. He goes on to say that a community may orient itself to a certain rationality or finality. Thus, one can sometimes see that 'a kinship group is like a community and on the other hand, it functions and is seen as "associative" by its members'.[14] In this way, Weber underlines that there can be an evolution and a reversion from one form to another. It is of course understood that the community dimension is the founding moment; this is particularly obvious in the case of cities which are based on 'kinship groups' or on 'sectarian associations'. Therefore, we must consider both this movement and its foundations. Indeed, in the combinatorial logic from which social structures are constituted, the repositioning of such and such an element, or even its saturation, can lead to a significant qualitative difference.* Thus, the end of a certain form can help us to understand the resurgence of another.

Besides religion and the community as I have just described them, there is another notion which deserves consideration: the masses. This term may be used without attaching to it any particular connotation, just as one can use the word 'social' in its widest possible sense. One can also show that its acceptance may serve as an indicator of a series of practices and representations which are offered as alternatives to the political order. This is just what the 'populist' movement attempted. Amongst its many expressions, it is nineteenth-century Russian populism which best illustrates this current. It had its moment in the sun, its philosophers, and produced many economic-social accomplishments. Of course, it would soon be viewed, by Lenin especially, as the adolescent expression of true socialism, that is, scientific socialism. Explicable perhaps in the case of the peasant communes, there were hesitations apparent in Marxism which at the time was quickly hardening into dogmatism. I always get a special pleasure from quoting the famous letter of 8 March 1881 from Karl Marx to Vera Zasulíc in which he expresses his uncertainty with regard to the healthy populism existing in the Russia of the time. Indeed, one can make the case that the very reality of the people was completely foreign to the 'authoritarian tradition' (Marxism, Leninism, Stalinism) of the workers' movement and amongst those who formulated its theoretical expression. For, measured against the 'non-authoritarian' current (anarchist, federalist), the authoritarian perspective was essentially political. What is more, Marx had accurately assessed the debate with this statement: 'When one refers to the "masses", I wonder what kinds of dirty tricks are being played on the proletariat.' Parenthetically, since, whether in its reformist version or its revolutionary representation, the defenders of the proletariat in many cases held the reins of power and were well situated to speak with authority of the dirty tricks played on the masses![15]

Beyond the ukases to which it was subjected, populism was something much more than a drooling child awaiting maturity. One may postulate that it represented a prophetic form or, and it amounts to the same thing, a laboratory in which the economic-political significance was relativized. By emphasizing the central solidarity, the effects of community, the myth of the commune (the infamous Russian *obschina*) – in some cases by

---

* *Transl. note*: here Maffesoli is pursuing his 'chemical' metaphors referring to the 'combination' of various elements or their 'saturation'.

announcing that the machine would favour this community[16] – the populists could be very useful to anyone today who regards the present and the future in terms of autonomy or micro-societies. This populist perspective should be remembered when trying to understand the development of small businesses, cooperatives, the direct involvement which characterizes today's economy, in short, to understand the evolution from a *global economy to a global ecology*, which is less disposed to master the world, nature and society than collectively to achieve societies founded above all on quality of life.

In keeping with the spirit of the times, the last century and the beginning of this century saw *class* (or the proletariat) progressively take the place of the masses. This process, which occurred principally in relation to the prevalence of history and politics, is now well known. Increasingly, we are aware of the difficulty in defining a given class as well as recognizing that it is always *post festum* that we attribute a certain action or battle to the working class or the proletariat acting in full consciousness.[17] Moreover, most of the time this quality is only granted to those struggles that conform to the edicts of the political bureau. The remainder are variously termed provocations, compromises, betrayals or class collaborations. A parallel can be drawn between the fact that the working class is less and less liable to obey the various injunctions imposed on it, and an observably diminished belief in the governing force of History. *No future now:** the refrain of the younger generations has lesser but real reverberations on the whole of society. We may well ask ourselves if the harking back to the past (folklore, the revaluing of popular festivals, the return of sociability, a fascination with local history) is a way of escaping from the dictatorship of finalized, progressive history and thus a way to live in the present. This much is certain: in undercutting the majestic march of progress, the above-mentioned rejection of the future confers once more its letters of nobility on the masses. This is more than mere word-play: it brings out the aristocratic aspects of the masses.

Compared to the political order, this aristocraticism takes various forms: first of all, the scorn reserved for politicians of all stripes. I have already analysed this 'aloofness' of the people. There is much anecdotal evidence, many witticisms and remarks to attest to its veracity;[18] there is really no need to go on. On the other hand, the *versatility* of the masses is notable. This versatility, the flip-side of the 'aloofness', is a special form of insolence: we are interested in those who live by the *libido dominandi* only in so far as they are useful to us or can give us something. This includes the worldly religion as described above – *do ut des*: I give you my vote so that you can return the favour. But at the same time this demonstrates the clear non-adherence of the masses to the political domain. Their interest is entirely dependent on what they can get out of it.

---

* *Transl. note*: This expression appears in English in the text.

This insolent versatility is also a shield against all forms of power. Historians and sociologists continue to note the fact that the masses alternately worship then burn at the stake a wide variety of spokesmen and values; examples of this abound. The same could be said of ideologies and beliefs which are cast down by the same persons who only a short time ago were extolling their virtues.[19] Instead of getting bogged down in this paradox, it would be better to see this situation as symptomatic of a basic relativism with respect to overarching entities that have very little to do with the proximity in which the lines of solidarity are drawn. In the murky world of ideas and distant theories, all cats are black in the dark.

I previously mentioned the sacred duty of ensuring a continued existence. It is an embodied knowledge – in an animal way – that allows the masses to resist. In fact, what we call versatility could well be a way of guarding the essential and underplaying the factual, the *ad hoc*. The leadership battle in all its theatricality is not insignificant, especially as spectacle, however it is above all *abstract*, and most of the time without the positive and negative effects attributed to it. If the role of the politician is to excite – hence the required staging, the monumentality of the surroundings and the symbols in which he or she is draped – the role of the masses is simply to survive. Continued existence is all. It now becomes easy to understand the flip-flops and switched allegiances as a function of such a *concrete* responsibility. I will go a step further and say that, without burdening itself with excessive scruples or marginal uncertainties, *the people as mass* has as its central responsibility to triumph over ordinary death. This is a task undoubtedly requiring constant effort and a great reserve of energy. It is in this very aspect that we can speak of the nobility of the masses.

Going back to the dichotomy I posited between *power* and *puissance*[20] and playing around with the wording, I would propose a second law:

Power can and must deal with the management of life; puissance must assume the mantle of survival.

Naturally, I am playing with words here (which is necessary when one creates laws) and by 'survival' I mean that which at the same time founds, surpasses and guarantees life. Survival, in Cannetti's words, is 'the central situation of power' [i.e. *puissance*];[21] it signifies that permanent battle against a death in which we never wholeheartedly believe, whether that death is strictly speaking a natural one or whether it is a deathly imposition of the 'pro-jective' aspect of the political-economic order in whatever form it might take. One could compare this *puissance* to the *mana*, or other such expressions used to describe a collective force that transcends individuals or specific factions. In my opinion, I would draw a link between *puissance* and that 'most extreme concrete' (Walter Benjamin) which is everyday life. In the face of these histories made from both nothing and everything, Political History has no consistency for a collective memory that knows what is important.

Individual histories instead of History: this could well be the secret that explains the perdurability of societies. Beyond the political order, great cultural entities last across the centuries. The Greek, Roman, Arab and Christian cultures are, as far as we are concerned, based on an internal strength which is ever renewing, comforting and reinvigorating that which the powers tend to label, confine and, in the end, destroy. There is a collective will to live at work here that calls on the social observer to give it greater scrutiny. Simmel remarked that, in order to understand a political decision, one has to consider the whole life of the decision-maker and to 'judge those aspects of this life lying outside the bounds of politics'.

It is necessary *a fortiori* to surpass the confining framework of simple political finality in order to comprehend this ever-renewing basic decision known as the 'survival of the species'. The life of every man and woman, stubborn and irrepressible, forces us to do so. Must we see it, in the well-chosen words of Gilbert Renaud, as the expression of a 'recalcitrant sociality which resists domestication'?[22] In any case, I believe it will be difficult to avoid answering this question in the dying days of this century.

2. A natural 'familiarism'

Contrary to what is perhaps difficult to admit, it seems to me that there is a close rapport, with perverse overtones, between the individual and the political. Indeed, these two entities are the two essential poles of modernity. As I have already explained, the *principium individuationis* is the very thing determining the whole political-economic and techno-structural organization that was inaugurated with the rise of the bourgeoisie. Durkheim, who was certainly one of the great theorists of this process, noted peremptorily that 'the role of the state is in no way negative. It has the effect of guaranteeing the greatest degree of individualism the social state allows.'[23] The state as an expression *par excellence* of the political order protects the individual from the community. In an anecdotal way, it is interesting to note that those who were the most politicized in the sixties – those selfsame people who claimed that 'the personal is political' – also state with the same degree of conviction, and sectarianism even, the necessity of individualism. As far as they are concerned, there is no fundamental contradiction involved, but rather a difference in nuance.

Thus, it is fallacious to draw a parallel between the end of politics and the withdrawal into the self, or what is termed the return of narcissism. This is a short-sighted perspective; in fact, I would postulate that the saturation of the political form goes hand in hand with the saturation of individualism. Paying close attention to this fact is another way of investigating the masses. The conformism of youth, the passion for likeness within groups or 'tribes', the phenomena of fashion, standardized culture, up to and including the *unisexualization* of appearance, permit us to claim that what we are witnessing is the loss of the idea of the individual in favour of a much less distinct mass. This mass has no need of the notion of (individual, national, sexual) identity, which was one of the most important conquests of the bourgeois order. I believe that an investigation of the socio-anthropological basis of this fact can enlighten us as to the antinomic relationship that exists between the mass and politics. This being said, one must show that the mass has already existed, that it is a manifestation of the being-together and that it favours those elements that the political project (a tautology) omits or denies. First, we can highlight, if only cursorily, the changing and chaotic aspects of identity. In a Pascalian fashion, we can say that its truth varies according to temporal or spatial frontiers. This is an apt summary of a remark made by Weber: 'identity is never, from the sociological point of view, anything but a simply floating and relative condition'.[24] With great acuity, he notes that, according to the situation and the emphasis placed on a particular value, the relationship to the self, the other and one's surroundings can be modified. It is understood that 'identity' concerns the individual just as much as the grouping to which he or she belongs: it is when there is an individual identity at stake that a national identity can be found. In fact, identity in all its various manifestations is above all the willingness to be something determined. This acquiescence to be one thing or another is a process that generally arises later on in human or social evolution. The founding moments may be characterized by the pluralism of possibilities, the effervescence of situations, the multiplicity of experiences and values – all things which characterize the youthful stage of mankind and societies. For my part, I would say that this is a *cultural moment* of the highest order. On the other hand, the choice which eventually must be made in the development of a personal or social individuality and the fact that this effervescence and pluralism in its varied aspects are eliminated, generally leads to what may be called *civilization*. It is in the context of this second moment dominated by the morality of responsibility that politics thrives.

I am leaning here on the classic dichotomy of German thought formalized by Norbert Elias:[25] before civilizing and finalizing itself, a social structuring in whatever form it takes is a veritable cultural stockpot seasoned by all manner of additional ingredients. This stockpot is frothing, monstrous, exploding; but at the same time rich in future possibilities. We can make use of this image in order to show how the mass is self-sufficient; it does not project itself; is not finalized, politicized: it roils in its multiple experiences. This is why it is both cause and effect of the loss of the subject. In my own jargon, I would say that it is dionysiac, confusional. There are numerous contemporary examples which, with varying degrees of distinctness, support this view. At these moments, a 'collective spirit' is created in which aptitudes, identities and individualities dissolve; moreover, it in no way prevents this effervescent entity from being the site of a real reappropriation. Each and everyone participates in this global 'we'. Against the political, which paradoxically is founded on both the 'I' and the distant, the mass is constructed on the 'we' and on proximity. The development of life histories reinforces the fact that the subject often speaks in terms of 'we'.[26] Thus, the 'effervescent' community can signify both the loss of the individual and the reappropriation of the person.

We are beginning to touch on the distinction – classic since Mauss – between the person and the individual. Contemporary commentators such as Louis Dumont in France and Roberto Da Matta have looked at this question, with well-known results. In our own perspective, we can say that *de jure*, of course, the individual is free, contracting and joining in egalitarian relationships. This will serve as a basis for the project or, better still, the pro-jective attitude (i.e. politics). The person, on the other hand, is dependent on others, accepts a social context and joins an organic whole. In short, the individual has a function, whereas the person plays a role.[27] This distinction is an important one, for it allows us to understand that, just like the motion of the pendulum, the forms of aggregation may swing toward either the political or what I have been proposing for some time to call sociality. The mass, which has been called 'monstrous', belongs of course to the latter category.

However, this 'monstrosity' is worth noting, since it allows us to underline a not insignificant aspect of the mass, that is, its relationship to nature and the natural. The words cultural stockpot, effervescence and explosion have been used, all of which denote chaos and the uncivilized; and all of which re-emphasize the natural element that civilization attempts to deny. A short apologia by Walter Benjamin shows how the ability to recognize similarities seemed to him to be a vestige of 'the old compulsion to become the same as everyone else'. This resemblance could be either to people or to furniture, clothing, apartments, etc.[28] One can thus see how this *principle of similarity*, which is the basis of the 'we', the people and the mass, is an intermediary between the natural and the social worlds. There is no longer a separation between the cosmos and the social, nor within the social whole. On the contrary, we are witness to what may be deemed *the culturalization of nature and the naturalization of culture*.

Here one may find the origins of conformity, the significance of sentiment, whose impact on social life is only now beginning to be measured, or even a kind of ontological vitalism manifested in the ecological ambience of the moment. It seems to me that this desire for imitation and conformity – the above-mentioned vitalism, in short, the emerging and rather mystical 'correspondence' – may be one of the essential qualities of the popular mass. To return to the distinction mentioned earlier, it becomes possible to set against the unified individual the heterogeneous person capable of a multiplicity of roles.

> One may consider this person as nothing more than a *condensation* in perpetual disequilibrium; it is but one element of a phylum.

The poetic or later psychological assessment of the plurality of the person ('I is the other'), can in fact be interpreted from a socio-anthropological viewpoint as the expression of an infrangible continuum. We only have value in so far as we are tied to a group. Obviously, it matters little whether this link is real or imagined. Think of Proust who, after the death of his grandmother, imagines he sees her traits transferred to his mother. By taking up the image of the grandmother, by identifying with her, the mother assumes the role which must be perpetuated across the generations. With his typical sensitivity, Proust shows how death becomes part of an indestructible vitality. It is in no way a sign of a sociological imperialism to recognize as Halbwachs does that 'in reality we are never alone . . . since we feel inside ourselves a quantity of persons'.[29] Memory and collective remembrances, whether private, public or familial in nature, are what allow a neighbourhood or a town, *places* where lives are layered upon each other, to be inhabitable, indeed they make such places inhabitable, permitting the feedback* established between the group and the person. Naturally, this occurs in an organic way rather than according to the rational equivalency of the political order. Renan emphasized that for the early Christians the community's strength, and here I would use the term *puissance*, was based on the 'great founding men' (*megala stoikeia*). It is around their tombs that the first churches were constructed. In turn, Peter Brown has shown how such a sanctuary was simply called 'the place' (*o topos*) and that these places were progressively to become actual networks criss-crossing the lands of the Mediterranean. Whether in a religious or secular form, such a practice of foundation is found regularly throughout human history. Beyond the urban or rural monumentality (palace, church, various monuments), this feedback is expressed in all commemorative ceremonies. From the Cult of Auglaurus** of ancient Athens to all the national holidays of today, with the liturgical calendar of the Christian Church in between, the same process of anamnesis is at work: we exist as one body. In his analysis of Christian practice in Breton villages, the sociologist Yves Lambert notes a particularly revealing ceremony. In speaking of the recently departed, the priest sets the scene whereby the children of the village represent, *in equal number*, those who have passed away that year.[30] There can be no better illustration of the fecundity and the meaningfulness of the idea of the phylum. The social imagination constructs a history around it and is thus constituted as such.

We should examine in the light of these specific examples how all these groups are founded, in the simplest sense of the word, on the transcendence of the individual. This is what drives me to speak of an *immanent transcendence*, one which both surpasses individuals and springs from the continuity of the group. This is a mystical interpretation which can perhaps be compared to that other mysticism contained within a number of psychoanalytical traditions. For example, one could cite the case of Groddeck, whose vitalist roots are well known. 'We are experienced by the id', 'the id is a force', or 'the ego is nothing but artifice, a tool in the service

---

* *Transl. note*: 'feedback' appears in English in the text.
** Goddess of the City of Athens.

of the id' – many other similar examples could be cited.[31] It is sufficient to note that the 'id' in question can perfectly describe, in a metaphorical way, the mass, the people or the group at issue here; it is a force that acts, whereas we believe we act upon it; the ego is defined by it. Here we can find all the ingredients constituting the small contemporary masses. Furthermore, such an extrapolation allows us to highlight the close connection between these entities and the natural order. Thus, we can see this as something that goes beyond individualism in practice as well as in theory.

The collective memory is quite a good way to describe the symbolic system and the mechanism of the above-mentioned participation. Of course, the term is perhaps a bit clichéd or dated; but it clearly underlines the fact that, just as there is no individual existence, there can be no singular thought. Our consciousness is but a meeting ground, the crystallization of various currents which, with precise moments of symmetry, intersect, attract or repel one another. Even the most dogmatic ideologies are finished examples which can never be entirely unified. Thus we say that a personal thought follows from the 'inclination of a collective thought'.[32] This is confirmed in their own way by contemporary researchers in the areas of theoretical physics and biology, such as R. Sheldrake who uses the word 'chreode' (necessary direction) to describe the simultaneity of similar or close discoveries in laboratories more or less isolated from one another. These researchers have various starting points; but in sharing the same 'spirit of the times', they converge as a group – albeit a sketchy one – rippled with conflicts. We can say the same for the constitutive groupings of sociality; each, in its own way, creates its ideology and pieces together its own small history from disparate elements culled from the four corners of the Earth. They may be borrowed from local tradition or they may cut across these traditions. Nevertheless, their assemblage shows similarities which will constitute a sort of matrix, giving rise to and reinforcing individual representations.

It would seem that this way of posing the problem might allow us to go beyond the classic *pons asinorum* of the social sciences: is history determined by individuals or a collection of undifferentiated groups? Or expressed another way, is it providence's 'great man' or the blind action of the masses at work? On the one hand, we find reason and its piercing light; on the other we find instinct and its dangerous obscurity. Perhaps one can imagine a middle ground, a precise 'social form'[33] which can explain knowledge and eloquence as something other than an individual action or an imposed structure. The 'collective memory' (Halbwachs) and Mauss' *habitus* may be such a form constituted of both archetypes and the various intentionalities which allow us to adapt to these archetypes, to experience them, in a manner of speaking. This, precisely, is the spirit of the group, of the clan, whose synergy and juxtaposition produce the spirit of the times.

There is a continuous process of contact; an essential 'relationism' whereby 'the individual life history is corrected and expanded in the overall life history',[34] leading to the communal life. Interaction and inter-subjectivity create something qualitatively different from its constituent parts. The collective memory can thus serve, in the straightforward sense of the word, as a revelation of individual acts, intentions and experiences. It is a true sphere of communication, the cause and effect of the community. In this way, thought, which appears the most individualized, is but a part of a symbolic system at the very heart of all social aggregations. In its purely instrumental or rational aspect, thought individualizes, just as on the theoretical plane it dissects and discriminates; however, by being integrated into an organic complexity, that is by leaving room for affect and passion, as well as the non-logical, this same thought favours the communication of the being-together. In the first case this leads to political development as a factor uniting these disparate elements; in the second, one may highlight the pre-eminence of the group or the tribe, that is, not projected far into the future, but rather living for the most extreme concrete which is the present.

This is the simplest and most prospective expression of the saturation of the political and its supporting structure which is individualism. In their stead we see structures of communication which are both intensive and more compact. These affinity groupings revalue the ancient anthropological structure of the 'extended family'. This is a structure in which the negotiation of passion or conflict is carried out in close quarters. Without suggesting consanguinity, this grouping fits in nicely with the perspective of the phylum that is returning with the redeployment of naturalism. It is possible to state that the networks forming within our megalopolises are rediscovering a role for themselves of mutual aid, conviviality, commensality, professional support and sometimes even of the cultural rituals which characterized the spirit of the Roman *gens*.[35] Whatever name we give these groupings – kinship groups, family groups, secondary groups, peer groups*
– there is a process of tribalism at work that has always existed but which, according to the era, has been more or less valued. What is certain is that, at the present time, it is alive and well, holding sway in the cellars of our public housing projects or in the classrooms of the rue d'Ulm.**

Contemporary analyses such as those by Young and Willmot on the sociability of neighbourhoods in large cities, or those of Raynaud on the multiplicity of 'secondary groups', are ample evidence of the perdurability of an *esprit de corps*.[36] Such a spirit is both the cause and effect of interaction and reversibility, both of which are certainly among those elements most foreign to political life. It is to them, therefore, that one must look for the contemporary form which sociality is assuming.

In a single word, the *economy* of the political order, founded on reason, the project and activity, is giving way to the *ecology* of an organic (or holistic) order, integrating both nature and proxemics.

---

* *Transl. note*: 'peer groups' appears in English in the text.
** *Transl. note*: site of the prestigious École normale supérieure.

Although such a change may be cause for some disquiet in many ways, it is no longer possible to deny its reality. Durkheim attributed to secondary groups the dynamic which integrates individuals into 'the general torrent of social life'. Such an image has its own resonance. There is effervescence in the natural and social vitalism, especially at certain times when values and convictions seem less sure. Moreover, it is possible that these secondary groups which metastasize throughout the social body, while signifying by their presence the end of civilized modernity, paint a meaningful picture of the emerging societal form.

Notes

1. Z. Yavetz, *La Plèbe et le prince, foule et vie politique sous le haut-empire romain*, Paris, Maspéro, 1983. Cf. the many citations with respect to the distrust of the masses, for example p. 25; cf. again M. de Certeau, *Arts de faire*, Paris, Union générale des éditions, no. 10–18 (1980), p. 116 and P. Bourdieu, *Esquisses d'une théorie de la pratique*, Genève, Drez, 1972, p. 202. While accepting this idea of the people as 'myth', I think we must grant it the meaning Sorel does. Cf. J. Zylberberg, 'Fragment d'un discours critique sur le nationalisme', *Anthropologie et société*, vol. 2. no. 1 (1978); F. Dumont, 'Sur la genèse de la notion de culture populaire' in *Cultures populaires et sociétés contemporaines*, Québec, Presses universitaires du Québec, 1982, p. 33.

2. R. Nisbet, *The Sociological Tradition*, London, Heinemann Educational, 1970, p. 35. Also cf. G. Renaud, *A l'Ombre du rationalisme, la société québécoise de sa dépendance à sa quotidienneté*, Montreal, Editions St Martin, 1984, p. 182.

3. Cf. P. Brown, *The Cult of the Saints: Its Rise and Function in Latin Christianity*, Chicago, University of Chicago Press, 1981, p. 20, *et seq.* to see how popular religion is analysed from such a perspective.

4. F. Venturi, *Les intellectuels, le peuple et la révolution. Histoire de populisme russe au XIXe siècle*, Paris, Gallimard, 1972, p. 50.

5. This is one of Morin's expressions, *L'Esprit du temps*, Paris, Livre de Poche, 1984, p. 20; on the consequences for the researcher, cf. my book, M. Maffesoli, *La Connaissance ordinaire. Précis de sociologie compréhensive*, Paris, Librairie des Méridiens, 1985.

6. G. Le Bon, *The Crowd*, New York, Viking, 1960, p. 77.

7. E. Canetti, *The Conscience of Words*, transl. J. Neugroshel, New York, Seabury Press, 1979, p. 2.

8. K. Mannheim, *Ideology and Utopia*, New York, Harcourt Brace, 1954, p. 81.

9. Cf. K. Schipper, *Le Corps taoïste*, Paris, Fayard, 1982, p. 27. Basing myself on Van Gulik, I have shown that we can find popular explosions derived from Taoism up until the present day; M. Maffesoli, *L'Ombre de Dionysos. Contribution à une sociologie de l'orgie*, Paris, Librairie des Méridiens, 2nd edition, 1985, p. 67.

10. On the link between experience and symbolic wholes, cf. the reference to Dilthey by J. Habermas, *Knowledge and Human Interests*, London, Heinemann, 1978, p. 147.

11. On interiority and the soul, I am following the analysis of W. F. Otto, *Les Dieux de la Grèce*, preface by M. Detiennes, Paris, Payot, 1981; cf. p. 24 and the preface, p. 10; on the 'oracles', and the group vitality to which they lead, cf. P. Brown, *The Making of Late Antiquity*, Cambridge, Mass., Harvard University Press, 1978, p. 38.

12. On 'multidinousness', and sociality induced by popular religiosity, cf. E. Poulat, *Eglise contre bourgeoisie*, Paris, Casterman, 1977, pp. 21 and 24. Cf. also the good description of popular religion by Y. Lambert, *Dieu change en Bretagne*, Paris, Cerf, 1985, especially with respect to 'indulgences as a "spiritual insurance policy" ', cf. pp. 206–208.

13. E. Renan, *Marc Aurèle ou la fin du monde antique*, Paris, Livre de Poche, 1984, p. 354. For a critique of statism, cf. J. Zylberberg, 'Nationalisme-Intégration-Dépendance', *Revue d'Intégration européenne*, vol. 2, no. 2 (1979), p. 269, *et seq*.

14. M. Weber, *Economy and Society*, Berkeley, University of California Press, 1978, pp. 40–42 and also *The City*, Glencoe Ill., The Free Press, 1956.

15. Cf. K. Marx, *Collected Works of Marx and Engels*, New York, International Publishers, 1974, vol. 46, p. 71; F. Venturi, *Les intellectuels*, p. 45, outlines these hesitations with regard to the *obschina*.

16. Cf. again Venturi, ibid., vol. 1, p. 29.

17. On the substitution of the 'people' by class, cf. Mannheim, *Ideology and Utopia*, vol. 1, p. 60, *et seq.*; for a critique of the class struggle, cf. J. Freund, *Sociologie du conflit*, Paris, PUF, 1983, p. 72, *et seq*.

18. Cf. Maffesoli, *La Connaissance ordinaire*, p. 167, and *La Conquête du présent. Pour une sociologie de la vie quotidienne*, Paris, PUF, 1979.

19. Cf. Yavetz, *La Plèbe et le prince*, p. 38, *et seq*, p. 54 regarding the turnover of emperors, or the attitude towards Caligula; Le Bon, *The Crowd*, shows the same degree of versatility as to ideologies.

20. Maffesoli, La Violence totalitaire, Paris, PUF, 1979, Ch. I.

21. Cf. Canetti, *The Conscience of Words*, p. 16.

22. G. Simmel, *Les Problèmes de la philosophie de l'histoire*, Paris, PUF, 1984, p. 104, and Renaud, *À l'Ombre des rationalismes*, p. 257. His programmatic proposal as applied to sociality in Quebec seems to me full of promise.

23. E. Durkheim, *Leçons de sociologie*, Paris, PUF, 1969, p. 103. Also refer to M. Maffesoli, *La Violence totalitaire*, chapters 6 and 7 and *L'Ombre de Dionysos*, introduction.

24. M. Weber, *Essais sur la théorie de la science*, Paris, Plon, 1965; 'Essai sur quelques catégories de la sociologie compréhensive', 1913, French transl., p. 360.

25. Cf. N. Elias, *The Civilizing Process*, New York, Urizen Books, 1982.

26. I am referring here of course to Le Bon, *The Crowd*, p. 51 and J. Beauchard, *La Puissance des foules*, Paris, PUF, 1985. On life histories and the transition from the 'I' to the 'we', cf. M. Catani, *Tante Suzanne*, Paris, Librairie des Méridiens, 1982, pp. 15, 12. The term 'effervescence' is borrowed, of course, from Durkheim.

27. M. Mauss, *Sociology and Psychology*, London, Routledge and Kegan Paul, 1979, 'A category of the human mind: the notion of person'; L. Dumont, *Homo Hierarchus*, transl. M. Sainsbury, Chicago, University of Chicago Press, 1980. R. Da Matta, *Carnavals, bandits et héros*, Paris, Seuil, p. 210, *et seq*. On the Mafia cf. my article, 'La maffia comme métaphore de la socialité', *Cahiers Internationaux de Sociologie*, Paris, PUF, vol. 73 (1982).

28. W. Benjamin, *Sens unique*, Paris, L. N. Maurice Nadeau, 1978, p. 72.

29. M. Halbwachs, *La Mémoire collective*, Paris, PUF, 1950, p. 2.

30. Lambert, *Dieu change en Bretagne*, p. 45; Renan's analysis, *Marc Aurèle*, p. 126. On Brown's 'topos', cf. P. Brown, *Society and the Holy in Late Antiquity*, London, Faber and Faber, 1982, p. 6, *et seq*.

31. Cf. the fine presentation by M. Lalive d'Epinay, *Groddeck ou l'art de décontracter*, Paris, Editions Universitaires, pp. 24, 40.

32. Cf. Halbwachs, *La Mémoire collective*, p. 92.

33. In the sense used by Simmel, from whom I am borrowing liberally here. Cf. *Les Problèmes de la philosophie de l'histoire*, p. 74, *et seq*.

34. Dilthey, quoted by Habermas in *Knowledge and Human Interests*, p. 150, *et seq*.

35. Cf. the analysis by Durkheim to this effect, *L'Année sociologique*, vol. 1, pp. 307–332; 2, pp. 319–323 and C. Bouglé, *Essays on the Caste System*, Cambridge, Cambridge University Press, 1971, pp. 36, 50.

36. Cf. M. Young and P. Willmott, *Family and Kinship in East London*, Harmondsworth, Penguin, 1964; and E. Reynaud, 'Groupes secondaires et solidarité organique : qui exerce le contrôle social?' in *L'Année sociologique*, Paris, vol. 33 (1983), pp. 181–194. It is unfortunate that this second study implicitly relativizes the significance of recognized groups.

4

TRIBALISM

1. The affectual nebula

'Noi siamo la splendida realtà'. This slightly clumsy phrase was discovered in a lost corner of southern Italy, and without any claim to pretence, it sums up what sociality is all about. It contains in miniature all of sociality's various elements: the relativism of life, the grandeur and tragedy of the everyday, the burden of the world around us which we bear as best we can; all of which are expressed in that 'we' which forms the glue holding everything together. We have dwelled so often on the dehumanization and the disenchantment with the modern world and the solitude it induces that we are no longer capable of seeing the networks of solidarity that exist within.

In more than one respect, social existence is alienated, subject to the injunctions of a multiform *power*; however, there still remains an affirmative *puissance* that, despite everything, confirms the '(ever-) renewed game of solidarity and reciprocity'. This is a 'residue' that must be noted.[1] In short, it is possible to state that, in each era, a type of sensibility predominates; a style which specifies the relationships we forge with others. This stylistic view has become more and more pronounced (cf. P. Brown, P. Veyne, G. Durand, M. Maffesoli).[2] It allows us to account for the passage from the *polis to the thiase*, or from the political order to the realm of identification. Whereas the former favours individuals and rational, contractual associations, the latter places the emphasis on the affective, feeling dimension. On the one hand is the social, with its own consistency, a strategy and a finality, and on the other a mass in which aggregations of every order are crystallized – haphazard, ephemeral and hazily drawn. The establishment of the social and its theoretical acknowledgement were not easily won. The same applies today for that vague concept we call *sociality*. This explains the approximate, partial, and sometimes chaotic nature of any approach to the question, mirroring these uncertain groupings. But once again something important is at stake, and I would be willing to bet that the future of the discipline depends essentially on our ability to convey the frenzied activity under consideration.

In my opinion, the endless pointing to the examples of narcissism and the evolution of individualism, in a number of sociological or journalistic articles, represents thinking at its most conventional. They are of little merit unless to illustrate the profound upheaval occurring within the ranks of intellectuals who have difficulty understanding anything of the society which is their bread and butter and who thus try to impart a kind of meaning in terms appropriate to the moral and/or political realm in which they prosper. It is not my intention to fight a rearguard action; it is sufficient to show, however cut-and-dried it should appear, that *experiencing the other* is the basis of the community, even if it leads to conflict. Let me be perfectly clear: I have no intention of adding to the moral mush so trendy these days; rather, I would like to trace the outline of what could be a logic of identification. This identification is a certain metaphor, one that, in the case of the mass, can function without what is traditionally called dialogue, exchange, or other stuff and nonsense. The identification of the community can be completely disindividualizing by creating a diffuse union that does not require one's full presence for the other (referring to the political); it establishes rather a relationship in the emptiness – what I would call a *tactile relationship*. Within the mass, one runs across, bumps into and brushes against others; interaction is established, crystallizations and groups form.

We can compare this to Walter Benjamin's comments on Fourier's harmonious new world, a 'world in which morality no longer has any role', a world in which 'passions are engaged and become mechanized in their workings', a world in which, to use Fourier's own words, undefined and undifferentiated combinations and associations reign.[3] And yet, these tactile relationships, through successive sedimentations, create a special ambience – what I have called a *diffuse union*. I would like to suggest an image to help us in our reflections: at its beginnings, the Christian world was a nebula of entities scattered throughout the Roman Empire. This proliferation secreted that lovely theory of the 'communion of the saints'. This link was at once firm and flexible, but for all that, it ensured the solidity of the ecclesiastical body. It is this group effervescence and its precise ethos which was to give rise to the civilization of today. It is possible to imagine that we are face to face today with a sort of 'communion of the saints'. Electronic mail, sexual networks, various solidarities including sporting and musical gatherings are so many signs of an ethos in gestation. Such trends are the framework of this new spirit of the times which we call sociality.

Let us first specify that the phenomenological and comprehensive tradition has looked at this question in detail. I think particularly of Alfred Schutz who, in a number of his analyses, and especially in his article entitled 'Making music together', made a study of 'syntony' (*mutual tuning in relationship*) according to which individuals in interaction are epiphanized in a *vivid presence*.* Of course, at the root of this we find the face-to-face relationship; however, by a process of association, the whole of social existence is involved in this form of empathy.[4] Moreover, whether by contact, by perception or by look, the senses are always implicated in a

---

* *Transl. note*: The phrases in italic appear in English in the text.

syntonic relationship. As we shall later see, this sensitivity forms the substrate of the acknowledgement and the experience of the other. We may note here and now that from this sensitivity springs the 'meeting of minds', which is just another way of saying comprehension in its strongest sense. Although it should be the height of banality to say so, there is no harm in repeating that the originality of the sociological procedure lies in the fact that it is based on the *materiality* of the being-together.

God (and theology), the Mind (and philosophy), the individual (and economics) step aside for this regrouping. Man is never considered in isolation. And even when we grant, as I would tend to do, the prevalence of the imagination, it should not be forgotten that it derives from a social body and in return rematerializes there. It is not a case of self-sufficiency as such, but rather of constant retroaction. All mental processes arise from a relationship and its process of action and retroaction: the entire communicative or symbolist logic is founded thereupon. This is what Spann calls the 'idea of matching' (*Gezweiung*). This couple effect can be observed between parents and offspring, the master and his disciples, the artist and his admirers.[5] It is of course understood that this couple effect transcends the elements of which it is composed; this transcendence was a characteristic of the sociological perspective at its beginnings, only to be clouded by the medieval community. However, as the triumphant bourgeois order claimed individualism as a principal vector, this community model became increasingly left behind or served, *a contrario* only to justify the progressive and liberating aspects of modernity. It remains true nevertheless, that the corporatist and solidarist myths were present – for instance the statue of the Commander* – at the origins of these proceedings. Even Comte, the most positivist of sociologists, reformulates them in his religion of humanity. We are only too aware of his influence on Durkheim and French sociology; but what is less well known is that, through the work of W.G. Sumner, the solidarist myth struck a chord in American thought.[6]

Without labouring the point, we can demonstrate that solidarity or the religion of humanity can serve as the backcloth to the group phenomena we are witnessing today, especially in so far as the logic of identity is concerned. This latter phenomenon has served as the mainspring for the economic, political and social order which has reigned for over two centuries. But although it continues to function, its steamroller effect no longer has the same impact it once did. Thus, in order to seize the *shared sentiments and experiences* at work in the various social situations and attitudes of today, it is a good idea to take a different tack: the aesthetic angle seems to me to be the least bad. By aesthetics, I mean the etymological sense of the word, as the common faculty of feeling, of experiencing. Despite his rationalism, Adorno remarked that aesthetics could allow us to 'assist the non-identical in its struggle against the

---

* *Transl. note*: A character in Molière's *Don Juan*.

aggressive identification compulsion that rules the outside world'.[7] There is
no better way to sum up the efflorescence and effervescence of neo-
tribalism which, in various forms, refuses to identify with any political
project whatsoever, to subscribe to any sort of finality, and whose sole
raison d'être is a preoccupation with the collective present. All one has to
do is to refer to the research and monographs completed on youth groups,
affinity associations, small-scale industrial enterprises, in order to be
convinced. It only remains to conduct studies on telecommunications
networks to confirm the prospective aspects of syntonic relationships.

The many lamentations of politicians, church officials and journalists
over growing disindividualization are a clue to the 'supra-singular' or
'supra-individual' realities. Without being in any way normative, it is
necessary to be able to weed out the consequences of this. Based on
psychological experiments conducted in the sixties, Watzlawick spoke of
the 'ardent and unquenchable desire to be in agreement with the group'.
At present, it is no longer a question of desire, but rather an ambience in
which we bathe. What was once Californian experimentation is now the
ordinary reality of everyday life. Desire used to be understood in terms of a
subject's desire: this is no longer the case, however. The concern for
conformity is a consequence of massification and within this, in an
incidental and haphazard way, the groupings occur. I spoke earlier of the
'materiality' of the being-together; the oscillating mass-tribe is its illustration. It is possible to imagine, instead of a subject-actor, being confronted with *interlocking objects*; like a nest of Russian dolls, the large
object-mass conceals smaller object-groups which are diffracted to infinity.

In developing his ethic of sympathy, Scheler was careful to point out that
it is neither essentially nor exclusively social. It would be an all-
encompassing form, a matrix in a way. I in turn will form such a
hypothesis. Like the pendulum of human history, this form has now swung
back from the margins to the forefront. It favours the emotional function
and the subsequent mechanisms of identification and participation. What
he terms the 'theory of fellow-feeling as identification' explains the
conditions of identification: those moments of ecstasy which may be
haphazard but which also may characterize the climate of an era.[8] This
theory of identification and the ecstatic flight from the self is in perfect
harmony with the evolution of the image and the spectacle (from the
spectacle as such to political displays) and of course with that of sporting
crowds, tour groups or quite simply passers-by. All of these instances go
beyond the *principium individuationis* which used to be the touchstone of
any social organization and theory.

Is it necessary to establish, as Scheler proposes, a gradation between
affective 'identification', 'vicarious emotion' and 'fellow-feeling'? Far better,
in my opinion, if only for heuristic purposes, to take note of an 'affectual'
nebula, with an orgiastic or, as I have already analysed, dionysiac
tendency. Orgiastic explosions, cults of possession and situations of
identification have always existed; but sometimes they become endemic

and pre-eminent in the *conscience collective*. On whatever issue, we are stirred in unison. Halbwachs addresses this by speaking of 'collective interferences'.[9] That which we think of as a personal opinion belongs in fact to the group of which we are a member. Thus can be explained the rise of these *doxa* which are the mark of conformity, and which can be found in every group, even the one claiming to be the most detached: the intellectuals.

This 'affectual' nebula leads us to understand the precise form which sociality takes today: the wandering mass-tribes. Indeed, in contrast to the 1970s – with its strengths such as the Californian counterculture and the European student communes – it is less a question of belonging to a gang, a family or a community than of switching from one group to another. This can give the impression of atomization or wrongly give rise to talk of narcissism. In fact, in contrast to the stability induced by classical tribalism, neo-tribalism is characterized by fluidity, occasional gatherings and dispersal. Thus we can describe the street scene of modern megalopolises: the amateurs of jogging, punk or retro fashions, preppies and street performers invite us on a travelling road show. Through successive sedimentation, the aesthetic ambience mentioned earlier is constituted. It is within such an ambience that we can occasionally see 'instantaneous condensations' (Hocquenghem-Scherer), which are fragile but for that very instant the object of significant emotional investment. It is this sequential aspect that allows me to talk of the surpassing of the principle of individuation. Let us evoke an image: in describing the beauty of the American highway and its traffic, Baudrillard reports on this strange ritual and the 'regularity of these flux(es) [which] put an end to individual destinies'. For him, 'the only true society, the only warmth present, is that of a propulsion, a collective compulsion'.[10] This image can provide food for thought. In an almost animal way, we can feel a *puissance* which transcends individual trajectories or rather which situates them as part of a vast ballet. These figures, as stochastic as they may be, in the end form no less a constellation whose various elements fit together in a system in which neither will nor consciousness play a part. This is the arabesque of sociality.

A characteristic of the social: the individual could have a *function* in society, functioning in a party, an association, or a stable group.

[*A characteristic of sociality*: the person (*persona*) plays *roles*, both within his or her professional activities as well as within the various tribes in which the person participates. The costume changes as the person, according to personal tastes (sexual, cultural, religious, friendship), takes his or her place each day in the various games of the *theatrum mundi*.]

It is impossible to overstate the case: the dramatic authenticity of the social is answered by the tragic superficiality of sociality. I have already shown with regard to everyday life how there may be hidden depths to be plumbed beyond the surface layer of things. Thus may be explained the importance of appearances. I will not cover this as such in these pages, except to indicate that it is a vector of aggregation. In the above-mentioned sense, aesthetics is a way of feeling in common. It is also a means of recognizing ourselves. *Parva esthetica*? Be that as it may, the hodge-podge of clothing, multi-hued hairstyles and other punk manifestations act as a glue; theatricality founds and reconfirms the community. The cult of the body and other games of appearance have value only inasmuch as they are part of a larger stage in which everyone is both actor and spectator. To paraphrase Simmel and his sociology of the senses, it is a question of a stage 'common to us all'. The emphasis is less on that which distinguishes than on the overall effect.[11]

The nature of spectacle is to accentuate, either directly or by euphemism, the sensational, tactile dimension of social existence. Being-together allows us to touch: 'The majority of the people's pleasures are found in the pleasures of the crowd or the group' (A. Ehrenberg). We cannot comprehend this strange compulsion to group together without keeping at the forefront of our minds this anthropological constant. I will return to the dichotomy presented by Worringer between abstraction and *Einfühlung*: there are moments in time that are abstract, theoretical or purely rational, and others in which culture, in its broadest sense, is constructed from participation and 'tactileness'. The return of image and sensation in our societies is undoubtedly linked to a logic of touch.

Under this heading too must certainly be placed the resurgence, albeit in a commercialized manner, of popular festivals, carnivals and other effervescent moments. In a happy turn of phrase which is worth noting, Roberto Da Matta remarked that, at these moments, 'men are transformed and invent what we call the people or the mass'.[12] Invention must be understood here in its most literal sense: to contrive, to find (*in-venire*) that which exists. The paroxysm of the carnival, its exacerbated theatricality and tactileness clearly highlight the mechanism under review: the groundswell of the crowd and, at its heart, the small nodal points that form, act and interact upon each other. The spectacle, in various forms, assumes the function of communion. Circus and circle have the same etymological roots; metaphorically speaking, one can argue that they act as a reciprocal reinforcement of one another. For what characterizes our era more than anything is the supple intersection of a multiplicity of circles whose articulation takes the shape of sociality.

It is this theatricality, of the circus and the circle – the concatenation of circles – that characterizes another aspect of sociality, namely, *religiosity*. This term should be seen in the most elemental light, that of *reliance* (Bolle de Bal), and with reference to its etymological origins: *religare* – to bind together. I have no wish to place my sociological reveries in competition with the specialists. As I do not make a distinction between the religious as such and the 'religious by analogy' (J. Séguy), I shall use this term to describe the organic relationship in which we can see the interaction of nature, society, groups and the mass.[13] To use a previously evoked image, we are witness to a nebula that, like any (radioactive?) nebulosity, drifting in and out, is perhaps always present, but with varying effect, in the collective imagination. It is impossible to deny, however, that its effect these days is certain.

In order to be a little more precise, let me say that this religiosity can go hand in hand with de-Christianization or any other form of de-institutionalization. Sociality points to the cause as one of saturation of great systems and other macro-structures. But the fact of fleeing, or at the very least ignoring, institutions in no way means the end of the *religare*. It can be vested elsewhere. This question is topical and sociologists, such as Yves Lambert and Danielle Hervieu-Léger, continue to work away at it.[14] I would also add that this religiosity can accompany technological development, or even be reinforced by it (e.g. the microphone, the 'Minitel').*

Whatever the case, to get back to the main line of argument of these pages, I would say that there is a link between the emotional and religiosity; Weber devotes a paragraph in *Economy and Society* to the 'emotional community' and the 'congregational religiosity'. Among the characteristics he attributes to them are 'neighbourhood' and especially the plurality and instability of their expressions.[15] Would it be taking too many liberties with interpretation to relate this to proximity, the tactile and the ephemeral which drive our contemporary tribes? Regarding the new role of today's Christianity, it has been possible to speak of 'affinity parishes' (D. Hervieu-Léger). I would relate this to what I have termed 'elective sociality'. This is a paradigm which, as such, serves as a methodological tool. We can no longer do without the forms of fellow-feeling which, aside from the causal relationship, give a more complete vision of an increasingly complex world.

In fact, the symbolic relationship I have deliberately sketched out lies within a vitalist framework not far removed from Schopenhauer's will to live or Bergson's *élan vital*. Similarly, sociality and the tribalism it gives rise to are essentially tragic: the themes of appearance, the affective and the orgiastic all lead to the finite and precarious; but, as L-V Thomas has clearly pointed out, all death rites prepare for 'the passage back to life'.[16] This is the key to sociality which allows us to see a sign of the future in that which is an ending. The disillusionment with respect to everything that was meaningful in the bourgeois order should not mask the especially hardy forms which are emerging. Through one's own death, the individual permits the perdurability of the species. I will refer to the passage taken from *The Memoirs of Hadrian*:

> I believe it could be possible to share the existence of everyone, and this sympathy would be one of the least revocable types of immortality. (Marguerite Yourcenar, *Les Mémoires d'Hadrian*, Paris, Gallimard, 1951)

Similarly, in going beyond the category of individualism, sociality permits us to be aware of (and to be present at the birth of) its emerging forms.

---

* *Transl. note*: the French system of home mini-computers which hook into the nation's phone system and provide a huge variety of services from the home.

2. The 'undirected' being-together

Briefly, it is worth remembering, in order to serve as the basis of what might be deemed the socio-anthropological structure of tribalism, that social life can be determined only in relation to the group, whether directly or *a contrario*. Self-evident as this might appear, it bears repeating. Some have even claimed that medieval society as an organic organizational system constituted the model of 'sociological utopia'. Thus, considering just a few examples, we can show how this society formed a background to De Tocqueville's analysis of American democracy. Le Play also uses it to develop his concept of 'founding families'; the same can be said of Tönnies' 'community' or Durkheim's 'intermediate associations'.[17] It seems to me that, beyond its comparative uses, this medievalist nostalgia can serve to remind us that, as opposed to mechanical or individualist perspectives, which are the legacy of nineteenth-century positivism, the *organic* perspective cannot be totally discarded.

It has been said that Karl Marx was fascinated by the only revolution that, to his mind, had succeeded: the bourgeois revolution of 1789; his work, based on essentially bourgeois categories, shows the effects of this. It is perhaps even possible to make a similar claim for Durkheim with respect to medievalism: that is, while remaining a defender of the primacy of the role of reason and the individual in society, he cannot help but note, *de facto*, the importance of sentiment and community. I believe that the distinction Durkheim makes between 'mechanical solidarity' and 'organic solidarity', and especially his application of these concepts, is no longer highly pertinent. Rather, it is important to underline that he was truly obsessed by the reality represented by solidarity.[18] This is no trifling matter; indeed, although it has not been adequately analysed by those who hark back to the founder of the French School of Sociology, it is certain that the problem of the pre-rational and pre-individualist consensus is for him a basis on which society can and will be built. From this stems the importance he lends to the *conscience collective* or to specific moments (festivals, common acts) by which a given society will reinforce 'the feeling it has of itself'. Nisbet rightly insists on this, since we too often forget that this perspective of the *communitas* surpasses the utilitarian and functionalist aspect prevailing in the surrounding economic order.

Moreover, it is interesting to note that Halbwachs uses this perspective to analyse the permanence of the group, which is something other than 'an assemblage of individuals'. His comments about those educated at the 'École' (the École Normale Supérieure, rue d'Ulm, of course!) could just as easily apply to a study of Mafia figures. A community of ideas; impersonal preoccupations; a stability of the structure which goes beyond particularities and individuals: these are the essential characteristics of the group which are above all based on shared feeling. This analysis contains within it a somewhat mystical logic of depersonalization. The 'impersonal substance of lasting groups'[19] with its strong erotic and passionate connotations fits in well with the holistic perspective that is a feature of the organic community; everything contributes to its maintenance – dissension and dysfunctions included. We need only observe the organization of primary groups (family, friendship, religious, political, etc.) in order to be convinced of the pertinence of such a dynamic.

This surpassing or relativizing of individualism is to be found in German sociology (in Tönnies, of course, but also in Weber or Mannheim). It is also obvious in Simmel, who, especially with respect to secret societies, demonstrated both the affective and feeling dimension of social relationships, as well as its flowering within small contemporary groups. This may indeed be a highly interesting cultural fact in the comprehension of the communications future of our societies. The analysis of basic structures or social micro-groups allows us in effect to downplay the role of the individual, which has increased markedly in influence since the Renaissance – just like the frog in the fable who tries to minimize the fact that he plays a minor role, rather than a leading part, in the events around him. Indeed, to paraphrase Plato answering Protagoras: why is the individual the measure of all things, rather than the pig on which he has feasted? In fact, the logic of communication and the interaction that are especially visible within groups tend to favour the whole, the architectonic and its resultant complementarity. This is how we come to speak of a collective soul, a founding matrix that encompasses and embodies everyday life in its entirety.

Without being afraid of the simplicity of these remarks, or their repetitive nature, we can perhaps talk of a *natural sociality*, precisely by drawing attention to the paradoxical aspect of the expression. Indeed, despite the fact that it may take on the form of aggression or conflict, there is a propensity to form a group – what Pareto called the combining instinct, or the 'internal instinct', which, according to Locke, is at the heart of every society. Without commenting on the content of this inclination, we may consider that communication, both verbal and non-verbal, constitutes a vast web connecting individuals. Of course, the prevalence of a rationalist perspective used to mean that only verbalization was accorded the status of a social connection. That being the case, it was easy to recognize that many 'silent' situations were not included in this link. This is certainly one of the reasons advanced by the individualist ideology inherited from the Enlightenment and completely foreign to the popular way of life, the festive and daily customs and the *habitus* which lie at the deepest heart of everyday life, without necessarily ever being verbalized. Contemporary analyses of body language, of the significance of noise and music and of proxemics, are closely related both to the mystic, poetic and utopian perspectives of correspondence and architectonics, as well as to the reflections of theoretical physics on the infinitesimal.[20] What is there to say, but that reality is nothing other than a vast ordering of homogeneous and heterogeneous elements, of the continuous and the discontinuous. There was a time when we pointed out the distinctive features within a given whole – that which could be separated and particularized – whereas we are beginning to realize that it is better to consider the synchrony and the synergy of the forces at work within social life. Consequently, we find that the individual cannot be isolated, but rather he or she is tied, by culture, communication, leisure or fashion, to a community which perhaps no longer possesses the same qualities as during the Middle Ages, but has nonetheless the same form, a form which must be closely examined. Taking Simmel as my inspiration, I have proposed describing the form as the 'thread of reciprocity' that is woven through individuals. It is a kind of thread in which the intersection of actions, situations and affects forms a whole, hence the metaphor: dynamic in terms of the weaving; static in its social fabric. Thus, just as the *artistic form* is created from the variety of real or fantastic phenomena, the societal form could also be a specific creation based on the minuscule facts that make up everyday life. This process thus treats the common life as a pure form, of value in and of itself. This irrepressible and infrangible 'impulse to sociality' (*Gesselligkeit*) follows, according to the moment, either the royal route of politics and the historic event or the underground path of the equally intense ordinary life.

In this perspective, life can be seen as a collective work of art. Whether it is a work of bad taste, kitsch or folklore, or even one of the various manifestations of contemporary mass entertainment,* all this may seem futile and devoid of meaning. And yet, while it is undeniable that there exists a 'political' society, an 'economic' society, there is one unqualified reality, and that is the social existence as such which I propose calling sociality and which may be 'the play-form of socialization'.[21] In the framework of the aesthetic paradigm so dear to me, the play aspect is not bothered by finality, utility, practicality, or what we might call 'realities', but rather it is what stylizes existence and brings out its essential characteristic. Thus, I believe that the *being-together* is a basic given. Before any other determination or qualification, there is this vital spontaneity that guarantees a *culture* its own *puissance* and solidity. Later on, this spontaneity can become artificial, that is, *civilizing*, producing remarkable (political, economic, artistic) works. However, it remains necessary, if only to appreciate better the new orientations (or reorientations), to come back to the pure form of the 'undirected being-together'. Indeed, this can serve as the background, revealing the new lifestyles re-emerging before our very eyes. We are dealing with a new set of rules concerning the sexual market, the relationship to work, the sharing of ideas, leisure time, and the solidarity of basic groupings. In order to understand all of this, we need to apply the methodological tool which is the organic perspective of the group.

---

* *Transl. note*: 'mass entertainment' in English in the text.

3. The 'religious model'

In describing the *Elementary Forms of the Religious Life*, Durkheim was not trying to make an exhaustive analysis of the religion of Australian tribes; his ambition was to understand the social context. The same can be said of Weber: his Protestant ethic is open to numerous criticisms by the sociology or history of religion *stricto sensu*, but this was certainly not his subject. And what to say of Freud's *Totem and Taboo*? In each of these cases, with different aims, the writer is attempting to update a logic of 'social attraction'.[22] It is in this perspective that I mention the religious model. It is a perfectly metaphorical perspective, since it is true that, beyond all specializations, and without wishing in any way to invalidate them, it is important to use religious images in order to seize *in nuce* the forms of social aggregation. This transversal or comparative view recognizes that it is from a collectively experienced imagination that human history is inaugurated. Despite the caution we must exercise when dealing with etymology, religion (*religare*) – reliance – is a useful way of understanding social ties. Although it may annoy the purists, I still support Berger and Luckmann's proposition: 'the *sociological understanding of "reality"* falls somewhere in the middle between that of the man in the street and that of the philosopher'.[23] In addition, when one considers the significant caesuras in the history of attitudes, it is easy to notice that the effervescence which is their cause and effect is very often taken over by small religious groups living as a whole, living and acting from a point of view of totality. The political/ideal separation no longer makes any sense. Lifestyles are experienced for their own sake, like that 'most extreme concrete', according to Benjamin's expression, where the ordinary and utopia coexist on a day-to-day basis, along with need and desire, withdrawal into the 'family' and turning outwards towards the infinite. It has been said that the dionysiac 'thiases' of the late Hellenistic period or the small sects of early Christianity formed the basis of the social structures that were to follow. Perhaps one can make a similar case for the multiplication of affective-religious groupings which characterize our own era. The use of the religious metaphor can then be compared to a laser beam allowing the most complete reading of the very heart of a given structure.

All those interested in the cult of Dionysus have underlined his late arrival to the Greek pantheon, and his strangeness in many respects. As far as we are concerned, and while emphasizing his emblematic aspect, he can be considered the paradigm of the founding otherness: at the same time signalling the end and heralding a beginning. In this respect, it is interesting to note that these 'thiases', which are religious groups devoted to the cult of this strange and foreign divinity, have a double function. Thus, as opposed to traditional political cleavages, the thiases cut on the diagonal, rejecting social, racial and sexual discrimination, before becoming part of the religion of the city-state.[24] On the one hand, they coalesce, constituting new aggregations, new primary groups and, on the other, they revitalize the new society. This double attitude is the core of any foundation. It is a procedure repeated regularly, especially each time that one can observe the saturation of an ideology or more precisely a specific episteme.

Renan shows clearly how at first it was small groups that gave birth to what was later to become Christianity: 'only the small sects are able to found something'. He compares them to 'small freemasonries', and their effectiveness is primarily based on the fact that the proximity of their members creates profound bonds, which gives rise to a genuine synergy between the convictions held by one another.[25] Isolated or lost in a too-vast structure, which amounts to much the same thing, an individual and his ideal in the end carry little weight; but when tightly interwoven, their effectiveness is multiplied many times over by the other members of the 'freemasonry'. Moreover, this is what compels us to say that ideas have their own richness, which, generally speaking, the positivism of the nineteenth century in its various guises (Marxism, functionalism) called into serious doubt. It is true that the economic logic which prevailed during the modern era and which favoured both the political project and the atomization of the individual was incapable of integrating the dimension of a collective imagination. At the very most, it was able to conceive of this dimension as a spiritual supplement, a private and superfluous 'extra', leading, without any opposition, to the familiar 'disenchantment with the world' (*Entzauberung*) which particularly prevailed in social theory, obscuring the mythical (utopian) weight of the workers' movement.

The small group, however, tends to restore, structurally, the symbolic power. Step by step, one can see a mystical network being built, carefully yet solidly connected, leading one to speak of a cultural resurgence in social life. This is the lesson taught by these eras of the masses – eras based mainly on the concatenation of groups with splintered but exacting intentionalities. I propose calling this the re-enchantment with the world.

The sociologist Ernst Troeltsch has shown with great finesse the distinction between the 'sect type' and the 'church type'. By extending this typology still further, and perhaps by emphasizing its clear-cut nature, one can say that, just as there are eras characterized by the 'church type', there also exist eras specifically known as being of the 'sect type'. In the latter case, their founding aspect will be highlighted, since what characterizes this aspect is, on the one hand, the constantly renewed force of the being-together, and, on the other, the relativization of the future – the greater weight being granted to the present in the temporal triad. This is not without organizational consequences: thus, the sect is above all a local community which lives as such, and which has no need of a visible institutional organization. It is enough for this community to feel it is an active participant in the invisible communion of believers, referring to a mystical idea of the 'communion of the saints'. It is thus a small group operating on the basis of proximity and which is only a hazy part of a greater whole.

Another aspect of the 'sect type' is the relativization of bureaucracy. There may well be charismatic leaders and various gurus on the scene; however, the fact that their powers are not based on rational competence (theological knowledge) or on a sacerdotal tradition, renders them fragile and does not favour their longevity. This is perhaps why it is said that 'everything, in the sect, is everybody's affair'.[26] It is perhaps difficult to speak in this context of a democratic attitude; in fact, this is a hierarchical and organic system, in which every single person is made indispensable to the life of the group. What is more, it is this reversibility that guarantees the constant dynamism of the whole. The structures created by the mechanism of delegation which they then reinforce tend to favour a nonchalant attitude among their members. On the other hand, the 'sect type' makes each and every one of us responsible for one another, thus inevitably giving rise to conformity and conformism. The present, proximity, the feeling of being part of a group, responsibility – so many essential characteristics are at work in the group-sect. It is these characteristics that allow the groups under consideration to be constituted as a 'mass'. Indeed, the imperialism of the institution cannot be understood without a rigid structure, oriented towards longevity and directed by a solidly established power. If, on the other hand, localism prevails, it is entirely possible to accommodate other entities operating on the same principles. Thus we can explain the image of federalism or at least of cohabitation that the network structure generally provides.

Furthermore, it is interesting to note the popular basis of the 'sect type'. This is one observation on which everyone who has analysed this phenomenon can agree, from late Antiquity to our own day. It is especially evident when we look at the Christian sects during their first four centuries of existence. It is well known that, at first, Christianity attracted the poor and slaves. Moreover, in his efforts to suppress Christianity, Julian the Apostate thought he was dealing with uneducated groups, unsupported by any of the elites whom he considered to be the philosophers. The same holds true for the medieval sects: it would seem to be a constant. Indeed, we can say that the sectarian structure is opposed, or at least indifferent, to the clergy and the governing classes in general,[27] and this according to the previously mentioned ideology of proximity. We can find in the conformism and the reticence towards the overarching power the overall perspective of the anarchists' logic: order without the state.

Thus we can develop Troeltsch's proposition concerning a sectarian ideal type. It allows the social form of the network to be accentuated: an unorganized yet solid whole, invisible, yet forming the backbone of any entity. We know that, in general, historiography has reacted with supreme indifference to the goldfish bowl which is everyday history, to concentrate on just a few emerging crystallizations (men or events). The same can be said of the social sciences (political science, economics, sociology): they all ignore that which is unorganized, or worse still, deny its importance. The 'sect type', because of its popular dimension, underlines the existence of a mass Christianity that can be seen as a sort of wellspring, irrigating the roots of the particular institutions which may be represented by churches, sects or designated movements.[28] The resurgence of basic communities or affinity groups within contemporary churches shows just how far this spring is from being exhausted. There are times when it is not well cared for: when we misuse it by laying waste to it. At other, more 'ecological' times we realize how much we owe it, especially that solid bond formed by sharing and helping one another in disinterested solidarity. This permits the perdurability over a long period of sociality. The small group offers the finished model of such an architectonic structure – in it we find in miniature, and outside of all theoretical systematism, the realization of the above-mentioned characteristics.

The guilds, whose roots are as we know to be found in the religious brotherhoods, or those ancient parish subdivisions known as 'phratries', are based on fraternal sharing. Their etymologies insist particularly on conviviality, family solidarity – the small group that has its origins in the far-off division into clans.[29] Here again, perhaps under different names, this basic structure, after having been forgotten, has a new currency or form; however, its form remains essentially religious (*re-ligare*).

> That which has been called the 'sect type' can be seen as an alternative to the purely rational governing of the institution. Regularly returning to the fore, this alternative accentuates the role of feeling in social life, which will aid the action of proximity and the welcoming aspect of that which is nascent.

It is in this sense that the religious model is useful in describing the phenomenon of networks, which is not bound by any form of centrality, nor even, sometimes, rationality. Contemporary lifestyles – it is necessary to state over and over – are no longer structured around a single pole. In a rather stochastic manner, they branch out from tremendously varied occurrences, experiences and situations – all things that characterize affinity groups. It all occurs as if the 'crazy love'* and the 'objective chance' of Surrealism, the encounter and the 'aimless drift' of the Situationists, were progressively infiltrating the bloodstream of the social body.[30] The tableau of life is no longer the work of a select few; it becomes a mass process, given of course that the aesthetic to which this refers cannot be summed up as a question of taste (good or bad aesthetic taste) or of content (the aesthetic object). It is the pure aesthetic form which interests us here: the way in which the collective sense is experienced and expressed.

---

* *Transl. note*: cf. André Breton, *L'Amour fou*, 1937.

4. Elective sociality

It is from the idea an era holds of otherness that it is possible to determine
the essential form of a given society. Thus, correlative to the existence of a
collective sense, we shall see the development of a logic of the network,
that is to say, that these processes of attraction and repulsion will be a
matter of choice. We are currently witness to the development of what I
shall call an *elective sociality*. This mechanism has certainly always existed,
but, as far as modernity is concerned for example, it was tempered by the
political corrective that brought compromise and long-term finality into the
picture to supersede particular interests and localism. It is the thematic of
everyday life and sociality (versus the political and social). On the other
hand, it highlights the fact that the essential problem of the social reality is
relationism, which can be translated in a more trivial way as the companionship of individuals and groups. It is of course a given that the bond
itself is more important than the elements which are joined together. It is
less a case of the goal to be reached than the fact of being-together which
will prevail; in a Simmelesque perspective: the *für-mit-gegeneinander*.
Thus one can see the necessity of what I have called a formist sociology,
that is, a way of thinking that records forms and existing configurations
without in any way criticizing or judging them. Such a phenomenology is
the aesthetic attitude responding to an aestheticizing of contemporary life.
This characterizes a stochastic approach which, using examples taken from
various sources, is only a musical variation on the theme of *Zusammen-
sein*.[31] However, there is no need to be afraid of sounding a familiar chord,
of remounting the attack from all sides, for it is very difficult to understand
a group phenomenon with analytical instruments especially developed
from a political perspective. This, moreover, is the reason for a common
enough blunder being committed these days: analysing the retreat from the
political and the loss of a social sense in terms of a resurgence of individualism. Let us rather continue our meanderings, highlighting especially the
affective or 'affectual' (Weber) aspect of these groups.

It is striking that sociality in its founding moment is particularly intimist.
The same holds true when we try to tighten the bonds or remind ourselves
of what is common to all. In this respect, the meal is a true sacrament
'rendering visible an invisible grace', as the catechism tells us. In a more
modern manner of speaking, it is a symbolic technique *par excellence*.
From the eucharist to the political banquet table, by way of small titbits
between friends, the list of these anamnetical procedures which seal
alliances, soothe enmities and restore strained friendships is a long one
indeed. The meal is used here as a metaphor for those places created inside
cenacles during periods of effervescence. From the multiplication of
private cults to the tight fabric of cells which offered hospitality to the
leaders of the new Christian religion and the revolutionaries of modern
times,[33] the new social aggregations, the birth of alternative values, occur
thanks to what can be called the logic of the network, that is, something

that emphasizes affective warmth or at least shows how it is significant to the social structure or objective.

The existence of such an affectual drive is undeniable in the political realm, as has been frequently noted. It may be interesting to point out in passing that it also has its effects in the economic sphere. Célestin Bouglé analyses this in his essay on the caste system. In a similar perspective to the one that has been applied to professional bodies and trade associations, he shows how the caste is simply the paroxysmal 'petrified' form of the medieval guild. We are aware of the role played by the one and the other in the structure of Western or Hindu industry and economics. This role only exists thanks to the existence of convivial, solidarity or legal self-help practices and any other cultural and religious forms of expression.[33] The economic order is thus sustained by that which is usually assigned to the symbolic order. This example shows clearly how worldly society is a whole, which we in vain cut up into slices; and within this whole the convivial being-together – festive or ordinary – occupies a considerable place.

It is left only to Durkheim in his wisdom to recognize the role of the affect. I have already shown this (cf. *L'Ombre de Dionysos*) with respect to his analysis of the corroboree festivals in *The Elementary Forms of the Religious Life*. It is more surprising to see the place he accords it in *The Division of Labour in Society*. Thus, in a rather vitalist spirit, he attributes to the group a 'source of life *sui generis*. From it emanates a heat that inflames or reanimates hearts, that opens them up to sympathy.' One cannot be any more precise; and he predicts that 'outpourings of feeling' will also have their place in the 'associations of the future'. We can almost read into this an analysis of contemporary networks. What is certain is that this famous theory of intermediate associations, which is perhaps Durkheim's greatest contribution, is totally incomprehensible if we fail to integrate this affective dimension. Moreover, it is obvious that the emphasis on the group is a deconstruction of the individualism which seems to prevail in those who claim Durkheimian positivism as their inspiration. This individualism exists, to be sure, allowing early sociology to explain the inner dynamics of modernity, but at the same time it is balanced by its opposite, or more precisely by the remanence of alternative elements. What is more, this paradoxical tension is the best guarantee of the tonicity of a given society.

One must thus understand the vitalism which occurs again and again in the work of Durkheim. Is this a nostalgia for the community? Perhaps. In any case, it underlines the fact that, mirroring the individual body, the social body is a complex organism in which function and dysfunction fit together as best they can. Hence his comparison between the division of social labour and the division of physiological labour: 'it never appears except in the midst of polycellular masses which are already endowed with a certain cohesion'. This is a most organic concept that does not hesitate to base itself on an 'affinity of blood' and 'an attachment to the same soil';[34] the call to spontaneity, to the impulsive forces which go beyond simple contractual rationality, thus places the emphasis on relationism, on the linked series of attractions and repulsions and basic elements of any social entity. It has been possible to analyse the erotic constructions of the divine Marquis de Sade as so many chemical compounds prevailing over each of their elements. This paroxysmal metaphor may be useful for our investigations: eros or passion favours the grouping of elements, according to the 'valency' inherent in each of these. There may be saturation; we then witness the emergence of another compound. Thus, within the orbit of spontaneous vitalism, we can see at work the conjunction and/or the paradoxical tension of the static – the community, space – and the dynamic – the birth and death of groups forming the community and living in this space. The old debate on structure and History is now being replaced by the debate on chance and the necessity of everyday histories.

Society thus understood cannot be summarized by any old rational mechanism; it is experienced and organized, in the strongest sense of the term, through encounters, situations, experiences within various groups to which each individual belongs. These groups cross each others' paths and constitute both an undifferentiated mass and highly diversified polarities. Remaining in the vitalist framework, we can speak of a protoplasmic reality issuing from the close conjunction between the nourishing substance and the cell's nucleus. These images have the advantage of highlighting both the importance of the affect (attraction–repulsion) in social life, as well as showing that it is 'non-conscious', or to sound like Pareto, 'non-logical'. It is necessary to insist on such an organicity, for that is what conditions many of the attitudes deemed irrational which we see around us today. And without being able to define it exactly (hence my use of metaphor), it is from such a nebula that we can understand what I have for the past several years been proposing to call sociality.

Just as I spoke of a remanence with reference to Durkheim, we can also say that Hegelian Romanticism contains a theoretical constant based on a nostalgia for the community. Beyond egalitarianism and the social contract, he has a 'concentric' view of society; that is, the different circles of which it is constituted fit together and have value only inasmuch as they are linked. Thus, for Hegel the state is a sort of *communitas communitatum*; it is not individuals that come first, but rather the relationships between them.[35] This idea of interconnection is a remarkable one, for it favours the cementing role that the affective plays – this close companionship, in other words. In this way, as opposed to the traditional reading, the Hegelian state may only be a hollow shell, a theoretical proposition whose sole function is to highlight the spontaneous organization of the various elements that, bit by bit, constitute the whole. Of course, this organization is far from uniform; it is in many respects very chaotic, yet it testifies well to a society which, while not ideal, exists *as best it can*. Indeed, the logic of the network and the affect which serves as its vector are essentially relativist. Must we then say, as is generally claimed, that the groups constituting contemporary masses are without ideals? It would perhaps be better to note that they have no vision of what should constitute the absolutes of a society. Each group is its own absolute. This is the affective relativism that is particularly translated by the conformity of lifestyles.

However, this supposes that there is a multiplicity of lifestyles – a kind of multiculturalism. In a both conflictual and harmonious way, these lifestyles confront and oppose each other. This self-sufficiency of the group may give the impression of restriction. What is certain is that the saturation of a projective attitude, an intentionality oriented toward the future – 'extensive' – is balanced by an increased quality of relationships which are more 'in-tensive' and immediate. Modernity, by multiplying the possibilities of social relationships, partly drained them of any real content. This was a particular characteristic of modern cities and has played a considerable part in the gregarious solitude we have rambled on about so much. For its part, postmodernity has tended to favour within megalopolises both the withdrawal into the group as well as a deepening of relationships within these groups, given that this deepening is in no way synonymous with unanimism, since conflict also has a role to play in them. Besides, that is not the issue; one need only remember that attraction and repulsion are cause and effect of *relationism*. It is this relationism that serves as a vector for the above-mentioned 'concentric' (Hegel) or 'polycellular mass' (Durkheim). Naturally, this structuring into affinity networks no longer has anything to do with the voluntarist presupposition generally found at the root of the politico-economic association.

Indeed, what must be realized is that the 'affective' ('affectual') nebula being described does not imply either a humanist or an anthropomorphic bias. This is of course my *delenda est Carthago*: the individual and its diverse theories have nothing to do with it; no more so even than the action of this same individual on History in progress. Within the framework of the dionysiac thematic, whose paroxysmal expression is confusion, the effervescent masses (sexual, festive, sporting, promiscuous) and the everyday masses (crowded, ordinary, consuming, following blindly . . .) go well beyond the characteristics of the principle of individuation. To be sure, it is not wrong to say that individual intentionalities play a certain role in the process of interaction, but this should not prevent us from seeing that as a social 'form', this process is made up of a 'multitude of minuscule canals, the existence of which is unknown to individual consciousness'. Simmel called this an 'effect of composition' (*Zusammenschluss*).[36] Indeed, without being able to say which is foremost, it is true that the pre-eminence of the group and the importance of the affect show how the density of everyday life is above all the product of impersonal forces. Moreover, this also explains its denial by the intellectuals who have been reflecting on social existence since the eighteenth century.

And yet, this everyday life, in all its frivolity and superficiality, is truly what makes any form of aggregation possible. I have said it before: the *exis* and the *habitus* so ably described by Mauss determine the mores and customs that constitute us. They are nothing less than conscious. *They exist*; imperative and constricting in their massiveness. We experience them without verbalizing them; perhaps – and we should not be afraid to say it – we lead what is quite an animalistic life. We are thus reminded of the logic of networks at work within contemporary masses. The depersonalization, or rather the disindividuation which it induces, is moreover perceptible in the fact that more and more situations are being analysed from the perspective of atmosphere. It is less identity and the specific trait which prevail than the vague and ambiguous – the qualifying terms of 'trans' and 'meta' come to mind, in many domains as well, such as fashion, ideologies, sexuality, and so on.

The explosion of scientific research or journalistic treatments referring to 'ambience' (*feeling*, *Stimmung*) is illuminating in this regard. This is not without consequence for our analytical methods, particularly as concerns the theoretical modesty which increasingly characterizes them. It is not necessary to delve into this question in these pages; it is sufficient to point out that it is as a result of this trend that a self-confident (and self-conscious) civilization, a set of representations dominated by the clarity of concepts and the certainty of reason, is at present giving way to what I shall call the *twilight of organizational models and ways of thinking of the world*. As with any twilight, this one is not without its charms; but it also has its own laws, which cannot be ignored if we wish to find our way.

5. The law of secrecy

One of the characteristics, and by no means the least, of the modern mass is surely the law of secrecy. In penning a little sociological satire,[37] I tried to show how the Mafia could be considered as a metaphor of sociality. It was more than a simple inside joke; specifically, in that it emphasized the protective mechanism with respect to the outside world (i.e. in relation to the overarching forms of power), as well as pointed out that the secrecy it engenders is a way of confirming the group. In translating the image onto a slightly less immoral plane (or at least one whose immorality will not be unduly exploited), we can say that the small tribes with which we are familiar – structural elements of contemporary masses – show similar characteristics. In my opinion, the theme of secrecy is surely a preferred way of understanding the social context before us. It may appear paradoxical when one knows the importance of appearances or theatricality on the daily scene. The kaleidoscope of our streets must not allow us to forget that there may be a subtle dialectic between display and concealment; just like Poe's *Purloined Letter*, the most overt display may be the best guarantor of remaining undiscovered. In this respect, we can say that the multitude and the aggressiveness of urban *images*, resembling the Mafia's *borsalino*, is the clearest sign of the secret and dense life of contemporary micro-groups.

In his article on 'La Société secrète', Simmel emphasizes the role of the mask, which we know has the function, among others, of integrating the persona in an overall architectonic. The mask may be an elaborate or colourful hairstyle, an original tattoo, the recycling of retro fashions or even the conformity of the 'preppy' style. In all of these examples, it subordinates the person to this secret society which is the chosen affinity group. Here we can find an example of 'disindividuation', participation, in the mystical sense of the word, in a greater whole.[38] As we shall later see, the mask makes me a conspirator against the established powers, but as of right now, this conspiracy unites me with others, and in a non-accidental, structurally effective way.

It is impossible to stress enough the unifying function of silence, which has been seen by the great mystics as the ultimate form of communication. And while their etymological relationship may be subject to some controversy, one can point out that there is a link between the mystery, the mystic and the mute; this link is one of initiation which permits the sharing of secrets. Whether it is anodyne or even objectively non-existent, this is of no consequence. It is enough that, even on the plane of fantasy, these initiates are able to share something. This is what gives them energy and makes their actions dynamic. Renan clearly demonstrated the role of secrecy in the establishment of the Christian network at its beginnings, which was not without cause for concern but at the same time attracted and played a considerable role in its success.[39] Every time one establishes, re-establishes or corrects a structure, a community, one starts from the foundation of secrecy, which confirms and reinforces the basic solidarity. This is perhaps the sole point those who speak of the 'retreat' into everyday life have got right. However, their interpretation is wrong: the refocusing on that which is close and the initiatory sharing which characterizes it are in no way a sign of weakness; in fact, they are the surest sign of a founding act. The silence surrounding politics highlights the resurgence of sociality.

In ancient sodalities, the common meal implied that one was able to maintain secrecy with respect to the outside. 'Dirty linen', whether in the case of families strictly speaking or the extended family or even the Mafia, is simply not laundered in public. Many policemen, educators and journalists have come across this secrecy in the course of their work. Certainly, the misdeeds of children, village crimes or a multitude of events are never easily accessed. The same may be said to apply to sociological inquiry. If only allusively, it is necessary to point out that there is always a reticence to submit oneself to a stranger's scrutiny, and it is important to take this parameter into account in these analyses. Thus, I would answer those who dispute (even if only semantically) the 'retreat' into everyday life, that we are in the presence of a 'collective privacy',* an unwritten law, a code of honour, a clan morality, which, in a quasi-intentional way, is protected from anything that is outside or overarching.[40] This attitude will be especially pertinent to these remarks.

---

* *Transl. note*: This phrase appears in English in the text.

Indeed, the essence of this attitude is to favour self-preservation: a 'group egoism', with the result that the group can develop almost autonomously within a larger whole. This autonomy, as opposed to the logic of politics, is neither 'pro' nor 'con'; it is intentionally situated *on the sidelines*. This is expressed by a distaste for confrontation, by a saturation of activism, by a distancing from militancy – all things which can be seen in the general attitude of the younger generation with respect to politics. And within this generation can be found the thematic of liberation, represented by the various feminist, homosexual or ecological movements. There are many fine thinkers who label this as compromise, degeneracy or hypocrisy. As always, the normative judgement holds little interest; it does not let us seize the vitality at work within the *avoidance* lifestyles. Indeed, this avoidance, this relativism, may be the tactic which guarantees the only thing for which the mass feels responsible: the perdurability of the groups of which it is constituted.

In fact, secrecy is the paroxysmal form of the *aloofness* of the people whose socio-anthropological continuity I have already shown.[41] As a social 'form' (without mentioning its specific actualizations, which may be the exact opposite), the secret society allows for resistance. Whereas power tends to encourage centralization, specialization and the establishment of a universal society and knowledge, the secret society is always found on the margins; is secular, decentralized, without the baggage of dogmatic and intangible doctrines. It is on this basis that the resistance resulting from the people's aloofness can continue, invariably, across the centuries. Specific historical examples, such as Taoism,[42] show the link between these three terms: secrecy, the people and resistance. What is more, the organizational structure of this conjunction happens to be the network, the cause and effect of a parallel economy, society and even administration. Thus, there is especially fertile ground for exploration here, even if it is not expressed in the way to which we have been accustomed by modern political science.

This line of inquiry could prove richly instructive, although (and because) it is rarely considered. I propose calling this the *hypothesis* of the *underground centrality*:

> Sometimes secrecy can be the way to establish contact with the other within the confines of a limited group; at the same time it conditions the attitude of the group towards whatever external force there may be.

This hypothesis is the hypothesis of sociality; its expressions may of course vary widely, but its logic is constant: the fact of sharing a habit, an ideology or an ideal determines the being-together and allows the latter to act as a protection against any imposition, from whatever outside source. As opposed to an imposed and external morality, the ethic of secrecy is both federative and *equalizing*. Even the rough-hewn Chancellor Bismarck, in speaking of a homosexual organization in Berlin, noticed this 'equalizing effect of the collective practice of the forbidden'.[43] Homosexuality was not in fashion then and neither was equality; and when one is aware of the sense of social distance among the Prussian Junkers, one is more ready to appreciate, as I have just pointed out, the nature and the role of secrecy in this homosexual group.

The confidence established between the members of the group is expressed through rituals: specific signs of recognition which have no other goal than to strengthen the small group against the large. The same double movement mentioned earlier applies; from the academic cryptospeak to the 'verlan'* used by young toughs, the mechanism is the same: the secret sharing of the affect, while reinforcing close ties, helps resist attempts at uniformity. The reference to the ritual underlines that the essential quality of group and mass resistance is to be cagey rather than to go on the offensive. Consequently, it can be expressed through practices reputed to be alienated or alienating. This is the eternal ambiguity of weakness behind whose mask can hide an undeniable force, like the submissive housewife who has no need of outward signs of power, assured as she is of her status as veritable domestic tyrant. Or, as Canetti analyses with respect to Kafka: how an apparent humiliation assures in return a real force to he who submits to it. In his battle against the conjugal plans of Felice, Kafka practises an untimely obedience. His taciturn ways, his secrecy 'have to be viewed as necessary practices of this obstinacy'.[44] This is a procedure we find at work in the group practice. Ruse, silence, abstention – the 'soft underbelly' of the social – are fearsome weapons that one would be wise to regard with suspicion. This applies to irony and laughter, which have destabilized, either medium- or long-term, the most solid oppression.

Resistance takes a low profile with respect to the requirements of a full frontal assault, but it has the advantage of encouraging complicity among those who practise it – this is the essential point. Combat always tries to go beyond itself, beyond those who lead it: it always has its own goal. However, *practices of silence* are above all organic, that is, the enemy is less important than the social glue which the group secretes. In the first case, we are in the presence of a history in the making, either alone or in a contractual association; in the second, we are dealing with a fate which we confront collectively, even if only by force of circumstance. In this latter case, solidarity is not an abstraction or the fruit of rational calculation; it is an imperious necessity which causes us to act with passion. It is exacting work, giving rise to the above-mentioned obstinacy and ruse; for, without a precise goal, the people has only one essential objective: that of ensuring the long-term survival of the species. Of course, this instinct for preservation has nothing conscious about it; therefore, it does not involve rational action or decision. However, in order to be as effective as possible, this

---

* *Transl. note*: a form of backwards slang, in which the order of syllables is reversed. Thus, 'verlan' is 'à l'envers' (reversed).

instinct must be active at the deepest level. This is precisely the justification for the link I have been proposing between small groups and the mass.
It also explains how what we call 'lifestyles', which are of the order of
proxemy, are as topical as they are.

This question should be re-examined in greater detail; however, one can
already remark that the conjunction of 'group preservation–solidarity–
proximity' has found its favoured expression in the notion of family, which
should be taken in the sense of extended family. In this respect, it is
striking to note the effectiveness of this anthropological constant, despite
the failure of social historians and analysts to pick it up. From the cities of
Antiquity to the modern urban agglomerations, the 'family', as we
understand it, has had the role of protector, limiting incursions by the
overarching powers, serving as a bulwark against the outside. The whole
thematic of the *padroni*, of clientelism and the various forms of the Mafia
find their origin here. Returning to the period of late Antiquity – so
relevant to these remarks – we can highlight how Saint Augustine
envisaged his apostolic role as such: the Christian community as the *familia
Dei*. In part, the spread of the Church in its early days was dependent on
the quality of its leaders and the networks of solidarity which were able to
protect it from the demands of the state.[44]

However, although this social structuring is particularly well represented
in the Mediterranean basin and although it took on paroxysmal forms
there, it is in no way limited by them. It must be forcefully stressed that,
although they have been tempered by a concern for objectivity, the social
structures that history describes to us, until and including the most contemporary or the most rational, are all marked by the affinity mechanisms
mentioned earlier. Familialism and nepotism, in either the strict sense or
the metaphorical sense, have their place here; continually, through 'bodies',
schools, sexual inclinations and ideologies, they recreate protective niches
– individual territories within great political, administrative, economic or
labour entities. This is the eternal question of the community or 'parish'
which dares not make itself heard. And, naturally, in order to do this, no
means are spared, no matter how dishonourable: many studies have
updated the informal process of 'pulling strings' in favour of the 'family'.
And from the top-level executives turned out by the 'Grandes-Écoles' of
Paris, to the dock workers of Manchester working through the trades union
network, mutual aid is the same and, as far as we are concerned here, is the
firm expression of a mechanism of ruse reinforcing a specific sociality.[46] It
would be interesting to highlight this *illegalism* at work inside the social
circles that claim to be the guardians of the purest morality: senior civil
servants, the *haute* intelligentsia, journalists of record and other influential
figures. It is sufficient to note that there are no 'just', in the eyes of the
'Universal' – it is as well to have no illusions on that score. I would add that
this is certainly fortunate, since, after all, as long as they counterbalance
each other, these various illegalities, mirroring the war of the gods so dear
to Weber, relativize and neutralize one another. To quote Montherlant,

there is always 'a certain morality contained within immorality . . . a certain morality that the clan has forged for itself alone', the corollary of which is an indifference to morality in general.[47]

The reflection on secrecy and its effects, even if anomic, leads to two conclusions which may appear paradoxical: on the one hand, we are witness to a saturation of the principle of individuation, with the attendant economic-political consequences and, on the other, we can see the increasing development of communication. It is this process which may give rise to the belief that the multiplication of micro-groups can only be understood in an organic context. Tribalism and massification go hand in hand.

At the same time, within the sphere of tribal proximity, just as in the organic mass, there is ever greater recourse to the 'mask' (in the above-mentioned sense). The further one proceeds masked, the more the community bonds are strengthened. Indeed, in a circular motion, in order to recognize oneself, symbolism is required, that is, duplicity, which in turn engenders recognition.[48] Thus it becomes possible, in my opinion, to explain the development of *symbolism*, in its various guises, which we can observe around us today.

> The social is based on the rational association of individuals having a precise identity and an autonomous existence; as to sociality, it is founded on the fundamental ambiguity of symbolic structuring.

In pursuing the analysis still further, the autonomy that is no longer in the realm of the individual will relocate to the 'tribe', the small community group. Many analysts do not hesitate to point out this runaway autonomization (usually a cause of great concern to them). Thus, secrecy may be considered as a methodological lever for understanding contemporary lifestyles, for, in the succinct words of Simmel: 'the essence of a secret society is autonomy', an autonomy which he likens to anarchy.[49] One has only to remember that, above all else, anarchy seeks an 'order without the state'. In a way, this is what stands out in the architectonic at work inside the micro-groups (tribalism), and between the various groups which inhabit the urban space of our megalopolises (mass).

In conclusion, one can state that the 'disturbance', or perhaps it would be better to say the deregulation, introduced by tribalism and massification, the secrecy and the clientelism that characterize this process, should be considered neither as something entirely new, nor in purely negative terms. On the one hand, it is a phenomenon which is found frequently in human history, particularly during periods of cultural change (for example, the period of late Antiquity); on the other hand, by breaking the unilateral relationship to the central power, or to its local delegates, the mass via its groups will make use of competition and reversibility: competition between groups and, within these, competition between the various 'bosses'.[50] It is this polytheism, moreover, that may lead us to believe that the mass is rather less homogenous than it is dynamic. Indeed, the fact of being 'on the outside', as may be observed in the social networks, does not imply the end of the being-together, but quite simply that this being-together is invested in forms other than those recognized by the instituted legality. The only serious problem is that of the threshold at which abstention, the fact of being 'on the outside', sets off the implosion of a given society. This is a phenomenon which has already been observed,[51] hence not surprising to the sociologist who, beyond his or her preferences, convictions or even sense of nostalgia, is above all fully aware of what is about to be born.

6.   Masses and lifestyles

Whether one uses the term lifestyles or even (the sociology of) everyday life, it is certain that this thematic can no longer be given cursory treatment. We can no longer be content to critique it, whether this 'criticism' is done in the name of a non-alienated life or in the interest of a logic of what ought to be. For my part, I believe that this (re)surgence is a clear indicator of the paradigm shift going on today. More specifically, I would postulate that the societal dynamism which, in a more or less underground fashion, runs through the social body should be set in relation to the ability of micro-groups to create themselves. This is perhaps a case of *creation par excellence*: – pure creation. In other words, the 'tribes' we are considering may have a goal, may have finality; but this is not essential; what is important is the energy expended on constituting the group *as such*. Thus, developing new lifestyles is an act of pure creation of which we should be aware. It is important to insist on this fact, for it is a 'law' of sociology to judge all things as a function of what is instituted. This is a heavy charge which at times causes us to pass over that which is newly emergent. The movement between the anomic and the canonic is a process much of whose richness remains to be uncovered. Thus, to be more explicit, I would say that the *constitution of contemporary micro-groups in a network is the most final expression of the creativity of the masses*.

This brings us back to the old notion of community. It would seem that at each founding moment – what I will call the cultural moment in opposition to the civilizing moment which follows – the vital energy is concentrated on the creation of new community forms. Here I call upon the historians: does not each great caesura in human evolution – revolution, decadence, the birth of empire – see the rise of an array of new lifestyles? These may be effervescent, ascetic, oriented toward the past or the future; they have as their common characteristic on the one hand, a breaking with the commonly held wisdom and, on the other, an enhancing of the organic aspect of the social aggregation. In this sense, the 'fused group' of the founding moment is marked by the previously mentioned symbolism. Mirroring the city transported to the countryside in the work of the famous humorist Alphonse Allais, we can see the rise of what might be called 'villages within the city', that is, the face-to-face relationships that characterize the basic cells; it may be the result of solidarities, everyday life, religious practices or even small professional associations.

On these various points, historical analyses may allow us to shed some light on the evolution of contemporary megalopolises and metropolises.[52] Indeed, the so-called 'Crisis of Western civilization', may perhaps be none other than the end of great economic, political and ideological structures. Moreover, in each of these domains we need only refer to the varied experiences, decentralizations and other minuscule autonomies, to the explosion of knowledge and the performative entities on a human scale, in order to appreciate the pertinence of the *tribal paradigm* I am putting forward. This paradigm, it must be underlined, is completely foreign to the individualist logic. Indeed, as opposed to an organization in which the individual can (*de jure* if not *de facto*) be sufficient unto himself, the group can be understood only within a whole. This is an essentially *relationist* perspective; whether the relationship is one of attraction or repulsion makes little difference. The organicity we are examining here is another manner of speaking of the mass and its equilibrium.

Going beyond a dominant school of thought that accentuates the macro-political and economic perspective, the research on contemporary urban life would be well advised to bring up to date the symbolic relationship which is (re)structuring our neighbourhoods – and not grudgingly, but willingly. The breakdown and uprooting of the nuclear family, the resulting sense of isolation – all of these analyses no doubt motivated by the best reformist or revolutionary intentions – cannot resist unbiased observation and urban decay. One has only to look at the 'genuine surprise' of Young and Willmott who, in their research carried out in the East End of London, remarked upon a 'quasi-tribal family and community system'.[53] This very prudent 'quasi' is no longer appropriate, now that ideological barriers are falling away and tribalism is confirmed on a daily basis – for better or worse, it must be said – since, although the tribe is the guarantee of solidarity, it also represents the possibility of control; it can also be the cause of village racism and ostracism. Being a member of a tribe may require self-sacrifice for the other, but also a degree of open-mindedness in so far as the chauvinism of the small shopkeeper allows. The caricature of the 'brother-in-law' by the cartoonist Cabu is a perfect example.*

Whatever the case, putting aside any judgemental attitude, tribalism in its more or less brilliant aspects is in the process of infiltrating lifestyles to a greater and greater degree. I would be tempted to say that it is becoming an end in itself; that is, through interposing groups, clans and gangs, it reminds us of the importance of the affect in social life. Thus a pertinent

---

* *Transl. note*: Cabu: the French cartoonist who has made a career of attacking the traditional institutions of work and family. *Mon Beauf* (1976) gives a stereotyped view of a conventional, even racist white male.

recent study on 'secondary groups' points out that single mothers, feminists and homosexuals are not seeking a 'temporary resolution of individual situations'; it is rather an 'overall reconsideration of the rules of solidarity' that is at issue.[54] Gain is secondary; it is not even sure that success is desirable, since it risks draining the warmth out of being-together. What has just been stated with regard to the organized movements in question is even more true in the case of the multiplicity of scattered groups whose sole purpose is to share warmth. It so happens that such a gradual goal does not fail to rebound on the social whole.

It is precisely this network which binds, as I have said, the group and the mass. This bond is without the rigidity of the forms of organization with which we are familiar; it refers more to a certain ambience, a state of mind, and is preferably to be expressed through lifestyles that favour appearance and 'form'.[55] It is a case of a kind of *collective unconscious (non-conscious)* which acts as a matrix for the varied group experiences, situations, actions or wanderings. It is striking in this regard to note that contemporary mass rites are the result of micro-groups that are both highly distinctive at the same time as forming an indistinct and rather muddled whole – to which we are referred by the orgiastic metaphor and the surpassing of individual identity.

Let us pursue the paradox further: these tribal mass rites (mass rites *and* tribal rites) are perceptible in the various sporting gatherings which, through the influence of the media, take on a familiar significance. We can see them at work in the consumer (consuming?) frenzy of department stores, supermarkets and shopping centres which of course sell products but secrete even more a symbolism, that is, the impression of participating in a common species. It can also be seen in those aimless wanderings along the avenues of our great cities. When we pay close attention, this indistinct companionship, resembling nothing so much as animal migrations, is in fact constituted of a multitude of small cells that interact with each other. It is also permeated by a whole series of recognitions, of people and places, which turn this maelstrom of cultural signs into a well-ordered whole. Of course, our eye needs to get used to this incessant flux; but if, like a hidden camera, it can both take in the bigger picture and focus on detail, it will not fail to appreciate the powerful architectonic which structures these wanderings. Let us remember that these phenomena are nothing new: the agora of Antiquity or, closer to home, the *passegiata* of Italy, or the evening promenade in the south of France all present the same characteristics, and are considerable sites of sociality.

Finally, in the same vein, the rituals of evasion known as summer holidays offer the spectacle of crowded beaches, prompting many chagrined observers to deplore the promiscuity and discomfort engendered by such cramped conditions. Here again, one must remember that these conditions allow a kind of euphemized communion, and as Dorflès remarked, they 'remove any distance between oneself and others, [and] construct a unique amalgam'.[56] On the other hand, such cramped conditions are subtly differentiated and tastes in clothing or sexuality, sports, groups and regions, have to share the same coastal terrain, recreating a community whole with diverse and complementary functions. In a country such as Brazil, where the beach is a veritable public institution, monographs have noted that in Rio the numbering of 'blocks' (security posts spread over all the beaches) lets you know where you are (X – leftist, Y – homosexual, Z – golden youth, etc.). In Bahia too, the different sections of beach are like so many meeting places, according to the group to which you belong.

What should be retained from these few anecdotes is that there is a constant movement back and forth between tribes and the mass, which is part of a whole that fears emptiness. This *horror vacui* which manifests itself for example in the non-stop music on the beaches, in the stores and in many pedestrian streets, is an ambience perhaps reminiscent of the permanent noise and the disordered restlessness of Mediterranean and Eastern cities. Whatever the case, no domain is spared by this ambience. By way of summing up, if we are to grant that the theatre is a useful mirror for appreciating the state of a given society, then it is appropriate to remember both what the restlessness of our cities owes to the various street spectacles, and the development of the 'primitive theatre' and the various (re)surging cults of African, Brazilian and Hindu origin. I have no intention of analysing these phenomena here; I only wish to show that they are all based on a tribal logic which itself can exist only by invading, through the concatenation of the network, the mass.[57]

These are all things that contravene the spirit of seriousness, the individualism and 'separation' (in the Hegelian sense) which characterize modern productivist and bourgeois perspectives. These characteristics of modernity have tried their best to control or sanitize the dances of possession and other forms of popular effervescence. Perhaps we should see here the revenge of the values of the South over those of the North: 'choreographic epidemics' (E. de Martino) are breaking out. It should be remembered that they had an aggregative function. The act of lamenting or enjoying *in a group* had the effect of looking after as well as reintegrating the sick member into the community. These phenomena common to the Mediterranean basin (maenadism, tarantism, various bacchanalia), to India (Tantrism), or to the African or Latino-African cultures (candomblé, shango) are of the greatest interest in understanding group therapies, parallel networks of medicine and the various manifestations of what Schutz called 'making music together',* as well as the development of sectarianism: all things which are the contemporary signs of 'the choreographic epidemic'.

In fact, it is not a given lifestyle that can be considered prophetic; it is the jumble itself that is prophetic. Indeed, although it is impossible to tell what will arise to form a new culture, one can nevertheless state that it will be structurally pluralistic and full of contradictions ['contradictoriel']. In the

---

* *Transl. note*: This phrase appears in English in the text.

caste system Bouglé saw union in the cult of division. This paradoxical tension has not failed to give rise to intense collective sentiments 'which emerge above the mass of castes'.[58] Such a fine insight can surpass moral judgement to see the solid organicity of the whole. For our part, we might say that modernity has experienced another paradox: that of uniting by blurring differences, and the division that this engenders. At the very least, it attempts to attenuate their effects, which, it will be agreed, is not without a certain grandeur and generosity. *The entire political order is built on this.* But, mirroring other eras and other places, it is possible to imagine that the bond holding a given entity together might in fact be constituted of that which divides (cf. the conjugal polemic). The tension between heterogeneities could be said to guarantee the solidity of the whole. The master craftsmen of the Middle Ages knew a thing or two about this, and built our cathedrals on this principle. This is the *order of the mass*. Thus, lifestyles which are foreign to each other can sketch the outline of a way of living together. And this occurs while remaining curiously faithful to the specificity of each. From this arose the richness of the great cultural moments, at their very founding.

Notes

1. On the power-*puissance* relationship, cf. M. Maffesoli, *La Violence totalitaire*, Paris, PUF, 1979, pp. 20–69, especially p. 69.

2. On style, cf. P. Brown,*The Making of Late Antiquity*, Cambridge, Mass.; Harvard University Press, 1976, p. 1. G. Durand, *La Beauté comme présence paraclétique, Eranos, 1984*, Frankfurt, Insel Verlag, 1986, p. 129; M. Maffesoli, 'Le Paradigme esthétique: la sociologie comme art', *Sociologie et Sociétés*, Montréal, vol. 17, no. 2 (October 1985), p. 36.

3. Cf. W. Benjamin, *Essais*, Paris, Denoël-Gonthier, 1983, p. 40.

4. A. Schutz, 'Faire de la musique ensemble. Une étude des rapports sociaux', French transl. in *Sociétés*, Paris, Masson, 1984, vol.1, no. 1, pp. 22–27. Excerpted from 'Making music together' in *Collected Papers*,vol. 2, The Hague, Nijhoff, 1971, pp. 159–178.

5. Cf. for example Gumplowicz, *Précis de sociologie*, Paris, 1896, p. 337, *et seq*; on O. Spann, cf. the analysis by W. Johnston, *L'Esprit viennois, une histoire intellectuelle et sociale, 1848–1938*, French transl., Paris, PUF, 1985, p. 365.

6. On sociology's fascination with the medieval community, cf. R. Nisbet, *The Sociological Tradition*, London, Heinemann Educational, 1970, p. 15; for a precursor of American sociology, cf. P. St-Arnaud, *W.G. Sumner et les débuts de la sociologie américaine*, Québec, Presses de l'Université Laval, 1984, p. 107.

7. T. Adorno, *Aesthetic Theory*, London, Routledge and Kegan Paul, 1984, p. 13; cf. my definition of aesthetics, Maffesoli, 'Le Paradigme esthétique', pp. 33–41.

8. Cf. P. Watzlawick, *La Réalité de la réalité*, French transl., Paris, Seuil, 1978, p. 91 and M. Scheler, *The Nature of Sympathy*, London, Routledge and Kegan Paul, cf. especially pp. 72, 51, *et seq.*, p. 55. On crowds, cf. J. Beauchard, *La Puissance des foules*, Paris, PUF, 1985. On sport, cf. A. Ehrenberg, 'Le Football et ses imaginaires', *Les Temps modernes*, November 1984 and P. Sansot, *Les Formes sensibles de la vie sociale*, Paris, PUF, 1986. On tourism, cf. *Sociétés*, no. 8, Paris, Masson, vol. 2 no 2, (1986).

9. Scheler, *The Nature of Sympathy*, pp. 96–99. On the dionysiac tendency, cf. M. Maffesoli, *L'Ombre de Dionysos, contribution à une sociologie de l'orgie*, Paris, Librairie des Méridiens, 2nd edition, 1985 and K. Mannheim, *Ideology and Utopia*, New York, Harcourt Brace Jovanovich, 1954, who speaks of 'orgiastic chialism' (p. 190); M. Halbwachs, *La Mémoire collective*, Paris, PUF, 1968, p. 28, on 'collective interferences'.

10. Cf. G. Hoquenghem and R. Scherer, *L'Ame atomique*, Paris, Albin Michel, 1986, p. 17. Cf. J. Baudrillard, *L'Amérique*, Paris, Grasset, 1986, p. 107. Cf. also the work of A. Moles, Institut de psychologie sociale, Université de Strasbourg I, on street-life, on fire-eaters, etc.

11. On appearance, refer to my analyses: M. Maffesoli, *La Conquête du présent, pour une sociologie de la vie quotidienne*, Paris, PUF, 1979; cf. also P. Perrot, *Le Travail des apparences*, Paris, Seuil, 1984. On the 'Parva esthetica' cf. Hoquenghem and Scherer, *L'Ame atomique*, p. 25. On perceptions, see Sansot, *Les Formes sensibles*. For an approach by the sociology of the senses, cf. G. Simmel, *Mélanges de philosophie rélativiste*, Paris, Félix Alcan, 1912.

12. R. Da Matta, *Carnaval, bandits et héros*, Paris, Seuil, 1983, p. 116; cf. also Ehrenberg,'Le Football et ses imaginaires', p. 859.

13. On the organic connection, see my analysis: M. Maffesoli, *La Connaissance ordinaire. Précis de sociologie compréhensive*, Paris, Méridiens, 1985. On J. Séguy's distinction, cf., C. Lalive d'Epinay, 'La Recherche aujourd'hui, pistes et contacts' in *Sociétés*, Paris, Masson, vol. 2, no. 2 (1986), no. 8, p. 29. For my part, I consider the 'return of the gods' to be less in the minds of researchers than in the minds of the people, which is why it becomes problematic for the researcher. On *reliance*, cf. Bolle de Bal, *La Tentation communautaire*, Editions Université de Bruxelles, 1985.

14. Y. Lambert, *Dieu change en Bretagne*, Paris, Cerf, 1985 and D. Hervieu-Léger, *Vers un nouveau christianisme*, Paris, Cerf, 1986, p. 49, on which she details specific traits of working-class religiosity, and p. 217, on which she observes an affinity between the modern world and religiosity; on 'affinity parishes', cf. p. 12.

15. Cf. M. Weber, *Economy and Society*, Berkeley, University of California Press, 1978, pp. 452–456.

16. L.-V. Thomas, *Rites de mort*, Paris, Fayard, 1985.

17. On medievalism and sociology, cf. the analysis and examples by Nisbet in *The Sociological Tradition*, pp 14–15.

18. With respect to Karl Marx, cf. F. Lévy, *K. Marx, histoire d'un bourgeois allemand*, Paris, Grasset, 1973. On Durkheim, cf. Nisbet, *The Sociological Tradition*, pp. 84–86. On the problem of mechanical and organic solidarities, cf. Maffesoli, *La Violence totalitaire*, p. 120.

19. Cf. Halbwachs, *La Mémoire collective*, pp. 119–120. On non-individualism in Simmel, cf. my article, 'Le Paradigme esthétique'.

20. Cf. B. Nicolescu, *Nous, la particule et le monde*, Paris, Editions Le Mail, 1985; on synchrony, cf., E. T. Hall, *Beyond Culture*, Garden City, New York, Anchor/Doubleday, 1976, p. 61; on the *habitus*, cf. Maffesoli, *La Connaissance ordinaire*, p. 225, *et seq.*; on the thomist origins of the *habitus*, cf. G. Rist, 'La Notion médiévale d'*habitus* dans la sociologie de P. Bourdieu', *Revue européenne des Sciences Sociales*, Genève, Droz, vol. 22 (1984), no. 67, pp. 201–212.

21. Here I am basing myself on a very pertinent analysis by G. Simmel, *Sociologie et epistémiologie*, Paris, PUF, 1981, p. 125. Unlike Madame L. Gasparini, I propose to translate the term *Geselligkeit* as sociality and not sociability.

22. It is not very useful to cite the works of Durkheim, Weber and Freud. I am borrowing this expression from P. Tacussel, *L'Attraction sociale*, Paris, Librairie des Méridiens, 1984.

23. P. Berger, and T. Luckmann, *The Social Construction of Reality*, New York, Anchor Books, 1967, p. 2.

24. Cf. M. Bourlet, 'L'orgie sur la montagne', *Nouvelle Revue d'Ethnopsychiatrie*, Paris, no. 1 (1983), p. 20. For a more general use of the figure of Dionysus, cf. Maffesoli, *L'Ombre de Dionysos*. Cf. also G. Renaud, *A l'Ombre du rationalisme*, Montréal, Editions St Martin, 1984, p. 171: 'La confrontation à l'étranger, à l'Autre . . . interroge l'appauvrissement d'une identité nationale qui se ferme de plus en plus sur elle-mème.' (The confrontation with the stranger, the Other . . . questions the impoverishment of a national identity increasingly closed in on itself.)

25. E. Renan, *Marc Aurèle ou la fin du monde antique*, Paris, Livre de Poche, 1984, pp. 317–318.

26. J. Séguy, *Christianisme et société, Introduction à la sociologie de Ernst Troeltsch*, Paris, Cerf, 1980, p. 112. Cf. his analysis of the 'sect type', p. 111, *et seq.*

27. Cf. Gibbon, *The History of the Decline and Fall of the Roman Empire*, London, Methuen, 1909, Vol. 2, Ch. 23, p. 456, *et seq.* On medieval sects, cf. Séguy, *Christianisme et société*, pp. 176–179.

28. The expression 'wellspring' was applied by E. Poulat to popular Catholicism in *Catholicisme, démocratie et socialisme*, Paris, Casterman, 1977, p. 486. On the permanency of the 'real country', of the Catholic base, cf. E. Poulat, *Eglise contre bourgeoisie*, Paris, Casterman, 1977, p. 155. Cf. also the work of Prof. Zylberberg and Madame P. Côté, Université Laval, Québec, Faculty of Social Sciences.

29. On the guilds, cf. the article by A. Guedez, 'Une société en clair obscur : Le compagnon français', *Revista de Ciencias Socias*, Universidade Federal do Ceará, Fortaleza, Brazil, vol. 5, 2nd edition (1974), p. 36. On the 'phratries', cf. Lambert, *Dieu change en Bretagne*, pp. 40 and 264.

30. One may interpret in the light of everyday history such historicist concepts as 'situational determination' or 'seat in life' proposed by P. Berger and T. Luckmann in *The Social Construction of Reality*, p. 7. On surrealism and situationism ethics, cf. also Tacussel, *L'Attraction sociale*.

31. While recognizing the primacy of relationism in Simmel, I am opposed to Séguy's individualist interpretation of it: 'Aux enfants de la sociologie des religions: Georg Simmel', *Archives de sociologie des religions*, Paris, C.N.R.S., 1964, no 17, p. 6. With respect to aestheticism, cf. my article, 'Le Paradigme esthétique'. Cf. also Y. Atoji, 'La Philosophie de l'art de Georges Simmel: son optique sociologique', *Sociétés*, Paris, Masson (forthcoming). The term *reliance* is borrowed from Bolle de Bal, *La Tentation communautaire*.

32. Concerning the example of private worship, cf. E. R. Dodds, *The Greeks and the Irrational*, Berkeley, University of California at Berkeley, 1956, p. 242. Cf. also P. Brown, *Augustine of Hippo*, Berkeley, University of California Press, 1967, on the Manichaean networks (p. 46).

33. Cf. C. Bouglé, *Essays on the Caste System*, Cambridge, Cambridge University Press, 1971, pp. 32–35. On the 'play of human passions in Québec society', cf. Renaud, *A l'Ombre du rationalisme*, p. 167.

34. E. Durkheim, *The Division of Labour in Society*, New York, Free Press, 1964. On the group as a 'source of life', cf. the preface (p. 26). Concerning the intermingling of groups, cf. Halbwachs, *La Mémoire collective*, p. 66.

35. Cf. Nisbet's sociological analysis in *The Sociological Tradition*, p 55.

36. G. Simmel, *Les Problèmes de la philosophie de l'histoire*, Paris, PUF, 1984, p. 75.

37. M. Maffesoli, *Cahiers Internationaux de sociologie*, vol. 73 (1982), p. 363.

38. Refer to my chapters on theatricality in Maffesoli, *La Conquête du présent*. On secrecy, see Simmel's remarkable article 'La Société secrète' in *Nouvelle Revue de Psychanalyse*, Paris, Gallimard, no. 14 (1976).

39. Cf. Renan, *Marc Aurèle*, p. 294.

40 On the 'foreign' sociologist, cf. E. Morin, *La Métamorphose de Plozevet*, Paris, Fayard, 1967, p. 37. On sodality, cf. E. Poulat, *Intégrisme et catholicisme intégral*, Paris, Casterman, 1969. On the reductionist fantasy of the sociologist, cf. Renaud, *A l'Ombre du rationalisme*: 'Society becomes a laboratory and must conform to reality as defined by the sociologist' (p. 235).

41. Cf. my book, *La Conquête du présent*. On the 'egotism of the group', cf. Simmel's article, 'La Société secrète', p. 298.

42. Cf. K. Schipper, *Le Corps taoïste*, Paris, Fayard, 1982, pp. 28–37. It shows how secret societies depend on the 'real country'.

43. Cf. Bismarck's memoirs as quoted by G. Simmel, 'La Société secrète', *op. cit.*, p. 303. For a good introduction on homosexuality, cf. G. Ménard, *L'Homosexualité démystifiée*, Ottawa, Leméac, 1980.

44. E. Canetti, *The Conscience of Words*, transl. J. Neugroshel, New York, Seabury Press, 1979, p. 115.

45. Cf. the remarkable biography by P. Brown, *Augustine of Hippo*, p. 194.

46. I would refer the reader to the study of executives carried out by A. Wickham and M. Patterson, *Les Carrièristes*, Paris, Ramsay, 1983. On the dock workers, cf. the studies cited by M. Young and P. Willmott, *Family and Kinship in East London*, Harmondsworth, Penguin, 1964, p. 97, *et seq*. On perversity as ruse, cf. Renaud, *A l'Ombre du rationalisme*, p. 186.

47. Cf. H. de Montherlant, and R. Peyrefitte, *Correspondance*, Paris, Plon, 1983, p. 53.

48. On the duplicity of the symbol, besides what is already known as regards the Western tradition, one might also refer to the function of its Chinese equivalent expressed in the word 'fool'. Cf. Schipper, *Le Corps taoïste*, p. 287, note 7.

49. Simmel, 'La Société secrète', p. 293.

50. On the link with Antiquity, cf. P. Brown, *Society and the Holy in Late Antiquity*, London, Faber and Faber, 1982, p. 116.

51. On the consequences of the phenomenon of the 'group apart' on Roman society for example, cf. Renan, *Marc Aurèle*, p. 77.

52. On the 'fused group', cf. of course J. P. Sartre, *Critique of Dialectical Reason*, London, Verso, 1976, p. 358. Concerning the creativity of communal forms in Antiquity, cf. Brown, *The Making of Late Antiquity*, p. 6. On perdurability and the attention paid to solidarity, cf. Renaud, *A l'Ombre du rationalisme*, p. 179.

53. Young and Willmott, *Family and Kinship in East London*, p. 12. Cf. also a more recent study: S. Rosenberg, *Annales de la recherche urbaine*, no. 9 (1981). On religious groups in Paris and Recife, cf. M. Aubrée, 'Les Nouvelles tribus de la chrétienneté', *Raison Présente*, Paris, no. 72 (1984), pp. 71–87.

54. E. Reynaud, 'Groupes secondaires et solidarité organique : qui exerce le contrôle social?' in *L'Année sociologique*, Paris, vol. 33 (1983), p. 184. On the significance of gangs, cf. E. Morin, *L'Esprit du temps*, Paris, Livres de Poche, 1983, p. 310.

55. Cf. my article, 'Le Paradigme esthétique'. Cf. also *La Connaissance ordinaire*, Ch. 4: vers un 'formisme sociologique'.

56. G. Dorflès, *L'Intervalle perdu*, French transl., Paris, Librairie des Méridiens, 1984, p. 30, *et seq*. It goes without saying that I do not share Dorflès' fear concerning contemporary tribalism and its 'fear of the void'.

57. On the 'primitive theatre', cf. the references and studies cited ibid., p. 163. Tarantism has been thoroughly analysed by E. de Martino, *La Terre du remords*, French transl., Paris, Gallimard, 1966. On the *candomblé*, please refer to R. Da Matta, *Cidade e Devoçao*, Recife, 1980 and 'Le Syllogisme du sacré' in *Sociétés*, Paris, Masson, no. 5 (1985), and V. Costa Lima, *A Famiglia de Santo nos candomblés, jeje-nagos do Bahia*, Salvador, 1977. Schutz's 'Making music together' is also translated in the journal *Sociétés*, Paris, Masson, vol. I, no. 1 (1984). On Tantrism, cf. J. Varenne, *Le Tantrisme*, Paris, 1977. On sects, cf. the fine article by J. Zylberberg and J. P. Montminy, 'L'Esprit, le pouvoir et les femmes', Polygraphie d'un mouvement culturel québécois, *Recherches sociographiques*, Québec, Université Laval, vol. 22, no. 1 (1981), pp. 49–104. Cf. also the thesis of P. Côté, 'De la dévotion au pouvoir: les femmes dans le Renouveau charismatique', Québec, Université Laval, 1984.

58. Bouglé, *Essays on the Caste System*, p. 142.

5

POLYCULTURALISM

1. Of triplicity

While modernity has been obsessed with politics, it may be equally true that postmodernity is possessed by the idea of the clan, a phenomenon which is not without its effect on the relationship to the Other and, more specifically, to the stranger. Indeed, from the political perspective, a mechanical solidarity tends to predominate between rational individuals and between them as a group and the state. On the other hand, with the clan we are faced with an organic solidarity that mainly accentuates the whole. To quote Simmel, in the individualist (and political) perspective, the general principle is 'that in which we take an active role, rather than that which is common to all'.[1] It is this 'common to all', while being shared by small groups, that seems pertinent today. Consequently, beyond a surface individualism or narcissism, we shall pay closer attention to the group attitudes that develop in our societies – attitudes which, in my opinion, are in harmony with the dionysiac logic of sociality. It is perfectly obvious that the multiplication of small affinity groups in our modern megalopolises raises the question of their more or less conflictual relationships. In any case, this neo-tribalism reminds us that consensus (*cumsensualis*)* is not uniquely rational, something that is too often forgotten.[2] To be sure, this hypothesis of 'shared sentiment' obliges us to rethink the role of the third person or outsider, that is, of the plural in the societal structure. The conjugal relationship of the individual–state may be characterized as turbulent, however its orbit used to be well delineated. The intrusion of the outsider puts us square in the centre of a storm whose results are difficult to foresee. It would be interesting to examine some of the essential elements of this effervescence.

Julien Freund, like Schmidt and Simmel before him, pointed out on numerous occasions the importance of the figure three in social life. Since then, the notion of the third person has had an epistemological dimension which disclaims reductionist simplifications.[3] With the figure '3', society is born and therefore sociology. I have no intention of confronting this question head-on here; I shall limit myself to saying that from anthropological research (Lévi-Strauss, Dumézil, Durand) to the psychological experiments of the Palo Alto School, one can find evidence of the strength

---

* *Transl. note*: 'with the senses' (rather than the usual Latin derivation of consensus: *consentire*).

of triadism.[4] In the strongest sense of the word, cultural and individual dynamism are based on the tension between heterogeneous elements. This is a perspective that takes on increasing significance at the same time as a symbolist vision of the world is resurgent.[5] We are now far, to be sure, from the unity that has been, from the dawn of modernity, the goal of Western rationalism. The metaphor of the triad lets us highlight the paradox; the splintering; the break-up; the contradictory in action – in short, the constitutive plurality of this contemporary neo-tribalism.

Thus, succeeding the dream of unity is a sort of *unicity*: the adjustment of diverse elements. In the image of the coenesthesia which is able to integrate, within the framework of conflictual harmony, bodily functions and dysfunctions, the notion of the outsider emphasizes the founding aspect of difference. What is more, this is not due to the unanimist perspective of tolerance, but is caused by what might be called the organicity of opposites; the famous *coincidentia oppositorum* of ancient wisdom that, from medieval alchemists to Far Eastern Taoists, has given birth to many organizations and many social representations. Especially for Taoism, in its description of the 'interior country', the field of cinnabar, the root of man is situated '*three* inches above the navel in order to express the *trinity* of Heaven, Earth and Man'. To highlight its richness still further, the Tao sees the three as that which gives birth to the 'Ten thousand ones'.[6]

The preceding has often been analysed; it is enough just to touch on it, if only allusively, in order to insist on the fact that multiplicity is the vital principle. As for the upholders of monist or dualist systems, it is well to remind them that effervescence and the imperfection of the three are what account for its prospective sharpness and dynamism.

There are times when this pluralism is either denied or forgotten; we are then witness to the creation of entity-types, conceived on the basis of homogeneous models: unified nations, historical subjects (the proletariat), linear progress, and so on. But these hypostases cannot weather the winds of change and its harsh laws; whether in the case of the masses and their behaviours or political structures, differential realities win out in the end. And many are the examples which show that, following a process of centralization and unification, there is a swing back to particularism and localism, and in all domains. The example of French political history is particularly instructive in this regard. Any unified entity is temporary. Furthermore, accounting for diversity and complexity is a mark of common sense too infrequently adopted by intellectuals – on the grounds that it contravenes the simplicity of the concept.

Infinity begins with the third person. With the plural, the living is integrated into sociological analysis. Of course, this does not simplify the task at hand, since, to quote Morin, the pluralism at work among the people causes the latter to become 'polyphonous, even cacophonous'.[7] However, the risk must be assumed, since, on the one hand, unanimity and unity are quite often pernicious for the structuring of the city (cf. Aristotle,

Politics, II, 1261 b–7); and on the other, although we are now sensitive to the spirit of the times, we cannot help but acknowledge the irrepressible growth of the *plural* in all its forms in our societies. The resultant pluriculturalism is certainly not without risk, but arising as it does out of the conjunction of a principle of logic and a principle of reality, it is in vain that we deny its significance; especially since, as for all periods of effervescence, this heterogenization in action is the matrix for the social values of the future. Thus, in first recognizing this heterogenization, then by analysing its components, we are capable of listing all that makes up the social fabric of this *fin de siècle*; as well as that which is becoming clear in that nebula which can be called *sociality*.

Without having a definite sense of direction, let us point out once more the orientation that sociality may take. It would no longer be based on the Faustian monovalence of 'doing' and its flip-side, the contractual and finalized associationism I will sum up as the following: 'the economy-politics of the self and the world'. Quite on the contrary, in fact (hence the 'orgiastic' metaphor I keep using),[8] the sociality which is being defined integrates a good portion of passionate communication, pleasure in the present and incoherence – all things that are characterized by both acceptance and rejection. This ambivalence has often been analysed from a psychological perspective; it is appropriate to examine the social sub-clauses of this ambivalence and note that it adapts easily to technological change. We can indeed observe that, with the help of micro-electronics, these extending forms of association that are *networks* (contemporary neo-tribalism) are based on integration and the affective refusal. This paradox – a clear sign of vitality – is in any case one of the most useful keys to any comprehensive project.

2. Presence and estrangement

Thus, by relying on the classic dichotomy between culture and civilization, we may note that the former in its founding dynamism has no fear whatsoever of the stranger. On the contrary, it has always been able to flourish thanks to all that it gets from the outside while at the same time remaining itself.

In this regard, we must refer to all those examples given to us by human history; self-assuredness – which is a form of autonomy, hence the other's exclusion – favours the welcome of this other. In analysing the evolution of French culture and language in Europe, Louis Réau underlines with the utmost erudition that during the seventeenth and eighteenth centuries, foreigners in France were certain of receiving the 'most pleasant and flattering welcome. Never had xenophilia, I would even venture to say xenomania, been pushed further.'[9] This cannot fail to be instructive ('foreigners are spoiled'); and at the same time a specifically French way of life and of thinking was becoming hegemonic. It is this way each time something authentically strong is born. *Puissance*, as I have shown,[10] has nothing to do with power and all that surrounds it: that is, fear and anxiety both experienced and inflicted. Weakness leads to both the withdrawal into the self and aggressiveness; whereas civilization is barricaded behind a cold fear, culture can grow and accept the outsider. This surely explains what Réau highlights with astonishment (ibid., p. 314): no effort was made to spread the use of French in the eighteenth century, yet we know how phenomenally its use increased during this era. From ancient Athens to contemporary New York, by way of Florence in the quattrocento, we can constantly see such poles of attraction that function in fact like processes metabolizing foreign elements.

Thus, it has been possible to make a connection between the vitality of a region like the Alsace and 'the constant arrival of new blood'. According to F. Hoffet, it is this mixing that explains the 'major works' produced in this country.[11] Certainly, although a tragedy of the border (*Grenze Tragödie*) exists, it does not fail to be dynamic: bridges and doors, to use an image of Simmel's. The border countries live life in a major key, the consecutive mixing and imbalances following movements of populations. But at the same time, throughout the exogamy that this gives rise to, original creations are born, the best expressions of the synergy of the static and the labile qualities inherent in the social reality. This synergy is summarized in the expression 'dynamic rootedness'. It should not be forgotten that this 'border' tension explains the thinking of Spinoza, Marx, Freud, Kafka and others . . . all of whom were both integrated and distant. The strength of their thinking perhaps has its origin in the fact that they are founded on a double polarity:[12] presence and estrangement. These determined regions and works of genius experience or indicate, in a heightened way, that which otherwise constitutes, in a minor key, the everyday life of the people. Before becoming a racist or a nationalist, or, on a more trivial plane, the 'average bloke' so often described, the citizen 'knows' instinctively that short of, or beyond, lofty and more or less imposed ideals, his everyday life is composed of mixture, difference and mutual arrangement with the other; whether a foreigner or anomic figure with strange customs. Firstly, let us draw a link between the mass and culture at its founding moment. This is not an accidental or abstract link: every time an era begins, a city flourishes or a country is epiphanized, it occurs as a result of a popular *puissance*. Only later is there confiscation (of the era, the city, the country) by a few who appoint themselves managers, owners and clerks of legitimacy and knowledge. Secondly, let us recognize at this juncture a capacity both for absorption and for diffusion. The above-cited examples are abundant proof of a confident entity integrating and radiating. Let us venture an organic image: a body in shape can show great flexibility; there are no signs of rigidity or prudence – the stuff of precautions and pettiness! To use a term of Bataille's, there is a sort of sovereignty that wells up from this conjunction – a form of triumphant animality that 'feels' how to strike a balance between the particularity that preserves and the general that integrates us into a vast worldly evolution. It is a matter of to and fro between the nomadism and sedentariness that make up the human adventure; between the yes and the no at the heart of any representation.

Among the plethora of historical examples that come to mind, there is one particularly noteworthy one, that furthermore can be considered as instructive for our time: of the fight over Donatism that presented a difficult moment for early Christianity. In more than one aspect, it seems to me that this period called 'Late Antiquity' is not without similarity to our own. The historian Peter Brown in his remarkable work on Saint Augustine examined with great insight the reasons why the Donatists were opposed to the Bishop of Hippo.[13] In the framework of our reflections here, I will retain, in simplified form, only one essential element of the *disputatio*: according to the Donatists, it was necessary to isolate themselves, remain a Church of the pure, cut off from the world with all the consequences involved in such a choice. For Augustine, on the other hand, it was important to feel sufficiently strong to assimilate the 'other', to be flexible in order to win over the world; because he was certain of the validity, the universality and especially the prospective aspect of the evangelical message. Thus our Bishop, who as a Manichaean knew the delights of the utmost purism, did not hesitate to gather from the literary and philosophic heritage of the pagan world anything that could reinforce the message he heralded. At a time when a new world is being born, the question is significant: to the tranquil assurance of the self-contained sect, Saint Augustine preferred a wider *ecclesia* open to the effervescence of customs and men from all over the map. The city of God he sought to establish was measured against the scale of a vast world and it is normal that it should also embrace its turbulence. It is only by paying this price that it will perdure – such a vision of genius from a founder of a new culture!

Let us take another look at this phenomenon, but this time referring to another era: the mythical era (but is it any more so than the previous one?). By referring to the dionysiac theme, which is also applicable to our own era, we may note that in the city-state of Thebes – civilized, rationally administered and rather languid – the irruption of Dionysus is also the irruption of the stranger. Effeminate, perfumed, differently clothed: his appearance, habits and the ways of thinking that he disseminates are shocking in more than one sense.[14] The irruption of this foreign body corresponds to the passage from classical Hellenism to the Hellenistic period. Dionysus, latecomer god (demi-god?) upsets this period's perfection, but because of this, allows it to blossom. That which exhausts itself, even in its completeness, needs a dysfunction, even an external one, to come and recharge it. Moreover, most of the time, the foreign element usually only actualizes a potentiality that had been neglected or kept in check. In the above-mentioned logic, tension and paradox are thus necessary, a bit like a graft that allows worn-out trees to bear beautiful fruit once again.

This intrusion of the foreign element may function as an *anamnesis*: it reminds a social body that had a tendency to forget it, that it is structurally heterogeneous; even if for reasons of ease it tended to try to restore everything to unity. This reminder of the polytheism of values is particularly blatant in the case of dionysiac ceremonies. Dionysus, god from 'elsewhere', must integrate those 'others': the metic and the slave of the Greek city-state. It seems (cf. M. Bourlet) as if the thiase associated them with the citizens. Thus, although only haphazardly and ritually, the community performs as a function of the here and elsewhere. It will be remembered that the cult of Aglaurus celebrated the city as *unity*; the orgiastic thiase reminds that it is also unicity, i.e. the conjunction of opposites.

In short, to go back to our initial remarks, 'the languishing civilization requires barbarians in order to regenerate'.[15] Is it paradoxical to say that the stranger allows a new culture to be instated? The role of the Romans with respect to the Greek civilization, of the barbarians with regard to the end of the Roman Empire and, closer to our own time, the name 'Huns of the West' (*die Westhunnen*) that was given to the protagonists of the French Revolution, or even the rallying cry 'Hurray for the Cossack revolution', which was repeated by certain anarchists tired of bourgeois weakness – they all underline the cultural importance of the founding foreignness. Further, Mosco's recent film *Des terroristes à la retraite* shows easily how, during the Nazi resistance, many defenders of the idea of France, and among the most vigorous, were stateless persons who had arrived from disparate parts.* Less resigned than certain upstanding Frenchmen, they fought and offered their lives in the name of ideals that, for them, symbolized this country that they had chosen as the land of welcome.

What is certain is that all of the great empires of human history are the product of a familiar blending. These few cavalier remarks here refer to the work of historians who tackled this question and whose work may be summed up by the following quotation taken from the remarkable book by Marie-Françoise Baslez who, with nuance and erudition, emphasizes that 'many cities owed their fortune to a heterogeneous population'.[16] This statement can be supplemented by the hypothesis that it was the lack of openness, the cool fear shown towards the stranger that led many cities to their downfall. As we know, 'Rome is no longer in Rome';** but at a certain point, it must measure itself against the other, that is, its heterogeneous empire. I have tried to show that this was a matter of socio-anthropological structure. There is no need to return to Simmel's analysis of the stranger; it is well known. On the other hand, in order to remain faithful to the spirit (as well as the letter), the sociologist must be able to reconsider the importance of such a social 'form'. It is not merely the domain of the past;

---

* *Transl. note*: 'Terrorists in Retirement' (1983) is the title of a documentary by Mosco shown on French television. It recounts the role played by immigrant units in the Resistance.

** *Transl. note*: 'Rome n'est plus dans Rome, elle est toute où je suis' – Rome is no longer in Rome, it is wherever I find myself (Pierre Corneille, *Sertorius*, III, I).

the Chicago School and Sorokin have shown its immediacy for our modern era. Gilberto Freyre has also been able to underline how, taking the example of Portugal, Brazil has constituted itself and energized itself thanks to miscibility and mobility in all senses of the word.[18]

A fortiori, in so far as our postmodern era is concerned, it is time to deal with the consequences of the constitutive heterogeneity of our societies: what is more, a heterogeneity that is only beginning. In the cultural stockpots represented by today's megalopolises, it is no longer possible to deny the existence of the stranger, nor to disclaim his or her role. The historical and mythical examples I have provided are like so many metaphors allowing us to imagine the efflorescence of images, the hedonism and vitalism that can be qualified as dionysiac. These are all things that, because they are experienced in small groups, in a differentiated way; because they do not depend on a particular link and do not refer to unified representations, forbid us from seeking a one-dimensional explanation. The values of *Aufklärung* which, when exported, became the model for the whole world, seem saturated. And in their stead, as in other periods of history, we can see substituted a societal effervescence, favouring intermingling, miscibility, the blending of West and East, in short: the polytheism of values. It is a formless and indefinite polytheism, but one to which due attention should be paid, since it is charged with the future.

The barbarians are at our gates, but should we worry? After all, we are in part barbarian ourselves.

3.   The polytheism of the people, or the diversity of God

After having shown the significance that should be accorded the outsider, and after having given a few highlights of its role in the history of societies, it may be interesting to isolate one of its essential characteristics. It is a logical characteristic in a sense, and one that can for the best part be described by Weber's expression, the 'polytheism of values'. It is necessary to insist on this thematic, since it remains very poorly understood, desiring as we do to bring it back into the realm of politics. More specifically: the fact that a certain right-wing element uses, sometimes with conviction and talent, in its cultural and political battle, the polytheist mythology, is not enough to invalidate such a mythology nor to claim it as the property of a given camp. It even seems to me that polytheism goes beyond the political order; structurally, we might say, since the relativity of values results in *undecidability*. What can be more antithetical to the logic of politics? Moreover, if we wished to be even more precise, or more faithful to the spirit behind these reflections, then perhaps we should mention 'henotheism' as Bouglé did in writing about the Vedic religion in which 'all the Gods become sovereign in turn'.[18]

It is with such nuance and, let us stress once more, in a metaphorical way, that the gods are convoked to enlighten us about the social. Indeed, I have proposed linking the masses and the founding act of culture; it seems to me that this conjunction allows us to welcome the stranger while remaining ourselves (or even better, to nourish this self with the stranger). In consequence, it is possible to present polytheism as the surest sign of the 'non-racism' of the masses.*

Let us make another detour. The essential feature of Judaism and later Christianity was their intransigent monotheism. This is an essential demarcation line which does not bear reconsideration. On the other hand, it should be remembered that, once this principle has been defined in Christian life, there are a thousand and one ways to transgress it. From an anthropological point of view, Gilbert Durand made an extremely fine analysis, from his observatory in Savoy, of the popular faith and practices with which he is familiar. In my own way, I have also shown that the cult of saints may represent a polytheistic intrusion into monotheist rigour, since the theological distinction between the cult of 'latria', directed at God only, and that of 'dulia', centred on saints, is a casuistry with little effect on everyday life. Finally, religious sociology, with some mistrust to be sure, has not left this problem untouched either.[19] It is less a matter of meeting head-on than of stressing here that there is an actualization of the traditional *coincidentia oppositorum* at work, which like a thread weaves its way through religious and hence social life.

Christian mysticism and theosophy, to which Böhme and Meister Eckhart attest, have always kept this preoccupation alive. The recent thesis of Mrs M.E. Coughtrie, 'Rhythmomachia, a propaedeutic game of the Middle Ages' has shown that within the monastic tradition, games can be found that express this irreducible pluralism, such as rhythmomachia, which is based on highly formalized mathematics. Thus, in popular practices (pilgrimages, cults of saints), in mystic expression or in logical sophistication, alterity, the foreign or the stranger have had many havens, enabling a resistance to simplification and unitary reduction.[20] Ecstasy, like the union of votive holidays, has allowed the expression of both the identical and the different. The 'communion of saints' that is the basis of the monastic prayer and the effervescence of the masses refers in a euphemistic or actualized manner to a being-together that is in its construction both varied and polyphonous.

This perspective has never been lost in what has presented itself as Christian monotheism. Thus, in his analysis of nineteenth- and twentieth-century Catholicism, Emile Poulat, with his characteristic scrupulousness, asked the question of how the 'disparate coexists without conflict'. What then is the 'inheritance of this strange phylum, capable of taking such incompatible forms as the Catholic Counter-Reformation, Christian democracy and Christian revolutionaries?'[21] It is surely the idea of the

---

* I use this term intentionally, referring to Pareto's 'non-logic'. There may be something illogical in the 'non-logic', but it is not, in the strictest sense of the term, its essential *quality*. One could make an analogous case for 'non-racism'.

People of God, the perfect *analogon* of the *coincidentia oppositorum* of the divinity – 'popular Catholicism; inter-classist Catholicism', in the words of Poulat. And it is certain that beyond the various political expressions, this popular basis holds firmly to the plurality of ways of thinking and being. In this sense, it can be called a phylum, an infrangible and permanent bedrock. There is an assurance that life perdures, thanks to the multiplicity of its expression, whereas a hegemonic value, perfect or not, tends to exhaust it. One may link this structural *coexistence* to the contradictory thinking (Lupasco, Beigbeder) that is the logical form of polytheism. The institution of the *simultaneum*, which allows, in certain small villages of Alsace, Protestants and Catholics to pray, one after the other, in the same church, can be a good metaphor, beyond all the familiar contingent reasons, of this contradictoriness in action. Like polytheism *stricto sensu*, pluralistic Christianity shows us the importance of finding, over and over again, a *modus vivendi* for integrating 'the other'. The community, the communion of saints, the mystical body bear this price. As to the war between the different gods, or the sometimes bloody conflicts resulting from different interpretations of the same God, they all lead in the end to the strengthening of the social body. Here, mythology joins the results of the latest research in logic or cybernetics; dysfunction and contradictoriness have a far from negligible place in the structuring of reality and its representation. It also joins certain Weberian analyses, such as this well-known observation that bears repeating: 'popular wisdom teaches us that a thing may be true even if it is not and while it is neither beautiful, holy nor good. But these are only the most elementary cases of the war between the gods of different orders and different values.'[22] In this text, Weber, who makes explicit reference to it, closely links polytheism and the people. Perhaps we should say that there are periods in which the mass, saturated with rational, finalized, productivist and economistic explanations and procedures, returns to the natural, 'ecological' substrate of all social life. It is at this point that it finds the to and fro movement that is established between the variety of nature and the multiplicity of the divine. This does not occur without some cruelty, for whosoever says polytheism, says antagonism. Whosoever turns to nature, turns to its harsh laws, including violence and death. But the fights between the gods or of groups among themselves is at least better than the denial of the stranger. In wartime, he takes on a human face: he exists. And even if his customs are opposed to my own, even if I consider them to be neither 'beautiful', 'holy' nor 'good', I cannot prevent them from being. It is this recognition that lets us draw an analogy between religious categories and social relationships.

With the same theoretical sensitivity as Weber, the sociologist Simmel asks us to consider God as *coincidentia oppositorum*, a centre where the antinomies of life blend together. In the same passage he refers to the tribe ('the original religious community was the tribe') and to the dependence of the individual on the latter – the dependence on God being in effect a 'stylization' (that is, at the same time in-depth and euphemized) of the former.[23] The tribes and their battles, the tight interdependence that constitutes these tribes and at the same time the necessity of a God that unites opposites – such is the mythico-epistemological framework of the dialectic of 'love and [of] estrangement' that seems to be at the root of all social structuring. The fact that religion (*re-ligare*) is the expression of a plural society in the sense that I have just stated is in no way surprising. Indeed, let us remember that before becoming an institution, with its accompanying rigidification, religious gatherings served above all as a way of keeping warm, uniting against the harshness of the social or natural 'state of things'.

It is no less true that these gatherings and the interdependence they imply are a heady mixture of communication and conflict. To quote Simmel once again, the 'side-by-side' experience, the living-together and the 'all for one and one for all' can go hand in hand with a 'one against the other'.[24] We will come back to this later; however, harmony or equilibrium can be conflictual. In this perspective, the varied elements of the social whole (like the natural whole) enter into a tight, dynamic mutual relationship – in short, suggesting the lability synonymous with the living. The complexity with which Morin speaks to us possesses the same characteristics; and in this sense the detour I am suggesting is perhaps not as useless as it may first appear, since, at the same time as the fear or the reality of racism mounts, so does the growth of religious groups and pluriculturalism, and affectual networks take on an increasingly prominent place in the complexity of modern megalopolises. Obsessed by the individualist and economic model, which predominated during the modern period, we have forgotten that social aggregations are founded equally on affective attraction and rejection. Social passion, whatever some may think, is an unavoidable reality. By failing to include it in our analyses we prevent ourselves from understanding a multitude of situations that can no longer be passed over as so much trivia. This is especially so since, as in all moments of 'cultural' foundation, the multiracial event bursts in. Without trying to hide behind a founding father, we can read a part of Durkheim's *The Division of Labour in Society* in this perspective. Whether or not it pleases the epigones who invoke his spirit and set themselves up as guardians of the Temple, friendship, fellow-feeling and, naturally, their opposites enter, in a not insignificant way, into the analysis of solidarity. Witness Durkheim's following statements: 'Everybody knows that we like those who resemble us, those who think and feel as we do. But the opposite is no less true. It very often happens that we feel kindly towards those who do not resemble us, precisely because of this lack of resemblance' (*DLS*, p. 54). Or there is Heraclitus who maintains that 'contrariety is expedient and that the best agreement arises from things differing and that all things come into being in the way of the principle of antagonism. Difference, as likeness, can be a cause of mutual attraction' (*DLS*, p. 55). He says that 'both types' are necessary to natural friend-ships.[25] To suggest as an introduction to his work what I would call a contradictory friendship would explain this solidarity that lets us understand logically how that which differs also completes.

Certainly, there is an element of functionalism in this perspective; however, it is of little importance in so far as it does not eliminate the contradiction in an abstract way and in that it makes us think otherness, with its specific dynamic. Until now, anthropology or ethnology had the monopoly on researching the other, just as theology was supposed to be interested in the absolute other. It is difficult to maintain such distinctions today. The sociology of everyday life in particular has been able to draw attention to duplicity, the double aspect of every social situation, to the 'aloofness' and the intrinsic plurality of what appeared homogeneous. We will not return to this.[26] On the other hand, we can resolutely direct our reflections to the fabulous architectonic built on these duplicities and their synergies. This is full of vitality: disordered vitality, cacophonous, as I said earlier, as well as effervescent, yet difficult to deny.

I have already made reference to the period of Late Antiquity and its analysis as a paradigm for our own time. It was an era filled with 'oracles', as Brown indicates; and, he adds, when the gods speak, 'we can be sure we are dealing with groups that can still express themselves collectively'.[27] In these remarks, we can see that contemporary polyphony gives a good account of the plurality of gods at work on the ongoing task of creating the new 'culture'. I used the word paradigm in order to insist on the effectiveness of this historical reference, for we who have conquered space too often forget that it is also possible to reduce temporal distance as well. We can speak of an 'Einsteinized' time that at once lets us read the present by 'transporting images' (meta-phors) of the past. Thus, by emphasizing the vitality of the gods – their diversity – we only stylize the effervescence of our cities. But we should allow the poet to speak:

> It seems to me that man is full of gods like a sponge immersed in the heavens. These gods live, attain the summit of their strength then die, leaving their perfumed altars to other gods. They are the very principles of any transformation. They are the necessity of movement. Thus I walked drunkenly among a thousand divine incarnations. (Aragon, *Le Paysan de Paris*, Paris, Gallimard, 1926)

This movement from culture to civilization, then to the creation of culture, can be read into the polytheism (antagonism) of values in which we live today. Some would call this decadence, and why not, if by decadence we mean that death is redolent of birth. Flowers that fade, exhausted by their own perfection, bear the promise of beautiful fruit.

4. The organic balance

Cultures exhaust themselves; civilizations die; everything becomes inscribed in the mechanism of saturation ably described by Sorokin. This is nothing we do not already know. There is however a more interesting question: what is it that causes life to perdure? The glimmers of an answer may in fact be found in the Heraclitian or Nietzschean perspectives: destruction is also construction. If the tradition of political homogenization becomes saturated, by and of itself, through indifference or due to the intrusions of the stranger, then it is because it has outlived its usefulness. As a consequence, the equilibrium it set up ceases to be. This balance was put into place to the detriment of what we can call difference. We must now consider how this outsider or 'third person', an anthropological structure we have followed every step of the way, can be integrated into a new balance. Indeed, according to the logic of my arguments, and in reference to many historical situations, we can postulate the existence of an equilibrium that is founded on the heterogeneous. Returning to a balance I have already evoked earlier, we can say that the unity of bourgeois society is succeeded by the unicity of the masses: the masses not as an historical subject, as in the case of the bourgeoisie or the proletariat, but rather as a contradictory entity; or as a daily practice in which 'evil', the stranger, the other, are not exorcized but integrated, according to varied measures and norms, be they homoeopathic even.

Once again, in the perspective of social passion mentioned earlier, and which we cannot do without, the problem facing our societies will be to balance these opposing passions whose antagonisms are accentuated the moment we acknowledge a natural plurality, a plurality of natures.[28] This is what I mean by conflictual harmony, since an equilibrium is more difficult to attain when passion triumphs over reason; this is a phenomenon quite easy to observe in both everyday and civic life.

We can begin with a notion that is difficult to accept today, and that moreover is not even taken seriously: the notion of hierarchy. Bouglé remarked that the all-embracing pantheism of India and its real polytheism are tightly bound up in the caste system.[29] The welcoming characteristic and the doctrinal non-dogmatism of the Hindu religion is in fact based on its highly developed sense of hierarchy. This paroxysmal situation cannot be exported as such or even serve as a model; but it is a good example of how a society can construct an equilibrium based on the coexistence of differences, codifying them with an accustomed rigour and building upon this an architectonic not lacking in solidarity. For his part, Louis Dumont in his *Homo Hierarchicus* was able to show a real interdependence and the reconciliation of communities produced by this system. While it is true that he leaves no room for individualism, he introduces us, in an astonishing way, to a holistic understanding of society. These works are now well known and hence need no further comment; it is sufficient to use them as a support in understanding that the arrangement of small groups with different lifestyles and opposing ideologies is a social form that can be balanced.

What the caste system proposes in an extreme way can be found in a milder version in the theory of 'estates' in the Middle Ages. It was also a matter of doctrinal theorization, since it received reinforcement from

Thomist Catholicism for example, which proposed, based on the existence of these 'estates', an idea of democracy that, as Poulat remarked, is noticeably different from the meaning we give this term today. Thus, this 'democracy no longer pits the lower classes against the others any more than it advocates their harmonization, but is opposed to any social forces that compromise their harmony . . . it defends *proportional equality within the hierarchical order*, all the while making historical reference to the medieval tradition of the commune'.[30] I would say for my part that this is a social form found, apart from the examples already mentioned, in populism, in utopian constructions (like those of Fourier), in solidarity perspectives and in their concrete realizations that, in a more or less sophisticated way, have been strewn throughout our societies since the nineteenth century.

It goes without saying that, despite any precautions we take ('proportional equality', for example), we are far from the egalitarianism – at least stated – that has characterized modernity since the French Revolution promoted it as a universal ideal. It is nevertheless true that we can find both a real solidarity in this cultural span – even if limited to the group, or at least to the proxemic – as well as a way of living with antagonism. Fourier, we may remember, proposed in his phalansteries a 'pastry war', a form of culinary competition that symbolized the attraction/repulsion inherent in any sociality. This may even remind one of the ancient *philotimia*, minus the frivolous aspect. Indeed, it allowed the rich and powerful or the merely lucky to put back into the community a portion of their gains, whether through public building projects, the construction of shrines, or shelter for the needy. The *philotimia* also had a competitive side: favoured by fortune, they and their accomplices issued challenges that were difficult to refuse. Thus, the hierarchical order permitted nonetheless *an organic equilibrium*, that in a coenesthetic way responded to the needs of the community, representing a ritualized game of difference, in a manner of speaking. There is no question of a proclaimed and programmed equality, but rather of real adaptation, balance and, what is more, of a *libido dominandi* (legitimate violence) that can express itself at a lesser cost for the whole social body. Brown called this 'the model of parity'.[31]

This perspective has the advantage of accounting for the two elements of any worldly life: conflict and communication. Moreover, it offers a model of 'profitability' of their *joint* existence. In this way, it is not anachronistic; by applying it to the case of the development of Brazil, Gilberto Freyre even speaks of a 'process of counterbalancing'.[32] There is always the danger of watering down the model, or of justifying oppression: only a concrete analysis allows us to form an opinion; but in terms of logic, there is no reason to condemn it out of hand. In any case, as far as these reflections are concerned, we are thus able to understand how the negotiations between antagonisms can serve to balance the whole and, furthermore, how in the stranger confronting the citizen, the wanderer contacting the sedentary, the powerful and the client enter into a vast intercommunication crucial to each of them. This has the added advantage of acknowledging that something exists. For, although it may be codified in the caste system, theologized as conforming to the divine plan or craftily disguised by egalitarian rationalizations, we all notice the existence of hierarchy. We must observe it better in order to correct its most harmful effects. This correction is perhaps most effectively carried out within the social structures that think in terms of proxemics, that is, those that leave it to the groups concerned to find their own forms of equilibrium.

For in this case, by virtue of the interdependence of all social life, each of us knows that we shall need the other at one time or another. There is reversibility: I have no intention of contesting a privilege from which I may draw benefit either at some other time or in some other form. The necessity of privilege that plays such a large role in France (as many articles and successful books have recently pointed out) is thus justified. Incomprehensible in a mechanistic perspective, it finds its niche in an organic vision that encompasses all. But this means that the individual is not the be-all and end-all of the social whole; rather it is the group, the community, the collective totality that prevails. To borrow a concept from German philosophy, the acknowledgement of hierarchy, of difference, and the models of parity and reversibility that they engender, seems to refer to a *spontaneous regulation* (*Naturwüchsig*). Here once more is the vitalism referred to earlier. As opposed to the periods that accentuate rational activity, this regulation is the result of those who have greater confidence in the intrinsic sovereignty of each group. These groups, through a process of trial and error, and chaotic proceedings, are able to accommodate their goals to their ways of differentiation. Thus, paradoxically, the 'outsider' can more readily find a place in a type of society that does not deny *a priori* the hierarchical dimension of social existence.

Apart from clichéd examples found in history, this can also be found in many identifiable and observable social situations today, like Carnaval, for instance. Many useful analyses of this fact have been made; from a socio-anthropological perspective, I would single out the remarkable one made by Roberto Da Matta. I have no intention of restating his analysis; instead, I prefer to underline a few strong points that go some way to explaining my argument here. Firstly, I would mention the inclusion of festive activities within holistic and hierarchical societies. In so far as the 'Brazilian ritual triangle' is concerned, it shows that, next to Patriots' Day, which represents the national state and the army, next to Holy Week whose principal protagonist is the Church, the 'Carnaval' involves essentially the people, the mass.[33] This tripartite arrangement is interesting in more than one respect; it accounts for a coexistence that divides time. To be sure, this division is differentiated; but within the framework of a generalized theatricalization, it attributes a role to each group. I say *role* rather than *function*, which denotes a mechanistic, rational, goal-oriented social functioning. Role and theatricality, on the other hand, take their place in a cyclical time divided into moments. This cyclical evolution gives each group the assurance that it will be able to benefit once again from a moment in time that is reserved for it alone. In this respect, we need only know that the preparations for Carnaval are carried out by individuals well ahead of time. This assurance is significant when we know that time management is the primordial element in what I have called 'confronting destiny'. For a determined period of time and in relation to other moments, the people knows that it is capable of exercising its sovereignty.

This moment of popular sovereignty then allows for the integration of the anomic, the stranger. Da Matta speaks of 'periphery' and of 'edge' (p. 65). Referring to what I said earlier, it is a question of anamnesis. The bandit, the prostitute and even death (the absolute other) may be expressed as emblematic figures. The social body remembers that it is an inextricable blend of contradictory elements; and the multiplicity of guises and the situations to which they lead is illuminating. Also, it is quite common for an individual to change costumes on a daily basis: an external as well as internal multiplicity, in other words. In this way, the antagonists are played against each other in an entertaining way, or exhaust themselves in the contests put on by the samba schools and individuals whose primary concern remains the cost of the costumes. No one is immune to this competition; and there are many anecdotes and direct observations that will astonish the more calculating among us. The above-mentioned *philotimia* could here be applied to the mass: the expenditure, even by those who have nothing, is a way of putting back into the collective circuit all that had been privatized: money and sex. Just as the powerful of ancient times bought favour by constructing temples, here we are forgiven our normal individuality by constructing cathedrals of light at this festive time.

Furthermore, apart from the collectively played antagonisms, apart from the plurality of characteristics expressed in costume, we find the acceptance of the stranger. The fact that it is rendered emblematic is a way of acknowledging its presence. Thus, although racism is perhaps not absent from the everyday life of Brazil, the effervescence and theatricality of Carnaval are a way of relativizing it and tempering it, to some extent. Through these few characteristics of Carnaval, a form of organicity is experienced. The whole Carnaval is inscribed in the organicity of the tripartite festivities; within the Carnaval, we can find a specific organicity that leaves real room for the multiplicity of functions and characteristics. And the fact that this multiplicity is 'only' make-believe does not change anything. The imaginary is increasingly granted a role in structuring society.

This ritual effervescence and cyclical contradictoriness permits the reinforcement, in everyday life, of the feeling of participating in a collective body. Just as Carnaval permits us to play the role of a general or a count or some other prominent figure, we can later take glory in being this general's chauffeur; or, as Da Matta reports, see an entire household rejoice in the title of Baron being conferred on the boss.[34] There is almost a 'participation', in the mystical sense of the term. It accentuates the concrete, secondary effects (financial, privileges, favours), but also the symbolic ones. By making common cause with a superior entity, I am reinforced in my own existence. It leads us to attribute a wider spectrum to solidarity, and not to limit it to its sole egalitarian and/or economic dimension.

The difference experienced in the hierarchy may be the vector of the social equilibrium that so preoccupies us. Another everyday example can be the basic sociality; the neighbourhood life, the everyday life without quality that is seen as a non-entity in a macroscopic perspective, but that recovers its significance with the accentuation of proxemics. Here we can see the same mechanism of participation mentioned above. This participation can be in a neighbourhood, in a group, or in the form of an emblematic animal, a guru, a football team or a minor local leader. This is a form of clientelism in which hierarchy is called upon once more to play a role. We 'belong' to a place, a group, or a local personality who thus becomes an eponymous hero. Studies on the senior civil service, university and senior executives all highlight this process. The intellectual microcosm, formed as it is of perfect examples of 'free spirits', cannot escape it: in the scorn reserved for the work of competitors anathematized by the professor; in the low blows exchanged inside various commissions, and so on. It remains to *participate* in the glory and the wrath of the master. 'I am his man' is not a phrase often heard in French nowadays, even if the reality exists, whereas in Italy one can still frequently hear: '*Io sono di l'uno, io sono dell'altro*. I am from his clan, his group.[35] Should we regret it? Should we fight it? It is, in any case, interesting to observe its effects. Inasmuch as in a given domain, groups can relativize themselves; this clan process can admit the game of difference, the expression of everyone and thus a form of balance. I have already said of the Mafia that it may be 'a metaphor of society'.[36] When the rules of proper conduct are respected, there is regulation and organic order, which cannot fail to be beneficial to all.

All the actors are an integral part of the same scene, while their roles are different, hierarchical, sometimes conflictual. Reciprocal regulation is surely a human constant, an anthropological structure found in all large socio-cultural groups. This was highlighted by G. Dumézil and was rediscovered in its own way by modern physics: Einstein's theory of relativity is the proof. In each of these large groups we find a definite polytheism, whether it is affirmed or more or less hidden. Even when there is an apparent monovalence of a value (a god), one always finds an alternative value or several, existing *mezza voce*, which have their own effects on the social structure and its equilibrium. Thus, for example can be seen the many heretical movements that existed within rigid medieval Christianity or even the popular Hassidism that was to pierce the intransigent Mosaical monotheism.[37]

Just like chemistry, it is all a question of combination: through the differentiated association of elements, we obtain such and such a specific compound; but, with a minimal change or by moving an element, the entity may take on a new form. This is how, in the end, one social equilibrium passes into another. It is in the framework of such a combinatorial logic that we have tried to appreciate the role of the outsider; this third person forms societies but is too often forgotten. Theoretical or anecdotal historical references were meant to underline that his acknowledgement always corresponds to a founding moment, a moment of *culture*. On the other hand, the weakening of culture in civilization tends to favour the turning back to unity, to instill fear of the stranger. Another key idea is to postulate that the effervescence surrounding the outsider is correlative with an accentuation of the people, who are reinforced by the idea of difference, which they know to be beneficial to each and every one of them. Religious and mystical images are illuminating in this regard, for they remind us and embody, in a manner of speaking, at the everyday level, this collective utopia, this imagined celestial community in which 'we will all be identical and different, just as all points on the circle are identical and different with respect to the centre'.[38]

We can see that this allusive and metaphorical reflection is not unrelated to contemporary reality; I have shown this throughout my analysis. The sociality that is manifesting itself before our eyes is founded, with greater or lesser force, according to the situation, on the ancient antagonism between the wanderer and the sedentary. As is the case with any passage from one combinatorial logic to another, it is not without fear and trembling, even on the part of observers that remain social protagonists as well. But if we can create a work of lucidity which, outside of any judgemental attitude, is our sole requirement, then we will be able to recognize, to paraphrase Walter Benjamin, that 'every document of civilization is also a document of barbarity'.

Notes

1. Indeed, it seems necessary to me to reverse these Durkheimian concepts, cf. my proposals: M. Maffesoli, *La Violence totalitaire*, Paris, PUF, 1979, p. 210, note 1; G. Simmel, *Problème de Philosophie de l'Histoire*, Paris, PUF, 1984, p. 131. Cf. the idea of 'Heteroculture' introduced by J. Poirier.

2. Cf. the preface to the 2nd edition of M. Maffesoli, *L'Ombre de Dionysos. Contribution à une sociologie de l'orgie*, Paris, Librairie des Méridiens, 1985. On the 'we-Dionysus', I would also refer to the article by M. Bourlet, 'Dionysos, le même et l'autre', *Nouvelle Revue d'ethnopsychiatrie*, no. 1 (1983), p. 36.

3. Cf. J. Freund, *Sociologie du conflit*, Paris, PUF, 1983, p. 14. Naturally, one should also refer to *L'Essence du politique*, Paris, Sirey, 1965, Ch. 7. For a good analysis of the outsider, cf. J. H. Park, 'Conflit et communication dans le mode de penser coréen', Thesis, Université de Paris V, 1985, p. 57, *et seq.*

4. As an example of the contradictions of 'so-called dual organizations', Cf., C. Lévi-Strauss, *Structural Anthropology*, New York, Basic Books, 1976, p. 161; also G. Dumézil, *Jupiter, Mars, Quirinus*, Paris, Gallimard, 1941, and G. Durand, *L'Ame tigrée, les pluriels de psyché*, Paris, Denoël-Médiation, 1980, pp. 83–84, and the psychological experiment mentioned by P. Watzlawick, *La Réalité de la réalité*, French transl. Paris, Seuil, 1978, p. 90.

5. On triadism derived from a symbolist vision, cf. G. Durand, *La Foi du cordonnier*, Paris, Denoël, 1984, p. 90; also M. Lalive d'Epinay, *Groddeck*, Paris, Edition Universitaire, 1983, pp. 56–57 for this psychoanalyst's notion of trinitarian division.

6. Cf. K. Schipper, *Le Corps taoïste*, Paris, Fayard, 1982, p. 146 (my emphasis) and p. 16.

7. Cf. E. Morin, *La Nature de l'URSS*, Paris, Fayard, 1983, p. 181. On the differential 'realities', cf. G. Simmel, *Problèmes de la Sociologie des religions*, Paris, C.N.R.S., 1964, vol. 17, p. 13; for an analysis of Aristotle's text, cf. Freund, *Sociologie du conflit*, p. 36, *et seq.*

8. Cf. P. Tacussel's analysis of 'general communications' in *L'Attraction sociale*, Paris, Librairie des Méridiens, 1984.

9. L. Réau, *L'Europe française au siècle des Lumières*, Paris, Albin Michel, 1951, p. 303, *et seq.*

10. Maffesoli, *La Violence totalitaire.*

11. F. Hoffet, *Psychanalyse de l'Alsace*, Strasbourg, 1984, pp. 48, 38. One might also make reference to Sicily or to the actions of the Emperor Frederick II.

12. Cf. O. Revault d'Allones' note in *Musiques, variations sur la pensée juive*, Paris, Edition C. Bourgois, 1979, p. 47.

13. Cf. P. Brown, *Augustine of Hippo*, Berkeley, University of California Press, 1967, pp. 213–219.

14. I will refer here to a learned and exhaustive article that appeared after my work on the dionysiac, Bourlet, 'Dionysos, le même et l'autre', *Nouvelle Revue de l'ethnopsychiatrie*. On what he justly called 'the work of the exile', cf. G. Renaud, *A l'Ombre du rationalisme*, Montréal, Editions St Martin, 1984, p. 171.

15. M. Maffesoli, *La Connaissance ordinaire. Précis de sociologie compréhensive*, Paris, Librairie des Méridiens, 1985, p. 132. On the French Revolution, cf. Réau, *L'Europe française*, p. 368. Cf. also the work of Coeurderoy, *Hourra, la révolution par les Cosaques*, Paris, Editions Champ Libre, 1972.

16. M.F. Baslez, *L'Etranger dans la Grèce Antique*, Paris, Edition Les Belles Lettres, 1984, p. 75.

17. G. Freyre, *The Masters and the Slaves: A Study in the Development of Brazilian Civilization*, New York, Alfred E. Knopf, 1963, e.g. p. 219. Cf. also R. Motta, 'La Sociologie au Brésil', *Cahiers Internationaux de Sociologie*, Paris, PUF, vol. 78 (1985). For G. Simmel, cf. Grafemeyer, I. Joseph ed., *L'Ecole de Chicago* (Paris, Aubier, 1984).

18. C. Bouglé, *Essays on the Caste System*, Cambridge, Cambridge University Press, 1971, p. 189.

19. On this distinction and Christian polytheism, I refer to Maffesoli, *L'Ombre de Dionysos*. As to the work of Durand, cf. in particular *La Foi du cordonnier*. For an analysis of popular religion, see Y. Lambert, *Dieu change en Bretagne*, Paris, Cerf, 1985. We might retain one remark: 'the blunders made about popular religion would not be so persistent if most specialists did not limit themselves to questioning the activists, the officials . . . who are only too glad to oblige' (p. 17).

20. Cf. for example A. Faivre, *Eckartshausen et la théosophie*, Paris, Editions Klincksieck, 1969, p. 14 and M.E. Coughtree, 'Rhythmomachia, a propaedeutic game of the Middle Ages', University of Cape Town, 1985, p. 26.

21. E. Poulat, *Eglise contre bourgeoisie*, Paris, Casterman, 1977, p. 59 and p. 130 on the *Simultaneum*, cf. p. 87 and *Catholicisme, démocratie et socialisme*, Paris, Casterman, 1977, p. 486. I knew of such a village, Wangen, where the mass was celebrated in the protective shadow of a stained-glass window in which figured the eye of the Creator contained within an isosceles triangle – a masonic symbol if ever there was one and an able metaphor of triadism!

22. M. Weber, *Le Savant et le politique*, French transl. by J. Freund, Paris, Plon, 1959, p. 93.

23. These meanderings are based on Simmel's text, 'Problèmes de la sociologie des religions'.

24. Ibid., p. 17.

25. E. Durkheim, *The Division of Labour in Society*, New York, Free Press, 1964, pp. 17, 18, *et seq*. On difference in conjugal society, cf. I. Pennacchioni, *La Polémologie conjugale*, Paris, Mazarine, 1986.

26. On the everyday which 'hides a fundamental diversity' cf. M. de Certeau and L. Giard, *L'Ordinaire de la communication*, Paris, Dalloz, 1983, p. 21. On 'duplicity', see my chapter 'De l'apparence au cynisme' in *La Conquête du présent, pour une sociologie de la vie quotidienne*, Paris, PUF, 1979.

27. P. Brown, *The Making of Late Antiquity*, Cambridge, Mass., Harvard University Press, 1976, p. 38.

28. For a similar observation from a Freudian point of view cf. A.G. Salma, *Les Chasseurs d'absolu: Genèse de la gauche et de la droite*, Paris, Grasset, 1980, pp. 21, 22 and 24 on Heraclitus.

29. Cf. Bouglé, *Essays on the Caste System*, p. 55; L. Dumont, *Homo Hierarchus: the Caste System and its Implications*, Chicago, University of Chicago Press, 1980.

30. Poulat, *Catholicisme, démocratie et socialisme*, p. 85, note 33 and p. 86.

31. Brown, *The Making of Late Antiquity*, p. 35. Cf. his analysis of the *philotimia*. We are far from what G. Renaud in *A l'Ombre du rationalisme*, calls 'social-statism' (*social-étatisme*) cf. p. 215.

32. Cf. Freyre, *The Masters and the Slaves*, p. 93.

33. R. Da Matta, *Carnaval, bandits et héros*, Paris, Seuil, 1983, p. 57, *et seq*. On 'theatricality' and the 'confronting of destiny', I would refer to my book *La Conquête du présent*. Regarding the samba, cf. M. Sodré, *Samba o dono do corpo*, Rio de Janeiro, Codecri, 1979.

34. R. Da Matta, *Carnaval, bandits et héros*, p. 183 and the references to Machado de Assis, see note 2.

35. A. Médam, *Arcanes de Naples*, Paris, Edition des Autres, 1989, p. 78, provides a good analysis of clientelism in Naples. With respect to businesses, see A. Wickham and M. Patterson, *Les Carriéristes*, Paris, Ramsay, 1984. It contains a good analysis and classification of networks.

36. M. Maffesoli, 'La maffia comme métaphore de la socialité' *Cahiers Internationaux de Sociologie*, Paris, PUF, vol. 73 (1982), pp. 363–369.

37. Cf. the examples given by G. Durand, *L'Ame tigrée. Les pluriels de psyché*, Paris, Denoël, 1980, p. 143 and notes. On Einstein and general relativity, cf. J.E. Charon, *L'Esprit, cet inconnu*, Paris, Albin Michel, 1977, p. 56.

38. J. Lacarrière, *L'Eté grec*, Paris, Plon, 1976, p. 54 for an analysis of Greek mysticism.

6

OF PROXEMICS

1. The community of destiny

Obsessed as we have become with the great entities imposed on us since the eighteenth century – History, Politics, Economics, the Individual – it is difficult for us to focus on 'the most extreme concrete' (Walter Benjamin) that is the life of the ordinary person. It would appear, however, that this will be a crucial, or at least unavoidable, focus for decades to come. And it is not new. Within the framework of these pages, ever faithful to my cause, I shall try to show both its anthropological roots and the specific modulations that it displays today.

There are times when what matters is less a question of the individual than the community of which he or she is a member, or when the great history of events is less important than histories experienced every day: the imperceptible situations which constitute our community network. These two aspects seem to me to characterize what can be rendered by the term 'proxemics'. Of course it requires us to pay attention to the relational component of social life. Man in relation: not only as far as relations between individuals are concerned; but also those which link me with a landscape, a city, a natural environment that I share with others. These are the day-to-day histories: *time crystallized in space*. The history of a place now becomes a personal history. Through a process of sedimentation, the anodyne – made up of rituals, odours, noises, images, architectural constructions – becomes what Nietzsche called a 'figurative journal'. A journal which teaches what we must say, do, think, love. It is a journal that teaches us that 'here we may live, since here we are living'. Thus, a 'we' is formed that allows each of us to see 'beyond the ephemeral and extravagant individual life'; that allows us to feel 'like the spirit of the house, the family, the city'. There is no better way of describing the change in outlook which I believe we must make. In this different focus, an emphasis will be placed on what is common to all, on what is done by all, if only on a microscopic level: 'history from below'.[1]

It so happens that such an emphasis is expressed regularly. It may be that it is at these moments of fermentation that, great ideals being saturated, the ways of life that will govern our destinies are established through a mysterious process of alchemy. It is a question of transmutation, since nothing is created; such and such a minor element, once again comes to the foreground, takes on a particular significance and becomes determinant.

Such is the case for those various forms of primary groupings which are the basic elements of any social structure. In analysing the Hellenistic civilization, F. Chamoux observed that what we easily term a period of decadence was once considered the 'golden age of the Greek city-state'. This may no longer designate a History in progress, but its intense daily activity demonstrates a certain vitality, a specific force that invests itself in the strengthening of the 'community cell, upon which all civilization is founded'.[2] Indeed, the great forces may confront one another in order to run the whole world or to create History; as to the city, it is content to assure its perdurability, to protect its territory, to organize itself around common myths. Myth versus History: to return to a spatial image, the extension (*ex-tendere*) of History is confronted with the 'in-tension' (*in-tendere*) of myth which will favour that which is shared and its inherent mechanism of attraction–repulsion.

Moreover, this is one of the factors of polyculturalism which we have already touched on (Chapter 5). Indeed, the *territory-myth* pair that is the organizing principle of the city is both cause and effect of such a structure. That is, like a nest of Russian dolls, the city reveals other entities of the same type: neighbourhoods, ethnic groups, associations, various tribes that will organize themselves around (real or symbolic) territory and common myths. These Hellenistic cities are founded essentially on the double polarity of cosmopolitanism and rootedness (which, as we know, was to produce a specific civilization).[3] What does this say other than that all these groups, strongly united by common sentiments, will structure a collective memory which in its very diversity is a founding structure. These groups may be of many types (ethnic, social); structurally, it is their diversity that assures the *unicity* of the city. As Lupasco said of the physical or logical 'contradictoriness', it is the *tension* between the various groups that assures the durability of the whole.

The City of Florence is an illuminating example of this. When Savanarola wished to describe the ideal type of a republic, it was the Florentine structure that served as his model. And just what was it? Very simple, if the truth be told, and very different from the pejorative connotation generally given to the description 'Florentine'. So in his *De Politia*, he bases the architectonic of the city on the idea of proximity. The *civitas* is the natural combination of smaller associations (*vici*). It is the interplay of these elements that guarantees the best political system. In an almost Durkheimian way, he bases the solidity of the system on those 'intermediate zones', which escape extreme wealth as well as the direst poverty.[4]

Thus, the experience of the common life is the very foundation of the grandeur of a city. It is true that Florence has known glory; a number of observers have pointed out what this owes to an ancient 'popular civic tradition'. The classical humanism that produced the works we know today could also be fertilized by the culture of the *volgare*.[5] This fact should be remembered, for although the foreign policy of the city was not remarkable, its domestic vitality, in all domains, had an impact that was to remain significant for a long time. This vitality was founded on what could be called a micro-localism that created culture.

The 'natural combination' I mentioned previously is of course reasonably cultural, that is, produced from a common experience, from a series of adjustments that were more or less able to constitute a form of balance from very heterogeneous elements: conflictual harmony of a sort. This struck Weber as significant; in his essay on the city, he notes the to and fro movement which is established between the people (*popolo*) and the political structure. Of course, this is only a tendency; but is nevertheless instructive and accounts for the adjustment between the above-mentioned *civitas* and *vicus*. We can find in it something of the cosmopolitanism/rootedness dialectic of Hellenistic cities; but here the two poles would be the patrician family and the people. They neutralize one another to an extent; the 'chiefs of economically and politically powerful families . . . distributed the positions among themselves'.[6] As the political expression of the polytheism of values, this sharing of honours is a way of tempering power while distributing it. At the same time, thanks to this quasi-state structure, the city possessed its own autonomy (economic, military, financial) and could then negotiate with equally autonomous cities.

However, this autonomy was relativized within the city itself by the organization of the *popolo*. As a counterpoint to the patricians, the *popolo* represented the 'fraternization of professional associations (*arti* or *paratici*)'. This did not prevent it from recruiting a militia and paying its employees (the *Capitanus populi* and his band of officers).[7] One might say that this fraternization came out of proximity: neighbourhoods and associations represented *puissance*, the basic sociability of the cities in question. In this way, appearances to the contrary, the close and the quotidian are what assure sovereignty over existence. Such a statement is occasionally necessary, and there are several historical examples to illustrate it; but as always, what can be seen at these specific moments can only translate an underlying structure that in ordinary times guarantees the durability of a social entity, whatever it may be. Without giving it a too-precise political connotation, the 'mass' is constant; in its various guises, the simplest expression of the recognition of the local as the community of destiny.

The noble, through opportunism and/or political alliances, can vary, change territory; the merchant, by the demands of his profession, inevitably circulates; as to the mass, it guarantees stability. As Gilberto Freyre points out with respect to Portugal, the mass is the 'depository of the national feeling which was lacking in the ruling class'.[8] Of course, this remark is in need of nuance; but it is sure that faced with the frequent compromises of the governing classes, one finds a certain 'intransigence' in the popular layers. They feel more responsible for 'la patrie'; taking this term in its simplest meaning, the fatherland. This is easily understood: as the least mobile class, the mass is *stricto sensu* the 'genius of place'. Its day-to-day life assures a link between time and space; it is the 'non-conscious' guardian of sociality.

It is in this sense that we must understand the collective memory, the memory of everyday life. This love of the nearby and the present is moreover independent of the groups that invoke it. To express it in the manner of Walter Benjamin, it is an aura, an all-encompassing value, which I have already proposed calling an 'immanent transcendence'. It is an ethic that acts as a glue between the various groups that participate in this space-time. Thus, the stranger and the sedentary, the patrician and the ordinary man are, *volens nolens*, full participants in a force that surpasses and assures the stability of the whole. Each of these elements is for a time a prisoner of this *glutinum mundi* that, according to the alchemists of the Middle Ages, guaranteed the harmony of the global and the particular.

As I have said earlier, there is a tight link between space and everyday life, which is surely the repository of a sociality we can no longer ignore. Many studies of cities have highlighted this point; it comes across, albeit prudently, in the preface by Raymond to the book by Young and Willmott: 'we must believe that, in certain cases, urban morphology and working class lifestyle manage to form a harmonious whole'.[9] Of course, such harmony exists; it is even the outcome of what I am proposing to call the 'community of destiny'. And for those familiar with the inside of the *courées* of the north of France or the *bâtisses** of the south and central regions of the country, there is no doubt that this 'morphology' serves as a crucible for the adjustment between various groups. Naturally, and it cannot be emphasized enough, any harmony also brings with it a dose of conflict. The community of destiny is an accommodation to the natural and social environment, and as such is forced to confront heterogeneity in its various guises.

This heterogeneity, this contradictory mix, no longer belongs to a history that can be acted upon – especially through political action – but rather a history with which one must negotiate, with which one must work for better or for worse. And this cannot be judged from the point of view of a life that is anything but alienated, from a logic of 'ought'. Referring to the Simmelesque metaphor of the 'bridge and the door', which link and which separate, the emphasis on the spatial, on territory, makes relational man a mixture of openness and reserve. We know that a certain affability is often the sign of a powerful 'aloofness'. All of this serves to show that proxemics in no way means unanimity; it does not postulate, as history does, the surpassing of the contradictory, of that which embarrasses (or those who are embarrassing). As the trivial expression goes: 'let's make do', hence an *appropriation*, even if relative, of existence. Indeed, in not aiming for a possibly perfect life, a celestial or terrestrial paradise, we get used to what we have. It is true that, beyond the various and often poor

---

* *Transl. note*: *courée*: in the North of France, a small dark courtyard shared by several poor households; *bâtisse*: a building principally constructed of masonry.

statements of intention, the protagonists of present-day life have, in a concrete way, a highly tolerant attitude towards the other, towards others, and it shows. This, in a paradoxical way, is what explains the fact that dire economic circumstances can sometimes give rise to undeniable existential and relational wealth. Thus, examining proxemics may be the right way to surpass our normal attitude of suspicion, in order to appreciate the intense personal investment expressed in the tragedy of everyday life.

I use this expression advisedly, since relationships founded on proxemics are far from comforting. To return to a well-known expression, these 'urban villages' can hide relationships that are both dense and cruel. Indeed, not knowing everyone else but knowing something about everyone else inevitably has important consequences on day-to-day lifestyles. As opposed to an idea of the city formed of free individuals engaging in essentially rational relationships – just think of the adage that states that the spirit of the city liberates: *Stadtluft macht frei* – it would seem that contemporary megalopolises give rise to a multiplicity of small enclaves founded on an absolute interdependence. The autonomy (individualism) of the bourgeois model is being surpassed by the heteronomy of tribalism. Whatever it may be called – neighbourhoods, varied interest groups, networks – we are witnessing the return of an affective, passional investment whose structurally ambiguous and ambivalent aspects are well known.

Thus, as I have already stated, I am describing a matrix-like 'form'. Indeed, this affectual tendency is an aura in which we bathe but which can be expressed in an *ad hoc* and ephemeral way. This is also its cruel aspect. And it is not contradictory, as Hannerz says, to see the development within it of 'brief and quick contacts'.[10] According to the interests of the moment, the tastes and instances, the passional investment will lead to such and such a group, such and such an activity. I called this the 'unicity' of the community, or the outline of a union, naturally inducing adherence and distance, attraction and repulsion. This is not without all sorts of dislocation and conflict. We are, and it is a characteristic of contemporary cities, in the presence of the mass-tribe dialectic; the mass being the all-encompassing pole, the tribe being the pole representing a particular crystallization. All social life is organized around these two poles in an endless movement; a more or less rapid movement, more or less intense, more or less stressful, according to the place and the people involved. In a certain manner, the ethic of the moment created by this endless movement allows us to reconcile the static (spaces, structures) and the dynamic (histories, discontinuities) that are generally seen as opposites. Alongside those civilized entities, which are rather 'reactionary', that is, favouring the past, tradition, spatial definition, alongside other 'progressive' entities, which emphasize rather the future, progress and the race forward, it is possible to imagine social aggregations that ally 'contradictorily' these two perspectives and make the 'conquest of the Present' their essential value. The mass-tribe dialectic can help explain this concurrence (*cum-currere*).[11]

Returning once again to a thematic that since Durand and Morin has left no intellectual indifferent, it must be recognized that there is an endless process at work that goes from the culturization of nature to the naturalization of culture; this allows us to understand the subject in both his social and natural milieu. It is important in this respect to be sensitive to the changes under way in our societies. The purely rational and progressive model of the West, which spread over the world, is becoming saturated, and we are witnessing an interpenetration of cultures which recalls the third term (contradictoriness) I mentioned. Alongside this Westernization, which, since the end of the previous century has been accelerating, there are many signs around us that refer us to what may be termed an 'Easternization' of the world. This is expressed in specific lifestyles, new habits of dress, without neglecting to mention new attitudes towards the occupation of space and the body. On this last point especially, one must be aware of the development and the variety of 'alternative medicines' and various group therapies. Moreover, research currently under way highlights the fact that, far from being marginal, these practices, in various guises, are branching off into all parts of the social body. Naturally, this goes hand in hand with the introduction of syncretist ideologies, which, attenuating the classic body–soul dichotomy, surreptitiously encourage a new spirit of the times to which the sociologist cannot remain indifferent. One can find this intrusion of 'foreignness' occurring occasionally, as was the case with the Egyptomania as explained by Baltrusaïtis; but it would appear that the process it triggers is no longer the privilege of an elite; rather it gives rise to those small tribes that by concatenation and various intersections have a cultural impact.[12]

The essential quality of the above-mentioned signs is a new deal for the space-time relationship. To return to the notions I have been proposing since the beginning, the emphasis is placed on the near and the affectual: that which unites one to a place, a place that is experienced among others. By way of heuristic illustration, I would refer to Berque, who stated that 'it is not impossible that certain contemporary aspects of Western culture intersect with certain traditional aspects of Japanese culture'.[13] If one pays close attention to this analysis, one will discover that the highlights of this intersection are its emphasis on the global, on nature, on the relationship to the environment, which all produce a communal type of behaviour: 'the nature/culture relationship and the subject/other relationship are indissolubly linked to the perception of space' (p. 35). To abstract oneself as little as possible from one's milieu, which must be understood here in its widest sense, conjures up, *strictissimo sensu*, a symbolic vision of existence, an existence in which 'immediate perceptions and near references' (p. 37) are privileged. The link between the spatial, the global and the 'intuitive-emotional' (p. 32) are an indelible part of the forgotten, denied, decried tradition of sociological holism. Such a tradition of organic solidarity, of the founding being-together may never in fact have existed; but it remains nevertheless the nostalgic basis, either directly or *a contrario*, of many of our analyses. The thematic of *Einfühlung* (empathy), which comes down to us from German Romanticism, is the best way of expressing this course of research.[14]

Paradoxical as it may appear, the Japanese example could be a specific form of this holism, of this mystical correspondence that confirms the social as *muthos*.* Indeed, whether in business, everyday life or leisure, few things escape its reach. It so happens that the contradictory mix to which this leads is significant today at every level – political, economic, industrial – which causes a certain fascination for my contemporaries. Should we speak of a 'Nippon paradigm' to use Berque's words (p. 201)? Possibly, especially if the term paradigm, as opposed to model, describes a supple and perfectible structure. What is sure is that this paradigm adequately explains the mass-tribe dialectic that is my principal preoccupation here; this endless and rather undefined movement; this 'form' without centre and without border: all things composed of elements, which, according to situation and current experiences, fit together in changing figures and according to several pre-established archetypes. This ferment, this cultural effervescence, is enough to cause our individualistic and individualizing reason to hesitate. But after all, is there anything new in this? Other civilizations were founded on ritual games of disindividualized personae, on collectively experienced roles, and still produced solid and notable social architectonics. Let us not forget: the affectual confusion of the dionysiac myth has produced significant effects of civilization; it is possible that our megalopolises are the site of their rebirth.

2. *Genius loci*

Many times I have tried to show that the emphasis on the quotidian was not a narcissistic turning inward, an individualist gesture, but rather a re-centring toward something that is nearby, a way of experiencing in the present and collectively the anguish of time passing. Thus we can speak of the tragic (as opposed to dramatic, which is progressive) ambience that characterizes these eras. It is interesting to note also that they favour the spatial aspect and all of its many territorial manifestions. In a succinct way, we can therefore say that space is concentrated time. History is abbreviated to day-to-day histories.

An historian of medicine has remarked on an astonishing parallel between the 'innate Hippocratic warmth' and the fire of the Indo-European domestic altar. They are both felt, he states, 'as unusual sources of heat. They are both placed at central locations and dissimulated: the ancient altar dedicated to the family cult at the centre of the house and invisible from outside; the innate warmth proceeding outward from the

---

* *Transl. note*: 'muthos' = myth.

heart, hidden in the deepest reaches of the human body. And both symbolize the protective force.'[15] This relates to my hypothesis of the underground centrality that characterizes sociality, hence the importance of the 'genius of place'. This collective sentiment carves out a space, which has in turn an effect on the sentiment in question. This makes us aware of the fact that every social form is part of a pattern traced by the passage of the centuries, that it is an offshoot of this, and that the modes of living that constitute it can only be understood in terms of this substrate, in short, the entire thematic of the Thomist *habitus* or the Aristotelian *exis*.

This constitutes a common thread of ancient memory. The cult of Auglaurus, symbolizing the City of Athens, or the *lares* gods of Roman families, is testament to this. Renan makes the ironical point that what he calls 'civic childishness' impedes accession to the universal religion.[16] It is an easy irony, since it is cultural; this 'municipalization' had indeed a function of 'reliance', turning an indefinite whole into a harmonious system, in which all elements, in a contradictory way, fit together and strengthen the whole. Thus, by raising altars to the glory of Augustus, Romans were able to integrate conquered states into the solid and flexible network of the Roman Empire. Civil religion has, *stricto sensu*, a symbolic function. It expresses at best an immanent transcendence, which, while surpassing individual atomization, owes its overall character only to the elements of which it is composed. Thus, the 'domestic altar', whether a family or, by association, a city altar, is the symbol of the social glue. It is a place where space and time are easily discerned; a place which legitimizes over and over again the state of being-together. Each founding moment needs such a place: whether in the form of an anamnesis, such as various festive moments, or through scissiparity, in the case of the settler, or the explorer who takes with him a bit of native earth to serve as the foundation of what will become a new city.

It is well known that Christianity at its beginnings revalued this localism. It is around such collective spaces that it grew stronger; one has only to consult the work of Peter Brown in order to be convinced of this. He even speaks of 'a cult of the civic saints'. It is around a *topos*, a place where a holy man has taught and is buried, that a church is founded, built and propagates his message. These *topoi* then gradually became connected to one another through such flexible means as I have been discussing. Before it became the overarching organization that we now know, the Church was at first a voluntary, even federative alliance of autonomous entities with their own traditions, their own ways of expressing religion and even, sometimes, their own (theological) ideologies. 'Local associations remained very strong'; and even such and such a *topos* aroused 'intense feelings of local patriotism'. It is in these terms that Brown describes the growth of Christianity around the Mediterranean basin.[17] For him, it is precisely because of these *topoi* in which collective feelings were invested, because each community had 'its' saint, that the Church was able to implant itself and give rise to civilization. This localist tradition was to develop in a solid and lasting way, never to be entirely annihilated by the centralizing force of the institutional Church.

To give just a few examples, we are reminded of the fact that, later on, monasteries were to play the role of reference point, principally because they were the repositories of relics. Duby remarked that the saint 'kept up a corporeal residence through the vestiges of his earthly existence'.[18] It is mainly thanks to this that the monasteries became havens of peace; that they were able, on the one hand, to extend this function of preservation to the liberal arts, to agriculture and technology, and, on the other, to expand and build up a close network of houses that became sanctuaries of culture for what was to become the Christian West. It is worth reflecting on what is much more than a metaphor: preservation of the saint/preservation of life; the rootedness (more or less mythical, besides) of a saint turned into the refuge, in the strong sense of the term, of a history in progress. To play with words a bit, one can say that *location becomes connection* ['lieu devient lien']. This reminds us that we are perhaps in the presence of an anthropological structure that makes the aggregation around a space a basic given of all forms of sociality – space and sociality.

Be that as it may, within the framework of my reflections here, this relationship is the essential characteristic of popular religion. This is a term that should cause many to tremble, since it is true that the cleric, he who knows, always has difficulty avoiding an overarching view; avoiding abstracting himself from what he is describing. And yet this term popular religion is adequate; besides, it is almost a tautology, meaning as far as we are concerned whatever is proxemic. Before becoming a theology, or even a specific morality, religion is above all else a place: 'We have a religion just as we have a name, a parish, a family.'[19] It is a *reality*: just as I am a product of a nature in which I feel an active participant. We can find in this the notion of holism: religion defined on the basis of space is the glue assembling an ordered whole which is both social as well as natural. This constant is remarkable for its structural significance. Indeed, the cult of saints in popular religion may be a useful tool for understanding the contemporary effect of a given guru, football player, local star or even charismatic luminary – the list is far from a closed one. If we are to believe the specialists, popular religious practices: piety, pilgrimages, cult of saints are characterized by their local flavour, everyday rootedness and their expression of collective feelings – all things which are in the realm of proxemics. The institution may restore, regularize and manage the local cult of a given saint, and with greater or lesser success; but it remains nonetheless true that one of its primary characteristics is spontaneity, which should be understood as that which surges, expressing its own vitalism.

This living, natural religion can be summarized with a few words from Hervieu-Léger who sees it as the expression of 'warm . . . relations . . . founded on proximity, contact, the solidarity of a local community'.[20] There is no better way of describing the link between religion and space in a double polarity which founds a given entity. Physical proximity and daily reality have as much importance as the dogma which religion is supposed to convey. In fact, in this case it is the container that prevails over the contents. This 'religion of the soil' is of the utmost pertinence for appreciating the multiplication of 'urban villages', the revitalization of the neighbourhood and relations between neighbours which emphasize inter-subjectivity, affinity and shared sentiment. I spoke earlier of immanent transcendence; we could even say now that popular religion brings together the 'divine and the everyday mental horizons of man'[21] – something that opens up wide avenues of research. But more than anything else, these remarks emphasize the territorial constancy of the religious dimension. The soil is that which gives birth and where all social aggregations die along with their symbolic sublimations.

This may appear rather mystical; but as Ernst Bloch so capably demonstrated, it is a matter of spiritual materialism, well rooted, I might add; or, even better, it is a question of the inextricable mix of the collective imagination and its spatial surround. There is no pre-eminence then, but rather a constant reversibility, a series of action–retroaction between the two poles of existence. In order to illustrate this, let us say that social life is the current which, in an endless process, passes between these two banks. What can we say of this, except that the bond between the collective sentiment and space is the expression of a harmonious architectonic in which, to return to the image of the Psalmist, 'together all are as one'.

Without being knowledgeable enough to go into it in depth, I refer to the Brazilian candomblé,[22] less for its syncretist representations than its territorial organization. Indeed, the terreiro* is striking in its internal symbolic harmony. The layout of its houses, places of worship and education, the role played by nature, whether with a capital 'n', as is the case with the great terreiros, or on a smaller scale represented by a single room – all are evidence of the tight mix, the holism of the varied social elements. As much for those who live there, of course, as for those who only come on occasion, the terreiro is a point of reference. One 'is' from a given terreiro. It is interesting to note that the symbolism induced by this model is then diffracted in a minor way throughout the whole of social life. The cult paroxysm, in its various guises, even when not identified as such, informs a host of daily practices and beliefs in a transversal way: in all the cities and towns of the country. This process is worth noting, for in a country whose technological and industrial potential is now recognized by everyone, this 'holistic' perspective arising from the candomblé is far from being extinguished. To sound like Pareto, it represents an essential (quintessential) 'residue' for any social comprehension. In any case, it is a specific form of the space–sociality relationship, the traditional rootedness

---

* *Transl. note*: terreiro is a place for worship of the *candomblé*, from a small courtyard to an agricultural estate.

– the postmodern perspective, in short, of a contradictory logic of the static and the dynamic, which in this case is articulated harmoniously.

To come back to the material spirituality I previously mentioned, what does this logic teach us? Mainly, that space guarantees sociality a necessary security. We know that limits fence one in, but also give life. All of 'formist' sociology can be summarized by this statement.[23] Just like the rituals of anamnesis or the handful of land I just mentioned; just like the cosmic concentrate represented by the *terreiro*, the domestic Roman or Japanese altar, the stability of space is a focal point, an anchor for the group. It allows for a certain perdurability within the teeming and effervescent life in perpetual renewal. What Halbwachs said of the family space, 'the calming image of its continuity', can be applied to our contemporary tribes. By sticking to its space, a group transforms (dynamic) and adapts (static). In this way, space is a social given that makes me and is itself made. All individual or collective rituals, whose importance is again being recognized, are the cause or effect of such a permanence. It is really a question of a 'silent society', of the 'strength of the material milieu' (Halbwachs)[24] which is necessary to the existential balance of every individual as well as the group as a whole. Whether we are talking about the family property or the urban 'property', whether it limits my intimacy or is its architectural framework (familiar walls, houses, streets), it is all a part of a founding proxemics that accentuates the vividness of the spatial framework. All of this gives security as well as allowing for resistance; in the simple sense of the term, it is what allows us to perdure, to hold back the various natural and social impositions. This is the community of destiny. Thus, the 'genius of place' is not an abstract entity; it is also a cunning genius that continuously drives the social body and ensures the stability of the whole *above and beyond* the multiplicity of variable details.

This dialectic has curiously been ignored, especially considering how careful we have been to underline the *progressive* aspect of humanity. But to apply a distinction developed by Worringer, although there are moments when the social production, that is, accommodation to the world, is essentially 'abstractive' (mechanical, rational, instrumental), there are others when it returns to *Einfühlung* (organic, imaginary, affectual). As I have shown, there are eras during which, according to different balances, these two perspectives can be found occurring jointly. Thus, the architecture of cities, which must be understood here in the narrowest sense of the term, the fitting into a given space, can be both the application of a precise technological development as well as the expression of a sensitive being-together, the former referring to the dynamic, the latter favouring the social static. It is this second case that interests us here; what has been called the desire for security is a by-product of it. In a study which inaugurated his reflections on cities, Médam even speaks of 'the ancestral need for protection', which he moreover ties to the collective imagination and everyday life.[25] Shelter, the refuge as an underground but no less sovereign reality of all life in society, the *puissance* of sociality responding to, without necessarily opposing, the *power* of the socio-economic structure. In neglecting this paradoxical tension we risk forgetting that, alongside the abstract political responsibility which theoretically and practically has prevailed since the nineteenth century, there is a much more concrete responsibility which is that of the space we live in, the common territory. Of course, while the former is macroscopic, the latter is concerned with the small number, since it comes out of a shared experience, which I propose to call an existential *aesthetic*.

Such a perspective does not easily lend itself to individualist ideologies or to the theme of liberation which came out of Enlightenment philosophy. To return to an analysis of Bouglé's, the 'sense of common responsibilities' with respect to the land, and the solidarity that it induces, are not favourable to the 'independent initiatives of individuals'. This is a reflection on the caste system; but this valuing of proxemics in 'joint villages' can shed some light on the tribal resurgence. The same can be said for the infamous *obschina* of pre-socialist Russia. Just as was the case for the castes and their interdependence, this peasant community was linked to a feudal structure, and as such within the context of the increasingly rational world was deserving of destruction; but 'from the peasants' point of view' it was full of ideals of solidarity that were worth noting – which is in fact what the populists and anarchists did.[26]

In both cases, servitude or an alienating social structure are confronted collectively. And this community of destiny is founded on the common responsibility, whether symbolic or not, of a territory. One may make the hypothesis that dependence and servility may be completely secondary, once they are relativized, shared within the framework of an affectual network. I can just hear the cries of outrage of the conventional majority, denouncing such a hypothesis as at best anachronistic, at worst reactionary. What does this matter, for upon a clear-eyed contemplation of a number of social structures, one becomes aware that, beyond the claims of abstract autonomy, they are all characterized by a high degree of heteronomy which must be acknowledged. This negotiation may lead to a political confrontation (historical predominance); sometimes it may be invested in the establishment of collective refuges (spatial predominance). It is not up to us to decide which is best, but rather to point out that the latter attitude has its own advantages.

In this respect, there is a paradox worth noting. While we are able to pick up here and there reference to the relationship between the Jewish people and agriculture, it is generally recognized that this was not the dominant characteristic of their history, it being understood that this is the result of many causes which escape reductive simplification. Nevertheless, as F. Raphaël says, 'the relationship of the Jews to the land is both complex and more ambiguous'.[27] Indeed, they seem to be the protagonists *par excellence* of a dynamic (historical) vision of the world. This is in part true; but *at the same time*, the diaspora, the outsider status of the Jew, makes no sense without taking into account his relationship to the land of Canaan.

Here is a land which is, in the simplest sense of the term, 'mythical'. It is the basis of the union; it reinforces the community. The community may be scattered, it nevertheless remains in organic solidarity, thanks to a process of constant territorial anamnesis. This attachment to place was, *stricto sensu*, an ethos ensuring the perdurability of the community across many vicissitudes, and far from minor ones, as History shows. Here is the paradox: arising periodically throughout a long historical development, the 'mythical' land will be diffracted into a variety of territories that may be ephemeral, fragile, under constant threat, but which nevertheless constitute refuges, constantly being reborn, in which different Jewish communities will find energy.

In this respect, the ghetto is almost the archetype of what I am attempting to describe. Louis Wirth, in his now classic book, showed how, in both Europe and the United States, the ghetto offered a kind of security, this 'family fold' which, while reminding one of one's origins also had a recreational function. Thus, as contrasted with the formalism that governed the Gentile world, the Jew found in the ghetto a language, daily rituals, friendship; in short, the familiarity that makes life tolerable. The analysis emphasizes the 'small group' structure which prevails inside the ghetto, and the 'emotional' ambience that results.[28] To return to the image of a nest of Russian dolls, the ghetto is a part of the greater urban entity and serves itself as a shell encompassing a variety of sub-groups which gather according to their place of origin, their religious or educational preferences as so many tribes sharing a common territory.

What can be retained from this example is the convergence of, on the one hand, the spatial affiliation and, on the other, the emotional glue. Thus, the ghetto can allow us to shed light on a number of contemporary groups which define themselves in terms both of territory and of an affectual sharing. Whatever the territory in question or the content of the affection – cultural pursuits, sexual tastes, clothing habits, religious representations, intellectual motivations, political commitments: we can easily go on listing the factors of aggregation – they can also be circumscribed on the basis of the two poles of space and symbol (sharing, the specific form of solidarity, and so on). This is what best characterizes the intense communication which in many ways serves as a breeding ground for what I am calling neo-tribalism. Let us clarify that this fact did not escape Durkheim who, reflecting on 'secondary groups', noted both the 'territorial basis' and the 'material neighbourhood'.[29] This attention to proxemics at a time when *The Division of Labour in Society* was at its most influential should be pointed out. It shows how every society is founded on a kind of contract between the living, the dead and those who are to come. I mean by this that social existence is possible in any place only because there is a specific aura in which, *volens nolens*, we participate. The territory is the specific crystallization of such an aura. Neighbourhood life, with its small rituals, can be analysed from this strange phylum. This Durkheim, in hardly less metaphorical terms, calls holism.

The very force of everyday life, even when unperceived, is built upon this phylum. Sociality or proxemics is thus constituted of a constant sedimentation which lays down a path; which builds 'territory'. The stranger, the wanderer, is integrated or refuses this sedimentation – can even create a new one (cf. polyculturalism); but he or she is obliged to define him- or herself in these terms. For an image, I will borrow an aphorism from Ebner-Eschenbach: 'The ambrosia of past centuries is the daily bread of the times to come (*Die Ambrosie der früheren Jahrhunderte ist das tägliche Brot der späteren*).' The temporal triad is here summarized, and the aphorism accounts for the materialist spirituality which, in a non-conscious way, or without spectacle, deeply informs everyday life and collective experience. As I have shown many times before, this translates in a contradictory way the dynamic rootedness characteristic of every society.

The spatial affiliation and its symbolic or mystical connotation that I have just described are in the orgiastic-dionysiac tradition which, according to certain sociologists (Max Weber, Karl Mannheim, Max Scheler) is a social constant (let us not forget that Dionysus is a 'tree' divinity, rooted). The essential attribute of this tradition is its foundation on 'ex-stasis', the exit from the self. Scheler draws a parallel between this process and the process of identification. I identify with such and such a place, totem, stone, because they place me in a long line of ancestors; he even speaks of 'man-stones'. Of course, this identification is emotional and collective; it induces a 'symbolic identification'.[30] This is now a well-known theme, and the term 'dionysiac' itself is beginning (again), to the great annoyance of the theoretical curmudgeons, to appear in many sociological analyses. On the other hand, it is important to emphasize its chthonic aspect: these expressions refer to that which is territorialized, materialized or incarnate, in the strongest sense of the term. One ought even to see whether the theme of reincarnation, of resurrection, of metempsychosis, by postulating perdurability, by ensuring the stability of the phylum, does not compare with the heavily spatial procedures of identification. In any case, such mythico-anthropological perspectives should not fail to shed some light on the many ecstatic forms of contemporary effervescence (musical, sexual, consumer, sporting, etc.) which, in a more or less enduring way, 'are embodied', delineate a territory, in short, reinvest these archaic, primitive values of proximity that rationalism seemed to have destroyed so easily.

In summarizing the given notes and examples, we can say that there is a close relationship between territory and collective memory. This could lead Halbwachs to say that, as far as their cities, houses or apartments are concerned, the groups 'in a way trace their shapes in the earth and connect with their collective memories in the spatial framework thus defined'.[31] This is a strong expression which bursts through the too-strict barrier established between social history and its definition in a specific place. What is more, it illustrates precisely what I am trying to underline here: the revaluing of space is correlative to the revaluing of more restricted entities (groups, 'tribes'). Symbolic and spatial proxemics encourage the desire to leave one's mark, that is, to bear witness to one's durability. This is the true aesthetic dimension of a given spatial affiliation: to serve the collective memory that defined it. Afterwards, of course, these affiliations may be subject to aesthetic analyses *stricto sensu*, and become in this sense works of culture; but it must not be forgotten that they surpass, and by far, what is only too often an abstract and intellectual reduction. In this perspective, the cathedral is no more worthy than the kitsch decorations of a worker's garden plot; urban graffiti or stencils can be compared to prehistoric cave paintings.[32] In each case, a group declares itself, delineates its territory and thus confirms its existence.

Finally, whether or not it is possible to develop it precisely, a parallel must be drawn between proxemics and the (re)new(ed) importance of the imagination in social life. It is almost as if a sociological 'law' needed to be drawn up: each time that distrust of the imagination prevails (iconoclasm, rationalist monovalency) theoretical representations and social modes of organization with the common denominator of 'the distant' evolve; we are then witness to the dominance of the political, of historical linearism, which are all essentially prospective in nature. On the other hand, when image in its various forms returns to centre stage, localism becomes an undeniable reality.

To take only one historical example to serve as a springboard to my analysis, let us remember that at the time the Christian civilization was being established, iconoclasm was the ideological banner under which the believers in centralism marched, whereas iconodulism* is the domain of those who favour the expression of local feelings. Of course, there is a theoretical rationalization, theological in this case, that is given to this conflict; but it is essential to know what form the organization of society will take. Peter Brown, in analysing this conflict, even speaks of 'iconoclast jacobinism'. All means are valid for eradicating local cults, quite simply because they impede the activity of a central government. These local cults are organized around a holy man and a specific icon; they both 'were consecrated from *below*'. This was the basis of a complex system of interrelationships between the various *topoi* that constituted a skein of alternate power structures outside the confines of the centralized organization that was being established in its place.[33] From this process one should remember the role of the icon that legitimized the opposition energy of the holy man, and served as the crystallization of the feelings expressed by the local groups.

In brief, in the solitude inherent in any urban setting, the icon, familiar and close by, is a reference point that is imbedded in the daily fabric. It is the centre of a complex and concrete symbolic order in which everyone has a role to play in the context of an overall theatre. It thus allows for self-

---

* *Transl. note*: pertaining to the veneration of icons.

recognition, the recognition of oneself by others, and, finally, the recognition of others. This is the empathetic strength of the image that regularly returns in order to remedy the deadening effects of uniformization and the commutation it engenders. It would naturally be interesting to note the contemporary manifestations of what I have just called icons. They are varied, and each of them would require its own in-depth analysis. I have contented myself here with bringing out the inner logic or the 'form'. But this should allow us to accentuate the 'imaginary' function of a whole range of local emblems. As I have already remarked, they may be notabilities of whatever type, animals with which the group identifies, specific places or products of the land: each one being, of course, eponymous.

One may add that the significance of the emblematic image is increased by technological innovations. Indeed, the television or advertising image was initially suspect, especially inasmuch as it was the bearer of a unique and alienating ideological message. We can now see that advertising on the one hand takes its inspiration from several archetypal figures, and on the other, as a result, addresses 'target' audiences, what I am calling tribes, which give rise to and recognize, through various modes of representation and imagination, the products, goods, services and ways of being that constitute them as groups. Television, because of its diffraction, is no longer the standard-bearer of a unique message applicable to all. Indeed, although what I am advancing here is just a tendency, it must be recognized that it is addressed increasingly to particular groups: groups based on age, region, cities, even neighbourhoods. Examples such as buildings which receive cable TV can only reinforce this process. What can this mean, except that the image is no longer distant, overarching, totally abstract, but rather it is defined by proximity? For better or for worse, and whichever is beside the point, the image will play the role of familiar icon. A building or neighbourhood will offer up its own spectacle. In the megalopolis, the televised image will be part of a tactile, emotional and affectual experience; as a result, it will strengthen the tribe as such, while at the same time creating a zone of security for itself.[34] Admittedly, the theoretical stakes are significant, especially if we are careful to notice that it is from 'below' that these new manifestations of being-together will issue.

What is certain is that all of these tendencies come back to space: there is a territorial connotation to all of the preceding examples. Basing himself on linguistic research, Berque distinguishes between 'egocentric' languages and 'lococentric' languages.[35] It is surely possible to extrapolate his analysis and recognize that there are cultures that are primarily 'egocentric' and others that are 'lococentric'. The former favour the individual and his or her concerted actions, whereas the latter emphasize the natural or social environment. One might also envisage that, within one culture, one could find differential sequences, with an emphasis sometimes on that which individualizes, and at other times, the collective, disindividualizing aspects. This is, at any rate, my theory for our own culture. Thus, the valuing of space, through the image, the body and territory is both cause and effect of the submerging of the individual in a vast whole. A society founded on such a dynamic risks seeing its fundamental values turned upside-down; this is perhaps the contemporary challenge represented by all the experiences and all the social situations which are based on proxemics.

3.   Tribes and networks

Indeed, the emphasis on the spatial is not an end in itself: if we are to restore meaning to the neighbourhood, neighbourly practices and the affectual aspect that this will inevitably give rise to, it is above all because it allows for networks of relationships. Proxemics refers primarily to the foundation of a succession of 'we's' which constitutes the very essence of all sociality. To follow up on what has already been said, I would now like to highlight the fact that the constitution of micro-groups, of the tribes which intersperse spatiality, arises as a result of a feeling of *belonging*, as a function of a specific *ethic* and within the framework of a communications *network*. These may in fact be the bywords of this analysis.

Although it takes the form of a metaphor, these three ideas can be summarized by speaking of a 'multitude of villages' which intersect, oppose each other, help each other, all the while remaining themselves. We now have at our disposal several speculative analyses and field studies which go a long way to reinforcing this point of view.[36] The city-object is a succession of territories in which people in a more or less ephemeral way take root, close ranks, search out shelter and security. In using the term 'village', I have made clear that it was only a metaphor. Indeed, it can of course delineate a concrete space; but this can also be a *cosa mentale*, a symbolic territory, in whatever shape or form, but which is no less real for all that. One has only to refer to the 'fields' broken down by the intellectuals to create protected domains in order to understand that the metaphor of the tribe or the village is not without heuristic interest. In all domains then, whether intellectual, cultural, religious, commercial or political, we can observe these roots which allow a social 'body' to exist as such.

In addition, the feeling of tribal belonging can be reinforced by technological developments. In speaking of 'the electronic nebula', A. Moles, with some reticence it is true, suggests what could become the 'model of a new global village'.[37] This is primarily thanks to the interactivity which this model gives rise to. Indeed, 'cable TV', computer bulletin boards (for amusement, erotic or functional purposes) may create a communicational matrix in which groups with various goals will appear, gain strength and die; groups which recall somewhat the archaic structures of village clans or tribes. The only notable difference which characterizes the electronic nebula is of course the very temporality of these tribes. Indeed, as opposed to what is usually meant by this notion, the tribalism we are exploring here can be completely ephemeral, organized as the occasion arises. To return to an old philosophical term, it is exhausted in the act. As has become clear in many statistical reports, more and more people are living as 'singles'; but the fact of living *alone* does not mean living *in isolation*. According to the occasion – especially thanks to the computer services of the Minitel – the 'single' can join a given group or activity. The 'tribes' based on sports, friendships, sex, religion and other interests are constituted in many ways (the Minitel is just one), all of them having varied lifespans according to the degree of investment of the protagonists.

Indeed, just as there are successive truths in loving relationships, science is constructed from sequential approximations; it is possible to imagine a participation in these diverse 'forms' of sociality that would itself be differentiated and open. This is made possible by the speed of the supply–demand circuit inherent in the computerized transaction.

It remains no less true that although they are stamped with the seal of timeliness, with its inevitably tragic dimension, these tribes favour the mechanism of belonging. Whatever the domain, it is more or less required to participate in the collective spirit. Moreover, the question is simply not asked, and acceptance or rejection depends on the degree of feeling* felt both by the members of the group and by the applicant. This feeling will then be either reinforced or weakened by the acceptance or rejection of various initiation rites. Whatever the lifespan of the group, these rites are necessary. We can moreover observe that they take on an increasing importance in everyday life. Some rituals are more or less imperceptible, which allow one to feel at ease, to be 'a regular' of a given bar or nightspot. In the same way, one would never dream of transgressing them to get one's racing form or lottery ticket; it is the same if one wants to be served properly in the neighbourhood shops or to walk in a given street. The rituals of belonging are of course found in office blocks and factories and the socio-anthropology of work has paid considerable attention to this aspect. Finally, we may recall that leisure or mass tourism is essentially dependent on this tendency.[38]

One could continue with examples; however, one need only show how, alongside the resurgence of the image and the myth (a story told by each group) in the contemporary world, the rite is an effective technique which at best constitutes the ambient religiosity (*religare*) of our megalopolises. One can even say that the ephemeral and tragic aspects of these tribes deliberately emphasize the performance of rituals; the latter, by their repetitive aspect and their attention to the minuscule, attenuate the anguish inherent in 'presentism'. At the same time as the aspiration, the future and the ideal no longer serve as a glue to hold society together, the ritual, by reinforcing the feeling of belonging, can play this role and thus allow groups to exist.

It must be noted, however, that at the same time that it encourages attraction, even if plural, the feeling of belonging proceeds if not by

---

* *Transl. note*: The word 'feeling' is in English in the text.

exclusion then at least by exclusiveness. Indeed, the characteristic of the tribe is that by highlighting what is close (persons and places), it has a tendency to be closed in on itself. This suggests the metaphor of the door (*Tür*) so dear to Simmel. The abstract universal gives way to the concreteness of the particular, thus explaining the existence of these 'localisms' which have surprised more than a few researchers. Thus, within the neighbourhood itself, we can find a series of clubs; friendly gatherings take place within a strictly defined perimeter. Movement is confined to a limited number of streets. This kind of phenomenon is well known in the cities of the south of Europe, but the work of Young and Willmott has also shown how it applies to London.[39] Localism favours what can be called 'the Mafia spirit': in looking for lodgings, finding work and as far as all the other trivial daily privileges are concerned, priority will be given to those who belong to the tribe or those who travel within its spheres of influence. Ordinarily, this process is analysed within the framework of the family, but it is certainly possible to extend the notion of family; that is, to a relationship based on family ties but also on various friendships, clientelism, or reciprocal favours.

The term 'tie' (family, friendship, etc.) must be understood in its most commonly accepted sense: that of necessity, which the medieval guild system classified under the heading of 'obligation'. Mutual aid in all its forms is a *duty*, the linchpin of a code of honour, often unstated, regulating tribalism. This is what gives rise to this exclusivism which, in many respects, distrusts anything unfamiliar. In their work on 'everyday villages', Young and Willmott mention a remark which underlines this phenomenon: 'they are newcomers: they've only been here 18 years'. The contradiction is only apparent; it means that these 'newcomers' have other ties, other networks of mutual aid, participate in other groups. They function according to their own proxemics. This reality is particularly evident in big cities but it is, like any evidence, worth repeating. For its own security, the group constructs its own natural and social environment and at the same time forces, *de facto*, other groups to constitute themselves as such. Thus, the territorial demarcation (I repeat: physical or symbolic territory) is the structural foundation of multiple socialities. Alongside direct reproduction there is an indirect form of reproduction which does not depend on the will of the social protagonists but on the social effect represented by the duo of 'attraction–repulsion': the existence of a group founded on a strong sense of belonging requires that, for everyone's survival, other groups exist from a similar necessity.

The manifestations of this process are, when all is said and done, quite ordinary. One only has to observe the customers of certain cafés, the specificity of certain neighbourhoods or even the clientele of such and such a school, concert hall or public sphere in order to realize the importance of such a structure. Within these various spaces, one may notice other equally exclusive groupings, based on the subtle yet deep-rooted consciousness of the feeling of belonging and/or of difference. Perhaps we should see this, as

Bouglé proposes, as 'certain traces of the caste spirit'.[40] What is certain is that, alongside a surface egalitarianism, there has always been an extremely complex social architectonic whose various elements were at the same time completely opposed to one another as well as interdependent.

There may exist a *de facto* recognition of these groups between themselves. As I have stated, exclusivity does not mean exclusion, just as such a recognition leads to a specific mode of adjustment. There may be conflict, but it is expressed within the boundaries of certain rules, to the point of being completely ritualized. Let us remember the paroxysmal metaphor of the Mafia: the sharing of territories is in general respected and clan or 'family' warfare arises only at such time as the equilibrium of the 'honourable society' is ruptured. If we were to apply this model to our urban tribes, we would observe that there are highly sophisticated mechanisms of regulation in place. The role of the outsider so ably described by the political scientists (Freund, Schmitt) finds its application here. A system of differentiated alliances arranges for one of these tribes to be always in a position of mediator. The *ad hoc* aspect of these alliances makes the system one of motion while it remains perfectly stable. The role of the outsider is not in fact a single person's doing: it can be played by an entire group which acts as a counterweight, which plays the role of intermediary, which simply makes up the numbers, thus strengthening the balance of a given whole.

This can be linked to the function of 'proxemics' which existed in ancient cities. It is an intermediate function, a matter of forming a link between the various ethical and national groups which made up the city. By playing around with these words, we can say that the *proxenus* (close) brings closer. It is this perdurability that allows the stranger, while remaining foreign, to take an active part in the city. He has his place in the social architectonic. Is it moreover fortuitous if, as M.F. Baslez reports, the poet Pindar plays the role of *proxenus* at the same time as he composes the dithyramb in honour of the city? Indeed, one can imagine that the celebration of the city as a city owes much to its capacity of taming and integrating the stranger.[41]

Thus, the recognition of diversity and the ritualization of the discomfort that it occasions leads to a specific adjustment which in a way uses the trouble and the tension as useful balancing factors for the city. Here we find once more the contradictory logic analysed many times already (Lupasco, Beigbeder, Durand) and which refuses overly mechanical and reductive binary structures and dialectical procedure. The various urban tribes constitute a city because they are different and at times even opposed. Any effervescence is structurally foundational. This is a basic sociological rule that did not of course escape Durkheim; the trick is to know how to use this effervescence, how to ritualize it. A good way, in the above-mentioned logic, is to let each tribe be itself: the resulting adjustment will be all the more natural. As I have already explained elsewhere, the coenesthesia of the social body can be compared with that of the human body: function and dysfunction generally complete and counter-balance one another. It is a matter of getting the individual 'evil' to serve the overall 'good'. Fourier posited this homoeopathic procedure as the basis of his phalanstery. Thus, he proposed using what he called the 'small hordes' or 'small gangs' to the best of their abilities, even if they were anomic: 'My theory is limited to using (disapproved of) passions such as nature provides without any modification. That is the magic spell, the secret calculation of the Passionate Attraction.'[42]

It is possible that these careful and rather utopian calculations for his time are poised to be realized in our own. As heterogeneity is the rule and pluriculturalism and polyethnism best characterize our great cities of today, it is possible to believe that the *consensus is more the result of an a posteriori 'affectual adjustment' than an a priori rational regulation.* In this sense, a great deal of attention to what we too easily call marginality is indicated. It is certainly the laboratory of future lifestyles, but the (re)new(ed) initiation rites of the groups in question are only taking the place of old rites (which we no longer dared characterize as such) emptied of meaning by becoming standardized. Hasty condemnation is not enough, and neither is condescension. It must be understood that these rites are deserving of their own analysis. Their vividness translates the fact that a new form of social aggregation is emerging; it is perhaps difficult to conceptualize, but with the assistance of ancient figures, it is surely possible to trace its outlines, hence the metaphor of the tribe and tribalism that I am expounding here.

This metaphor ably translates the emotional aspect, the feeling of belonging and the ambience of conflict to which it leads. At the same time, it allows us to bring out, beyond this conflictual structure, the search for a more hedonistic everyday life, that is, less finalized, less determined by the 'ought' and by work. These are all things which the Chicago School noted several decades ago, but they now take on a much more unstable scale. This 'conquest of the present' is manifested in an informal way by the small groups whose 'activity simply involved roaming about and exploring the world'.[43] Naturally, this leads them to experiment with new ways of being in which the next 'trip', the cinema, sport, the communal meal, take on a predominant role. Moreover, it is interesting to note that with the help of age and time, these small gangs will stabilize as the (sport, cultural) clubs or the 'secret society' with a heavy emotional content. It is this passage from one form to another which speaks in favour of the prospective aspect of tribes. Of course, not all of these groups survive; but the fact that some of them assume the various stages of socialization creates a social 'form' of flexible organization which is rather uneven, but which responds, *concreto modo*, to the different constraints posed by the social environment and that particular natural environment which is the contemporary city. From this point of view, the tribe can cause us to propose a new social *logic* which risks challenging a good number of our most comfortable sociological analyses. Thus, what was in the not too distant past deemed 'marginal', can no longer be described as such.

Before the Chicago School, Weber had noted the existence of what I shall call a 'tribal romanticism' which valued the affectual life and the life experience. With nuance moreover, it can be used to separate the wheat from the chaff; however, unlike certain commentators, it seems to me that his analysis of small mystical groups contains, *in nuce*, a number of elements which can allow us to appreciate what is happening today. In this regard, the prudence of Jean Séguy seems closer to the mark, since, beyond the reserve of his time, his description of that which escapes the rationalizations of the world is in perfect harmony with the *non-rational* that is deeply seated in urban tribes.[44] This term must be emphasized: the non-rational is not the irrational; it is not even defined in terms of the rational; it establishes a logic other than the one that has prevailed since the Enlightenment. It is increasingly given that eighteenth- and nineteenth-century rationalism is just one model of reason inherent in social life. Other parameters such as the affectual or the symbolic can have their own rationality. Just as the non-logical is not illogical, we can state that the search for shared experiences, the grouping around eponymous heroes, non-verbal communication and bodily gestures are all based on a rationality that is no less effective and which is in many ways wider and, in the simplest sense of the term, more generous. This calls upon the social observer to be generous of mind; this can only make us more sensitive to the multiplication of tribes that are located not on the margins, but which are like so many points in a nebula that no longer has a clearly discernible centre.

Let us acknowledge the fact that there is a host of loci secreting their own values and acting as a glue for those who *make and belong to* these values. Nineteenth-century values referred to History, to what I called the extensive (*ex-tension*) attitude; the emerging rationality is principally proxemic, intensive (*in-tension*). It is organized around a mainspring (a guru, an activity, pleasure, space) which binds people together as well as liberates them. It is centripetal as well as centrifugal, whence the apparent instability of tribes: the coefficient of belonging is not absolute, and anyone can participate in a multitude of groups, while investing a not inconsiderable part of him or herself in each. This flitting about is surely one of the essential characteristics of the social organization which is becoming apparent. It is this which allows one to postulate, in a paradoxical way, on the one hand, the existence of the two poles of mass and tribe and, on the other, their constant reversibility: the coming and going between the static and the dynamic. Must this be linked to the 'objective chance' so favoured by the Surrealists? It is certain that, more and more, each person is enclosed in the circle of relationships; and at the same time, he or she can yet be struck by the shock of the unexpected, the event, the adventure. Hannerz thus describes the essence of the city: 'the act of discovering one thing by chance when one was looking for something else'.[45] This can also apply to these remarks; determined by territory, tribe, ideology, anyone may also, and in a very short time-span, sweep into another territory, another tribe, another ideology.

This is what brings me to consider individualism and its various theories as invalid. Each social actor is less acting than acted upon. Each person is diffracted into infinity, according to the *kairos*, the opportunities and occasions that present themselves. Social life is then a stage upon which, for an instant, crystallizations take place: *let the play begin*. But once played, the whole is diluted until such point as another nodosity takes its place. Such a metaphor is not extravagant, in so far as it can allow us to comprehend the succession of 'presents' (*no future now*) which, in a general way, best characterizes the ambience of the moment.

4. The network of networks

Although the social organization created by this paradigm may shock our too-mechanical representations, it is no less functional: it forms a structure. It is truly, in the sense I have shown, taking my inspiration from Simmel, a *form* in which various elements of a social given hold together, in which they are as one body. This is what has caused me to speak of organicity, to rethink the notion of organic solidarity, even if it should seem paradoxical: at the end of this reflection, we are only at the beginning of our quest. What is this *glutinum mundi* developing before our very eyes? We may note that some solid work has already been done on the question of networks: for instance, micro-psychology and mathematical formalization.[46] Moreover, it is possible that contemporary mathematics is perfecting, in a sophisticated way, its own model of interpretation – I have, however, neither the competence nor the desire to use their analyses. One need only remark that, although their methods are divergent, their objective is the same: to account for a nebula with its own logic. Indeed, that is how I would formulate the problem: *the interplay of the proxemic is organized into polycentric nebulae*. These latter allow one to express both segregation and tolerance. Social groups organize their territories and ideologies around the values which are their own, and then, through force of circumstance, are obliged to adjust themselves. This macro-social model is in turn diffracted, giving rise to the myriad of tribes obeying the same rules of segregation and tolerance, of repulsion and attraction, hence, to return to Hannerz's expression, this 'urban mosaic' whose analysis remains to be completed: 'no one group has his undivided allegiance'.[47]

To understand fully the teeming life that characterizes this nebula, let us take the example of gossip, a euphemized form of segregation and desire for death. It serves as a group's glue and allows one to deny the honour, the pertinence – the very existence even – of the other. At first, its practice of anonymous killing is used to strengthen the group in its belief in what it represents and in its activities. It alone possesses the truth – theoretical, existential, ideological; the error lies 'elsewhere'. But it is striking to note how quickly gossip spreads: each little milieu has its own rumour mill. Without studying these as such, it is possible to state that they are a perfect expression of the fact that, within a particular group, there are many members who belong to a multitude of other tribes: this is how a piece of gossip becomes a rumour. This interpenetration can also work between different groups. By way of illustration, one can say that such and such a pre-emptory judgement – definite, more or less well founded, negative of course – about a member of the scientific tribe will spread from university to laboratory, from committee to commission, from colloquium to conference, from journal to report, in a vast tour of academia. The means are variable: it may range from private diatribe to silence or published criticism. But the whole of this social body is rapidly involved. Next, from cocktail parties to working meetings, the piece of gossip does the rounds of the publishers and then spreads to the journalists. Sometimes the contamination even spreads to another tribe, such as senior government officials or social workers who are occasional consumers of theoretical works. Thus, we can follow, by successive concatenations, the efficiency of multiple allegiances. In this sense, the rumour mill is a good indicator of the network structure, and it is very difficult to find a circle that is exempt.[48]

In fact, the interlacing (what English-speaking theoreticians call connectedness) is a *morphological characteristic* of the social aggregation which concerns us here. One will remember in this context Milgram's experiments, which showed that, with the help of five or six relayers, one could establish contact between two people in opposite corners of the United States.[49] Relying on the research by Milgram, one notices that the chain linking the people in question is composed less of individuals than of 'micro-milieux'. In the above-cited example, as in Milgram's experiments, information circulates because it is transmitted from link to link; sometimes within the chain there is a larger link. Depending on the case, it may be a bar, a tavern, a respected university laboratory, a church – it matters little. This link structures the received information, corrects it, prunes it, invents a little low embellishment, then sends it on to the next link. At its extreme, the individual concerned by the information does not count for much, *a fortiori* the one who is transmitting it; they are both interchangeable pawns of a particular 'structure effect'. This explains why no one is responsible (or answers) for the information or the gossip: they are transmitted through the atmosphere, making and destroying the most fragile of reputations – *sic transit*.

The aforementioned examples, which are of course only general indications, are reinforced by the non-voluntary, non-active structure of the networks. We might almost say that this is a constraint, or pre-constraint. From here on in, its protagonists can also be thus qualified: they are less producers of information than acted upon by information. If we can forget for a moment our judgemental attitude, and without giving it a pejorative connotation, we can refer back to the dionysiac metaphor of confusion: things, people and representations relate through a mechanism of proximity. Thus, it is by successive associations that what we call the social given is created. By a series of overlappings and multiple interconnections, a network of networks is constituted; the various elements are maintained in relation to one another, thus forming a complex structure; however, timing, chance, the present all play a considerable part. This gives to our era its uncertain and stochastic flavour. This does not alter the fact, difficult as it is for us to see, that there is a solid organicity at work that can serve as the basis of new forms of solidarity and sociality.

To be sure, these owe nothing to the ideology of development founded on an individual master of himself or on continuous progress; these are all part of a linear perspective or a physics comprised of isolated, juxtaposed atoms. As is the case in other domains, it is necessary from time to time to instigate a truly Copernican revolution. Indeed, it would be judicious to write a new *De revolutionibus orbium . . .* which would apply not to the heavenly realm, but which would show the particular evolutions and revolutions of a shattered social world. Thus, the network of networks would no longer refer to a space in which various elements are added to one another, are positioned; in which social activities are ordered according to a logic of separation; but rather a space where everything is combined, multiplied and reduced, making kaleidoscopic figures with ever-changing and varied contours.

Perhaps we can compare it to what Berque calls the 'areolar space', a space which refers to area, as opposed to a linear space uniquely defined by a succession of points: 'linear space would be defined as more extrinsic, areolar space as intrinsic'.[50] I would like to extrapolate the author's notes on this topic which he applies to Japan. Indeed, it is possible to imagine that the emphasis placed on context, correlative to this 'areology', can help us to define more clearly the effectiveness of the local and proxemic. As I formulated earlier, ex-tension gives way to 'in-tension'. Consequently, instead of interpreting the logic of networks as arising from a rather causalist mechanics – a series of sequences – it can be seen holistically as the correspondence of differing areas. In the context of a complex society, everyone lives through a series of experiences which can only be understood in an overall sense. Participating in a multitude of tribes, which are themselves interrelated, allows each person to live his or her intrinsic plurality. These various 'masks' are ordered in a more or less conflictual way and fit together with other surrounding 'masks'. Thus we can describe to some extent the morphology of the network. This construction, like paintings within a painting, values all of these elements, no matter how minuscule or anodyne.

I return to my main hypothesis: there is (there will be) an increasing to and fro between the tribe and the mass; within a defined matrix, a multitude of poles of attraction are crystallizing. In both of these images, the glue of the aggregation – which we could call experience, the lived, sensitivity, image – is made up of proximity and the affectual (or the emotional), which is evoked by area, the minuscule and the everyday. Thus, the network of networks appears as an architectonic whose sole worth resides in its various elements. To come back to Troeltsch's typology, the sociality produced by the network would be of the mystical type.[51] This term offers a suitable description of the dominant character-istic of contemporary *reliance*. We can find in it the flux, the mobility, the experience and the emotional life. These are all things which, as I have tried to emphasize throughout this analysis, surpass the individual monad and strengthen the collective feeling. It would thus appear that, due to one of those frequent short-cuts in human history, postmodern sociality is reinvesting some rather archaic values to say the least. Referring to bourgeois monumentality, to its institutional expressions and its pro-jective preoccupations, these can be called 'non-contemporary' values. And yet, they are no less real and gradually spread throughout the societal whole in their entirety.

The paradigm of the network can then be seen as the re-actualization of the ancient myth of community; myth in the sense in which something that has perhaps never really existed acts, effectively, on the imagination of the time. This explains the existence of those small tribes, ephemeral in their actualization, but which nevertheless create a state of mind that, for its part, seems called upon to last. Must we see this then as the tragic and cyclical return of the same? It is possible, however, that it forces us to rethink the mysterious relationship uniting 'place' and 'we'. For, although it does not fail to annoy the upholders of institutional knowledge, the jarring and imperfect everyday life inescapably secretes a true 'everyday knowledge' ('co-naissance') that the subtle Machiavelli called 'the thinking of the public square'.

Notes

1. Nietzsche, cf. F. Ferraroti's analysis, *Histoire et histoires de vie*, Paris, Librairie des Méridiens, 1983, p. 32, *et seq.*

2. F. Chamoux, *La Civilisation hellénistique*, Paris, Arthaud, 1981, p. 211.

3. Ibid., p. 231, on another application of this polarity, cf. the ideal type of the city developed by the Chicago School, in particular E. Burgess in U. Hannerz, *Exploring the City: Inquiries toward an Urban Anthropology*, New York: Columbia University Press, 1980, p. 29.

4. For an analysis of *De Politia*, cf. D. Weinstein, *Savonarole et Florence*, Paris, Calmann-Lévy, 1965, pp. 298–299.

5. Ibid., pp. 44–45 and footnotes 18 and 19 on the influence of the city of Florence. On 'space as a category of understanding', cf. A. Moles and E. Rohmer, *Les Labyrinthes du vécu*, Paris, Méridiens, 1982; on the 'community of meaning', cf. J.F. Bernard-Bécharies in *Revue Française du marketing*, 1980–81, book 80, pp.9–48.

6. M. Weber, *The City*, New York, Free Press, 1958, p. 111.

7. Ibid., p. 159.

8. G. Freyre, *The Masters and the Slaves: A Study in the Development of Brazilian Civilization*, New York, Alfred E. Knopf, 1963, p. 209.

9. H. Raymond, preface to M. Young and P. Willmott, *Le Village dans la ville*, French transl. of *Family and Kinship in East London*, Paris, Centre Georges Pompidou, Centre de création industrielle, p. 9.

10. Cf. Hannerz, *Exploring the City* p. 6; on 'urban villages', c.f. H. Gans, *The Urban Villagers*, New York, Free Press, 1962. On attraction, cf. P. Tacussel, *L'Attraction sociale*, Paris, Librairie des Méridiens, 1984.

11. On this theme and its essential categories, I refer to my book, M. Maffesoli, *La Conquête du Présent. Pour une sociologie de la vie quotidienne*, Paris, PUF, 1979. I am using the term dialectic here in its simplest (Aristotelian) sense: continuous travel between two poles; on action–retroaction, or the 'Morinian' loop, cf. E. Morin, *La Méthode*, vol. 3, *La Connaissance de la connaissance/1*, Paris, Seuil, 1986.

12. By way of example, see the work under way at the Centre d'Étude sur l'Actuel et le Quotidien (Sorbonne-Paris V) by Pina Lalli on alternative medicine networks, by P. Gérome on the multiplication of bodily therapies, by S. Joubert and B.G. Glowczenski on astrology, and J. Ferreux on the representations of alternative groups. Also refer to J. Dumazédier's work, including *La Révolution du temps libre*, Paris, Méridiens Klincksieck, 1988.

13. A. Berque, *Vivre l'espace au Japon*, Paris, PUF, 1982, p. 34, cf. the analysis pp. 31-39.

14. I have already proposed reversing the Durkheimian concepts of 'organic solidarity' and 'mechanical solidarity', cf. M. Maffesoli, *La Violence totalitaire*, Paris, PUF, 1979; on *Einfühlung*, I refer to my book *La Connaissance ordinaire, précis de sociologie compréhensive*, Paris, Librairie des Méridiens, 1985. On the community nostalgia of the founding fathers, cf. R. Nisbet, *The Sociological Tradition*, London, Heinemann Educational, 1970.

15. C. Lichtenthaeler, *Histoire de la médecine*, Paris, Fayard, 1978, p. 100. I owe this reference to the thesis under way by T. Orel on vitalism.

16. E. Renan, *La Réforme* in *Oeuvres Complètes*, Paris, Calmann-Lévy, p. 230. Cf. also Gibbon, *The History of the Decline and Fall of the Roman Empire*, London, Methuen, 1909, vol. 1, p. 76: 'Augustus permitted indeed some of the provincial cities to erect temples in his honour, on condition that they should associate the worship of Rome with that of the sovereign' and p. 85 'many persons preserved the image of Marcus Antoninus among those of their household gods'.

17. Cf. P. Brown, *Society and the Holy in Late Antiquity*, London, Faber and Faber, 1982, pp. 276-281. Cf. also *The Cult of the Saints: Its Rise and Function in Latin Christianity*, Chicago, University of Chicago Press, 1981, Ch. 1: 'The Holy and the Grave'.

18. G. Duby, *The Age of the Cathedrals: Art and Society 980–1420*, Chicago, University of Chicago Press, 1981.

19. E. Poulat, *Eglise contre bourgeoisie*, Paris, Casterman, 1977, p. 112.

20. D. Hervieu-Léger, *Vers un nouveau christianisme*, Paris, Cerf, 1986, p. 109; cf. also pp. 107, 123 for references to the work of H. Hubert, R. Hertz and S. Bonnet.

21. M. Meslin, 'le phénomène religieux populaire' in *Les Religions populaires*, Québec, Presses de l'Université Laval, 1972.

22. Cf. for example the studies of R. Motta (Recife), 'Estudo do Xango', *Revista de antropologia*, São Paulo, 1982; V. de Costa-Lima (Salvador de Bahia), *A familia de santo nos candomblés jeje. Nagos a Bahia : un estudo de relaçoes intra-groupais*, Universidade federal do Bahia, Salvador, 1977; M. Sodré (Rio de Janeiro), *Samba o dono do corpo*, Rio, Codecri, 1979.

23. I have explored this in *La Connaissance ordinaire*.

24. Cf. the remarkable pages Halbwachs devotes to the collective memory of space, in *La Mémoire collective*, Paris, PUF, 1968, pp. 130–138.

25. Cf. A. Médam, *La Ville censure*, Paris, Anthropos, 1971, p. 103. On the distinction Worringer makes, cf. *Abstraction and Empathy : A Contribution to the Psychology of Style*, transl. M. Bullock, New York, International Universities, 1967. On the shared experience, cf. M. Maffesoli, 'Le Paradigme esthétique', *Sociologie et Sociétés*, Montréal, vol. 17, no. 2 (Oct. 1985), p. 36.

26. On these two historic examples, cf. C. Bouglé, *Essays on the Caste System*, Cambridge, Cambridge University Press, 1971, pp. 171–172 and F. Venturi, *Les intellectuels, le peuple et la révolution. Histoire du populisme russe au XIXe siècle*, Paris, Gallimard, 1972, p. 211.

27. F. Raphäel, *Judaïsme et capitalisme*, Paris, PUF, 1982, p. 201.

28. L. Wirth, *The Ghetto*, Chicago, University of Chicago Press, 1966.

29. E. Durkheim, *The Division of Labour in Society*, New York, Free Press, 1964, pp. 28–29.

30. M. Scheler, *The Nature of Sympathy*, London, Routledge and Kegan Paul, 1970, p. 19 (cf. also p. 20, note 1); on the orgiastic-dionysiac, cf. K. Mannheim, *Ideology and Utopia*, New York, Harcourt and Brace, 1954, p. 194 and M. Weber, *Economy and Society*, Berkeley, University of California Press, 1978.

31. Halbwachs, *La Mémoire collective*, p. 166.

32. On the art of stencils, cf. the studies of M. Deville, 'Imaginaires, pochoirs, tribus, utopies', *Sociétés*, Paris, Masson, no. 10 (1986); on graffiti, cf. J. Baudrillard, *L'Échange symbolique et la mort*, Paris, Gallimard, 1976, p. 118, *et seq.*

33. P. Brown, *Society and the Holy in Late Antiquity*, London, Faber and Faber, 1982, pp. 293, 297 and 298.

34. On these various points, cf. A. Sauvageot, *Figures de la publicité, figures du monde*, Paris, PUF, 1987; M. Deville, *Les Vidéo-clip et les jeunes*, Paris, Centre d'études sur l'actuel et le quotidien (C.E.A.Q.) C. Moricot, *Télévision et société, les immeubles câblés*, Paris, (C.E.A.Q.).

35. Berque, *Vivre l'espace au Japon*, p. 47.

36. The term 'multitude of villages' which is close to the Chicago School as I have shown, is borrowed from J. Beauchard, *La Puissance des foules*, Paris, PUF, 1985, p. 25; on the neighbourhood relations, and their conflicts or solidarity, one can refer to a study by F. Pelletier, 'Quartier et communication sociale', *Espaces et Sociétés*, no. 15 (1975). More recently, cf. the poetic analysis of an ethnologist, P. Sansot, *La France sensible*, Champ Vallon, 1985; cf. also Ferrarotti, *Histoire et histoires de vie*, p. 33.

37. A. Moles, *Théorie structurale de la communication et sociétés*, Paris, Masson, 1986, p. 147, *et seq.*

38. E. T. Hall, *Beyond Culture*, Garden City, New York, Anchor/Doubleday, 1976, p. 55 gives the example of factories in Japan. On tourism, I refer to the article (a study under way) by R. Amirou, 'Le Badaud, approche du tourisme', *Sociétés*, Paris, Masson, no. 8 (1986). Finally, on ritual in general, cf. L.-V. Thomas, *Rites de mort*, Paris, Fayard, 1985, p. 16.

39. Cf. M. Young and P. Willmott, *Family and Kinship in East London*, Harmondsworth, Penguin, 1964, pp. 105, 110, *et seq.* Also see my note on the Mafia, 'La maffia : notes sur la sociologie', *Cahiers internationaux de sociologie*, Paris, PUF, vol. 68 (1982).

40. Bouglé, *Essays on the Caste System*, p. 11.

41. I am freely interpreting here the analysis done by M.F. Baslez, *L'Étranger dans la Grèce antique*, Paris, Les Belles Lettres, 1984, p. 40, *et seq.* On the role of the outsider, cf. J. Freund, *L'Essence du politique*, Paris, Sirey, 1965 and J.H. Park, 'Conflit et communication dans le mode de penser coréen', thesis, Université de Paris V, 1985. On Mafia territory, cf. J. Ianni, *Des affaires de famille*, Paris, Plon, 1978.

42. C. Fourier, *Oeuvres Complètes*, Paris, Anthropos, 1966–67, vol. 5, p. 157; cf. also E. Durkheim, *The Elementary Forms of the Religious life*, New York, Collier, 1961; as to the uses of violence, I have already developed these in M. Maffesoli, *Essais sur la violence banale et fondatrice*, 2nd edition, Paris, Librairie des Méridiens, 1985.

43. Cf. the analysis of these ethnographers by U. Hannerz, *Exploring the City*, pp. 38–39. On the theme of the present, I refer to my book *La Conquête du Présent*. For more on the model of secrecy, cf. G. Simmel, 'Les Sociétés secrètes', *Revue française de Psychanalyse*, Paris, PUF, 1977. On the rites of adolescent groups, cf. Thomas, *Rites de mort*, p. 15. On a more general sense of the uses of leisure time, cf. the books of J. Dumazédier.

44. One might also point out that the normative reservations enunciated by Weber are found more in *Le Savant et le Politique*, French transl. Paris, Plon, 1959, p. 85, 105, *et seq.*, which does a better job of gathering together his 'educational' texts than does *Economy and Society*. On the 'emotional community' cf. Weber, *Economy and Society*, p. 455 and J. Séguy, 'Rationalisation, modernité et avenir de la religion chez M. Weber', *Archives de Sciences Sociales des Religions*, Paris, Centre national de la recherche scientifique, 1986, vol. 61, no. 1, pp. 132, 135 and notes. On the climate in which Weber wrote about the 'orgiastic' and the

proximity of the 'Baal school of priests', and the Klages circle, cf. W. Fietkan, 'À la recherche de la révolution perdue' in *Walter Benjamin*, Paris, Cerf, 1986, p. 291, *et seq*.

45. Hannerz, *Exploring the City*, p. 118.

46. Apart from the references given by Hannerz, one can refer to the thesis by S. Langlois, 'Les réseaux sociaux et la mobilité professionnelle', Sorbonne, 1980, which gives a fine summary as well as opening up new avenues of research.

47. Hannerz, *Exploring the City*, p. 63.

48. The question of gossip or rumour is worth another look. Apart from the studies by Morin and Shibutani (Cf. *Sociétés*, Paris, Masson, 1984), I would refer to the *thèse d'état* by F. Reumaux, 'Esquisse d'une sociologie des rumeurs, quelques modèles mythiques et pathologiques', Sorbonne-Paris V, C.E.A.Q.

49. S. Milgram, *The Experience of Living in Cities*. Cf. the analysis done by Hannerz, *Exploring the City*, p. 68.

50. Berque, *Vivre l'espace au Japon*, p. 119.

51. E. Troeltsch, 'Christianisme et société', *Archives de Sociologie des religions*, no. 11 (1961), pp. 15–34; cf. with regard to the nebula and the sectarian group, Hervieu-Léger, *Vers un nouveau christanisme*, pp. 145, 343, 353, *et seq*.

APPENDIX: THE THINKING OF THE PUBLIC SQUARE*

1. The two cultures

The existence of a 'savage thinking' is now taken as a given; fortified by experience acquired through contact with primitive societies, anthropology is turning its attention to the everyday life of contemporary societies, even to what has been called the 'enterprise culture', or other spheres that used to seem too close to be successfully analysed. It is the same for the culture of knowledge, which is beginning to admit the existence of *another culture*, that of collective sentiments. We can agree on this emergence; many analyses testify to this;[1] however, a certain distance remains between these two cultures which at times risks becoming an unbridgeable gulf. There is no question, of course, of trying to get around this difference, or even of denying the genuine consequences, whether in the realm of knowledge or the everyday; rather it must be acknowledged in order to master its effects. It is a matter of experiencing the paradoxical tension produced by the existence of these two cultures, a tension which can be summarized thus: how to combine into a thought perspective – a very general perspective – that which can be qualified as evanescent, *ad hoc* and ephemeral. It is a question of 'everyday knowledge' which, without losing any of its reflexive aspect, tries to remain close to its *natural foundation*, that is, the basic sociality.

On all sides, moreover, we can see the resurgence of many issues related to this natural foundation; this is what we could call, taking a famous precedent, the 'Nature Question'. However, as opposed to what was, from the grottos of Umbria to the communities of the Ardèche, the 'Franciscan'-thematic, such a question is no longer seen in cut and dried terms. There can no longer be a case of culture on one side and nature on the other, with all the consequences such a dichotomy implies. It must be seen that the essential consequence is the constant relativization of the natural pole. In various forms – popular, folklore, common wisdom and so on – it was for the most part marginalized. At best, it was seen as a stage to be passed through; the infancy of humanity, always reborn, which had to be completely eradicated, a task to which the great thinkers buckled down with relish. Thus, before demonstrating, or at least indicating the synergy

---

Dedicated to Franco Ferrarotti.

that is becoming clear these days between the natural pole and the cultural pole, an analysis, however brief, should be made of the constant scorn or neglect of popular thought: whether in the realm of mythology or the everyday.[2] This is a procedure stated *a contrario* which can be of enormous help to my arguments.

To return to a concept of Gilbert Durand's, it was not until recently that the 'anthropological trajectory' (which Berque called 'trans-subjectivity') between the aforementioned poles was called into question. Thus, in the cabbalistic tradition, alongside the 'tree of knowledge' grows the 'tree of life'. It is the schism between the two trees that, according to Scholem, allows evil to gain a foothold in the world.[3] In a metaphorical way, one can surely say that this is one of the sources of the separation between life and philosophy, their profound antagonism and the enormous difficulty the latter has in integrating the rich experience of the former. Very early on, we see the emergence of an important distinction between a 'philosophic-rationalist' culture and a 'populo-mythological' culture, a distinction which, like a thread, weaves its way through the fabric of humanity.[4] I have no intention of writing their history, which is worth doing, however; but rather of highlighting that, in the words of a well-known expression, there are various 'knowledge interests' (Habermas) which are bound to confront each other. One might also stress the fact that the popular sensibility has always provoked the discontent of the clerics.

This is an ancient paradox between that which attempts to explain (return to square one), to regulate life, and that very life itself which forever resists explanation. The first sensibility proceeds by distinction and by subsequent analysis; the second favours conjunction and the overall comprehension of various elements of the worldly reality. Historians and sociologists have often contested the equivalency (ideal-typical) established by Max Weber between the spirit of capitalism and Protestantism. In fact, in this book he stylized the essential characteristics of what can be called bourgeoisism. In particular, with respect to his episteme: to master nature (social and natural) through the rational and systematic application of the disjunctive attitude. Moreover, this can be summed up by what Mehl states with regard to the Protestant outlook which, as opposed to what seems 'at times to characterize Catholic thinking', proceeds by 'rupture, by refusing conjunctions'.[5] In this sense, bourgeois society and its Protestant ideology, or even the Anglo-Saxon attitudes which are its vectors, push the logic of distinction and separation to its extreme. These are things which characterized modernity in its best as well as worst aspects. By favouring the demonstration of a rational order of 'ought', it simply forgets to show [*monstrare*] a real order that is much more complex – something modern thought has often been incapable of understanding. Witness this warning by an historian of Russian populism, concerning intellectuals who 'lead the people in the name of abstract, bookish, imported ideas, but adapt themselves to the people as *it was*'.[6] But this transition from a logic of ought to an embodied logic is not a given when one remembers the scholar's scorn of the ordinary, everyday life which, despite differing political sympathies, continues to form the basis of a good number of analyses of social reality.

2. For the people's happiness

We shall not return to an old problem which has been the subject of many studies for over a decade. At a time when it was unfashionable to do so, I myself made a contribution to this debate. One must remember, however, that the people must always be brought to consciousness from *the outside*. Leninism took this perspective and, as we know, very few intellectuals escaped its grip.[7] And all those who, even today, distrust spontaneous sociology, everybody's sociology, take their inspiration from the same philosophy: that of scorn for anything which cannot be explained conceptually; perhaps for anything that is lived.

One may remember the Hegelian expression, 'The people does not know what it wants, only the Prince knows.' Bit by bit, this privilege of the Prince's was passed on to the upholders of the logic of politics, the intellectuals, as carriers of the universal and the founders of collective responsibility. From the princes of the mind from centuries past enacting laws or the royal march of the Concept, to their pale reflections today in the form of contemporary buffoons, builders of a media infrastructure, the mechanism is exactly the same: in all places and at all times it is a question of 'answering for'. In this respect, it is enlightening to see that, whether in a scholarly study or in the multitude of newspaper articles, the moral preoccupation remains the basis of much of intellectual analysis. As for those who refuse to go along with this trend, they are classified under the shameful heading of aesthetes!

It would be instructive to compile an anthology of the expressions of the scornful attitude with respect to the idiocy and the idioms of the people; in short, with respect to its attachment to particularisms. Whether in the case of Gorky observing that Lenin had the barine's* scorn 'for the life of the masses' or the type of *populo* of whom Sartre stated 'they always notice the bad in things' when it is equally possible to see the good, there are many who cannot let go of their critical *a priori* in order to seize the values which make for the quality of life above all concerned with 'proxemics'. This outlook can best be summed up in a quip of Paul Valéry: 'Politics is the art of preventing the senses from getting involved in what concerns them.'[8] Indeed, the above-mentioned failure to comprehend resides in the propensity of the *moral-political* logic to concern itself with the far-off, the plan, the perfect; in a word, with the 'ought'. On the other hand, what for lack of a better term we shall call the people or the mass can be characterized by that which is close by, by that structurally heterogeneous, monstrous

---

* *Transl. note*: a nobleman of pre-revolutionary Russia.

everyday; in short, by being the centre of an existence it is very difficult to summarize. This explains its quasi-conscious refusal to be anything.

To account for this, I have proposed the metaphor of the underground centrality, in order to underline the fact that many social phenomena, while not finalized, have their own specificity. Thus, in the hypothesis of neo-tribalism I am setting out, one can say that within a multiform mass there is a multiplicity of micro-groups that escape the normal predictions or commands to identity of the social analysts. Nevertheless, these tribes' existence is conspicuous; the existence of their cultures is no less real. Naturally, these cultures are not part of the politico-moral order; any analysis starting from such a premise is condemned to silence or, what is unfortunately more often the case, to verbosity. As I have said, it is impossible to summarize; even less is it possible to be reductive, or to make sociality subject to some form of determination, be it of the highest order. We are living through some of the most interesting times, in which the efflorescence of the lived gives rise to a pluralistic knowledge, in which disjunctive analysis, the techniques of separation and conceptual *a-priorism* are giving way to a complex phenomenology which can integrate participation, description, life narratives and the varied manifestations of collective imaginations.

Such a procedure, which takes life into account, may go some way in explaining the contemporary throng. As I have said before, we are far from an abdication of the mind – on the contrary! Indeed, it is possible that in so doing we are able to see a particular order at work in our own day. Thus, corresponding to a logical vitalism would be a societal vitality, in other words, a logic of passions (or of confusion) would replace the politico-moral logic to which we have become accustomed. In the words of Saint Athanasius, '*ou kairoi alla kurioi*', which could be translated as: 'not that which is present; but rather the gods'. Martineau proposes inverting the proposition: '*ou kurioi alla kairoi*', which we might translate as 'not overarching authority; but rather that which is there', the occasions, the moments experienced jointly.[9] This inversion is useful in understanding our own time. Religious or profane monovalency has had its day; it may be that the aforementioned tribes are more concerned with the time that passes and its true nature, with the occasions that arise, rather than overarching authorities, whatever shape they may take. It is no less possible that these occasions define an *order* which, for all that it is more stochastic or more latent, is no less real. These are the stakes claimed by the underground centrality: to be able to comprehend a differentiated architectonic, based on an internal order or *puissance* and which, while not being *finalized*, possesses an intrinsic force that must be acknowledged.

The vitalism produced by the approach I have just laid out is not an *ex nihilo* creation. This perspective recurs regularly, and has inspired important works. To cite but a few names from modern history, one might refer to Schopenhauer's 'will to live', to Bergson's *élan vital*, Simmel's *Lebensoziologie* or Lévi-Strauss' *vouloir obscur*. In each of these, the accent is placed on the *system of conjunctions*. Or, to employ a term in use to refer to the various cultural, social, historical and economic elements, the social whole [*tout social*]. This conjunction seems to be equivalent to the great sociological characteristics of the moment. One may discriminate, separate, reduce a world dominated by the object and the objective; it is not the same when one is confronted with what I would call the 'return of life'. This theme can be found recurrently in Weber in the highly formalized form of *Verstehen*. It is appropriate that we have been able to underline the central role that this notion has played between knowledge and everyday life. 'Despite the mystique with which the concept of *Verstehen* has been infected, there seems to be no reason to suppose that historical or sociological understanding is different from everyday understanding.'[10] In fact, there is a certain amount of the mystical in the notion of understanding, in the sense that it is founded on knowledge that is at the same time direct, intuitive and global. It gathers; it keeps together the various elements that the analytic moment had separated.

Let us consider the term 'mystical' in its widest sense: that which tries to understand how things stay together, even if in a contradictory way. This accounts for the conflictual harmony that is the attribute of every society. In short, it is this *glutinum mundi* that makes something exist. Mystical is the astonishment of the member of the *populo* who, confronted with Sartre's critical spirit, sees, smells, tells the 'good at work in all things'. The affirmative 'yes' is in opposition to the dissociative 'no'. Remember that the disjunctive procedure is the flip-side of the principle of individuation. The critical individual who separates is the same one who divides. While his entire *oeuvre* is part of this tradition, Adorno, when he lets go, remarks with lucidity that 'no one has the right through elitist pride to be opposed to the mass of which he or she is also a moment', or 'in many people it is already an impertinence to say "I" '.[11] In fact, the mystical attitude of understanding takes into account the discourse of the mass; it is just, the truth be told, a specific expression of it. In these fine words: 'Our ideas are in everyone's head.' In contrast to the exteriority mentioned earlier, understanding encompasses the whole and is itself situated within this whole.

This is a specific ambience which encourages interactivity, whether communicational, natural or spatial. By putting forward in a previous book the notions of correspondence and analogy as approaches adopted by our discipline, I sought to highlight the pertinence of the global perspective in a world where, precisely because nothing is important, everything is important; in a world where, from the largest to the smallest, all elements fit together. This was also a matter of emphasizing that, just like a monochrome painting, social life is founded on a subtle overlaying of experiences, situations and phenomena, one on top of another which are interrelated in an analogous way. Without going into the reasons behind it, one can describe such ambiguity. In his own way, Berque uses the notion of 'mediance', which connotes ambience while evoking the multiform effects mentioned earlier. There is a back and forth movement between the objective and the subjective, and between the search for conviviality and the metaphoric procedure. To be more precise, it is possible to speak of the contamination of each of these registers by the other. All of these things, if they do not invalidate, at least relativize both external scrutiny as well as any conceptual and/or rational monovalence.[12]

3. The order within

The surpassing of rational monovalence as an explanation for the social world is not an abstract process; in fact, it is tightly aligned with the heterogenization of this world, or what I have called social vitalism. According to Renan, the ancient god 'is neither good nor bad; it is a force'.[13] This power has nothing moralizing about it, but is expressed through a variety of characters, which should be understood in the strongest sense of the word, and which all take their place in the vast symphony of the world.

Such a pluralization forces social thought to break through the constraints of a one-dimensional science. This is the essential lesson of Max Weber: the polytheism of values creates a causal pluralism. Within the conceptual framework imposed by the nineteenth century, I have shown how a value was recognized as good, and the intellectual's goal was to ensure that this principle became law. This is the politico-moral perspective. The few ideologies that shared (conflictually) the market functioned according to the same mechanism. It can no longer remain so when totally antagonistic values burst onto the scene, relativizing, at the very least, the pretension to universality, just as this gives nuance to the overall influence of a particular morality or politics. This eruption is the foundation of conceptual relativism.

Such relativism is not necessarily a bad thing. In any case, its existence is clear, and one might as well take note of it. In order to better understand its effects, one might recall a statement of Brown's, in which he says that the history of mankind therefore is marked by 'a constant tension between theistic and polytheistic ways of thinking'.[14] For my part, I would say that there is a constant swing back and forth. According to Sorokin's law of saturation which he so capably applied to cultural entities, there are paradigms that favour that which unifies in terms of political organizations, conceptual systems and moral representations; there are others that, on the contrary, encourage explosion, effervescence and proliferation. From a purely spiritual God, powerful and solitary, we have moved to bodily idols, disordered and pluralistic. However, as opposed to a simplistic linearity which can only envisage the path from 'poly' to 'mono', it is easy to observe that human histories provide many examples of a back and forth movement between these two modes of social expression.

Many studies have underlined this phenomenon: Durand, an expert on mythology, has shown how Christianity itself, in its monotheistic intransigence, is incomprehensible without its syncretist substratum.[15] Even in our own day and age, the development of sectarianism, charismatic movements, charitable initiatives, fundamental communities, the many forms of superstition, can be interpreted as the manifestation of our old pagan, populist roots that have lasted, more or less, within popular religion and which have undermined the unifying shell developed by the institution of the Church over the course of centuries. In fact, it would be interesting to show how the unified aspect of the doctrine and the organization is less solid than at first appears; that it is still vulnerable to fracturing and is above all *ad hoc*. The varied schisms and heresies are a good illustration of this phenomenon. Even the doctrines which prove later to be the most solid supporters of monovalent positions, since they are opposed to intolerance, because they confront the unknown and because they are based on the thirst for freedom, are in their founding moments the most solid defenders of pluralism. Thus, if we follow Strohl, a great expert on the young Luther, we can see how Luther contrasted a macroscopic, institutional Church with an 'invisible Church . . . that acts through its witnesses'.[16] Thus he found that the essence of the *ecclesia* was constituted of small local entities mystically united in the communion of the saints. For him, against the institutional Church serving up an established doctrine there exists an essential instituting force: *puissance* versus *power*.

It is interesting to note that this pluralistic vision of the Church has as its corollary an intellectual framework that dissociates itself from scholastic rigidity. Luther learned to 'combine fragments of the Aristotelian system with those of the Augustinian, without worrying about the principles of these two systems . . . he could easily adopt ideas derived from foreign principles, but which could be assimilated to his own'. In both these aspects, Luther's example is illuminating, for the success of Lutheranism resides in the intuitive understanding of the pluralistic foundation which characterizes the masses. Strohl, moreover, goes on to highlight that Luther 'son of the people . . . has both his good and bad qualities'.[17] We shall leave the responsibility for such claims to himself; what is sure is that in his own time the popular levels of society were not wrong in following him enthusiastically and, taking his teachings to their logical conclusion, revolted against the established powers, until Luther, having achieved his goal of getting rid of the vizier to become the new vizier, called upon the nobility for help in quelling the disorder of the rabble. But the 'circulation of elites' is another story!

Above all, it is critical to bring out the fact that there is a refractory social foundation to unity: refractory to any representational or organizational one-dimensionality. This foundation seems to be functionally manifest at moments in which massification occurs together with an explosion of the values underlying this mass. As I have just shown for the Reformation, the same can also be said of the Renaissance during which, alongside a general tendency for the 'amalgamation of different levels of society', as Jacob Burckhardt, the great historian of this period remarks, there is a vitalist explosion in all domains: doctrines, arts, sociability, political structures, etc. This effervescence constitutes a new social deal, usually inviting other forms of interpretation. Durkheim also noted it in the case of the French Revolution (in underlining its religious aspect), and, more generally, in the case of any form of religion which, he says, 'is not reduced to a unique cult, but rather consists of a system of cults invested with a certain degree of autonomy'.[18]

What becomes clear through these few examples and quotes is that there are times when societies become more complex by making use of procedures that are themselves complex. Refined classicism is followed by the luxuriant baroque. Just as the classical is linear, visual, closed, analytical, and liable to be clearly analysed, the baroque is evolving, complicated, open, synthetic and evokes a relative obscurity, or at least an approach based on the chiaroscuro. Such research arguments put forward in art history by Wölfflin[19] can easily be applied to these epistemological considerations. In this case, the accent will be placed on the latter of these two groups of notions. The baroque sociality that is being born requires that we know how to decipher the logic of its internal mechanism. I repeat, there is a specific order to the underground sociality, an internal order that occasionally blossoms at times of fracturing, disturbance or effervescence, given that these may be completely silent, or at the very least very discreet, to the extent that they may escape the close analysis of the experts. Let us remember the adage of 'keeping one's ear to the ground'.

Jünger noted with astuteness that there is no allusion in Egyptian writing to Exodus.[20] This event must not have played a significant role in the internal politics of that country. Nevertheless, we know what impact this small escape by slaves had on the course of history, or, and it amounts to much the same thing, on the mythological construction underlying our history. Thus, there are times during which the supposedly unimportant, the unobserved, considered marginal, is both a place of real investment for the protagonists, as well as being consequential for social evolution. The order to which I am referring is an attempt to come to terms with this phenomenon.

It has already been analysed by way of notions such as the 'soft underbelly', 'aloofness' and ruse; I even proposed the category of *duplicity*[21] to account for the process of abstention. It must also be noted that this thematic, aside from its inherently prospective interest, opens up an epistemological line of inquiry. Thus, as Poirier remarks, the life narratives, which 'try to make the people of silence talk, in the words of their most humble representatives',[22] can be seen as belonging to this perspective. He notes the fact that there is an eloquent silence, and that it is not a matter of rushing it, but rather of interpreting it in order to bring out all its richness. Silence is very often a form of dissidence, of resistance or even internal distance. If we interpret this in the context of positivist norms, which can only see the positivity of things, then this silence will be seen as 'less', as a non-existence. As opposed to this attitude, one must say that such a procedure has its own strong points: the 'nothing' which serves as a foundation for a meaningful life. This is the Weberian expression: understanding reality from the characteristics of the unreal. In fact, the categories of opacity, ruse, duplicity, the mechanisms of silence and the chiaroscuro are above all the expression of a vitalism which assures the long-term preservation and self-creation of sociality. This leads us to the aforementioned epistemological situation.

Behind the practice of silence lies, as I have pointed out elsewhere, the question of survival. By survival I mean that faculty of adaptation which allows one to accommodate constraints without being overwhelmed by them. Therein essentially lies the problem of force or *puissance*, which must not be confused with power. I would also note that, in its sociological dimension, the survival of the Jewish people can be seen in the context of the strategies I have just explained. Its jokes, its puns, silences and consequent ruses are accompanied by a great respect for and love of life, as many commentators have not failed to remark.[23]

In the same order of things, one may pursue the detailed analysis of a polemical dialogue of everyday life and how only loving relationships that escape the injunction of speech, the therapy of confession, have a chance to survive.[24] I am intentionally using illustrations from a broad spectrum. They have nothing to do with one another, but they are able expressions of how all sociality is based on communion and reserve, attraction and repulsion, and by paying too much attention to the first of these pairs we risk losing sight of the richness of the second. In the nineteenth-century zeal to explain everything in terms of reason, to require explanations for everything, we have forgotten, in the lovely words of Silesius, that the 'rose knows no reason'. From an epistemological point of view, relying too heavily on the 'spoken' portion of social relationships has caused us to forget that they are also founded on the unspoken. Such empty space is a storehouse worth exploring. This perspective, well represented by the ancient wisdom of the *secretum meum mihi*, can form the basis of a concrete sociality which is more than the simple reflection of our ideas, but has its own consistency. This may be common sense, grudgingly recognized by academics who feel relativized, but it regularly re-emerges both in everyday life and in the world of ideas.

4.   Experience, proxemics and organic knowledge

Contrary to what is typically acknowledged, the end of the great narratives of reference is not the result of a lack of great thinkers. The quality of intellectual research is not necessarily worse than at other times. In fact, if there is a disenchantment with overarching and distant ideologies, it is because we are witnessing the birth of a multitude of ideologies which are lived from day to day, based on close, familiar values. Experience and proxemics: this sense of the concreteness of existence can now be considered as an expression of good health, of particular vitality. This vitalism secretes in a way an organic thinking with, of course, all its inherent qualities, that is, an insistence on intuitive perception – seen from inside; on comprehension – seen overall; the holistic appreciation of the varied elements of the given and on the common experience, which is felt, along with others, to constitute a lived knowledge. Some authors, few and far between, it is true, have emphasized such an organic way of thinking. One might refer in this instance to Dilthey, of course, but also to any thought inspired by Nietzsche which prefers the dionysiac and its tactile, emotional, collective and conjunctive aspects. One might also quote G.E. Moore and his *Defense of Common Sense* while insisting on the truths he nurtures. Moore notes with finesse that 'most philosophers . . . go against the common sense which they still practise in their daily lives.'[25] One could cite more authors who take the same line by focusing their investigations on a similar thematic, such as sociological phenomenology, whose epistemological and thematic interest can be seen in the work of Schutz, Berger and Luckmann. Indeed, what may be called vitalism and 'commonsensology' are linked, and their conjunction allows us to highlight their intrinsic *hic et nunc* quality, and the value of a presentism whose richness has yet to be fully explored.

It remains true, however, that this is something that is difficult for the intellectual procedure to admit, since its natural inclination (a structural bias?) compels it towards the distant, the normative, the elaboration of the general rule. These can all be subsumed in the expression 'the logic of the ought', with all tendencies taken together. In order to bring this to a close, we might say that all of these explanatory procedures are *centrifugal* – always in search of what lies beyond the object under consideration. Opposed to that is a comprehensive approach which is deliberately *centripetal*, which thus takes its object, even the most minuscule one, very seriously. Every thing is examined in and of itself, and there is no wish to go beyond its contradictions to an illusory synthesis. In the perspective initiated by Lupasco and Durand, there is what may be termed a 'contradictory logic'.[26] History, distance and explanation combine centrifugally, resulting in the 'ought'; myth, the nearby and comprehension are combined centripetally, to produce the contradictory.

It is interesting to note that the impulse to reconsider the categories of social knowledge comes in large part from those who are emphasizing the significance of space. I am thinking in particular of Berque's work which showed on the one hand how 'the inhabitant lives as such and not for an external viewer'; he develops the hypothesis of an areolar or cellular theory which operates on the collective, in the strictest sense of the term, rather than on the individual. This, on the other hand causes him to speak of an indistinctness between subject and object, the I and the other,[27] which is somewhat reminiscent of the procedures of metaphorical or analogical correspondence. Whatever the case, this conjunction permits one to isolate an *immanent order* linked to the 'physical milieu' and the 'concrete field' in which social life takes place.[28] This is the major element of these remarks: to understand the existence of a societal logic which, while not obeying the simple rules of mono-causalist rationalism, is no less real. To be more precise, one can say that there is an open rationality which makes coherent the various elements of social reality without reducing them to any sort of systematic vision. That is, to paraphrase Pareto, the logical and the 'non-logical' at work in these elements enter into synergy to create the familiar architectonic.

Indeed, except in schoolbooks, no part of social life is one-dimensional. In many aspects it is monstrous, explosive, forever escaping the grasp of our analysis. Pluralism is what drives it from its very core. This state of affairs must be understood for what it is. Such is the aim of a sociology of everyday life. Nevertheless, nothing could be more difficult than the intellectual work that this requires. As Outhwaite indicated with respect to the comprehensive ambition of Simmel, ' this is . . . merely to say that everyday understanding is a highly complex activity'.[29] This is because everyday life, outside of various rationalizations and legitimations, is studded with affects, with ill-defined feelings, in short, with all those obscure instants which cannot be put aside and whose impact on social life is increasingly significant. These are also things which accept with difficulty the simplicity of the ideal, the simplification of perfection, or the simplistic fantasy which reduces existence to what it ought to be.

It is indeed easy to reflect on or in the intelligible world. It is unfailingly malleable and capable of acrobatics, reversals and other conceptually violent acts. There is brutality in the pure act of the mind, and I will not tire of repeating that the logic of ought is the easy way, a stop-gap, a truncated version of knowledge. Knowledge is much more respectful of the complexity of life and thus refuses *a priori* definitions while creating the intellectual conditions of possibility which allow one to bring out (epiphanize) the various elements of this complexity. As I have already explained, these are the stakes of 'formism': to put into place a rigorous descriptive procedure which is in congruence with the heterogeneous appearance of societal life and which, at the same time, is able to show its epistemological pertinence.

One must remember above all that it is the given (cf. Schutz: *taken for granted*), the manifest that constitutes the basis of intellectual constructions, whatever they may be. We could take the example of the proverb which Durkheim sees as 'a condensed statement of a collective idea or sentiment', or everyday conversation, which sometimes contains a greater philosophy of existence and sense of the problems to come than many discussions among academics.[30] These are cultural manifestations, *strictissimo sensu*, i.e., that which founds society, and it is surprising that scholarly culture is so impermeable to such manifestations. Moreover, it may be supposed that this impermeability is the principal cause of the sterility which characterizes a large part of the social sciences.

In fact, what makes culture is opinion, 'the thinking of the public square', all things which constitute the emotional bond of sociality. It is only *a posteriori* that scholarly culture develops. I will use a distinction proposed by Fernant Dumont, who speaks of 'first culture', which surrounds us imperceptibly, and 'second culture', which ties me to a particular group.[31] In the context of these reflections, I would say that the former is in a way the ambience, the amniotic fluid of all life in society, and it gives birth to or at least permits the flourishing of various traditions which cannot last outside the common matrix. There are thus as many specific traditions as there are groups; the intellectuals are one such group, but it is only in an abusive way that it presents its learning as the most legitimate. In fact, we would be better advised to note the correspondence, the synergy and the complementarity that unites these diverse scholars than to establish prevalence and hierarchies. In so doing, we would be more aware of the richness of such learning. Naturally, to accomplish this it is necessary to diversify our criteria of evaluation. Indeed, if in order to judge the validity of a given statement or practice we employ the sole criterion of formal coherence or simple causalist logic, we are condemned to provide tautological analyses. As far as French sociology is concerned, Pierre Bourdieu is certainly the most significant example of this when he elaborates (or theorizes, according to one's point of view) on 'practical beliefs'. There is no point reiterating the scorn induced by such an attitude. It can be judged for itself and is above all an admission of impotence. In my opinion, it is no more fitting to speak of a 'popular theoretical sense', since here once more the common sense is judged by the sole yardstick of the theoretical perspective.[32] In both cases, one is dealing with a 'centrifugal' perspective whose reference lies beyond the object with a more or less explicit judgemental attitude.

Modernity's strength lay in having situated everything in the framework of History and historical development. 'Centrifugation' is nothing more than the intellectual translation of such a perspective. But what was once a strength has inevitably become a weakness. Indeed, History deprived histories of their place; it relativized experience. And these once-repressed experiences are resurfacing today with a vengeance. Their modulations are of all types, but with the common thread of favouring empiricism and proxemics. This is forcing us to reorient our analyses, to focus our scrutiny on 'the most extreme concrete' (W. Benjamin) that is everyday life. The complexity of everyday life, the 'first culture', deserves special attention. I have proposed calling this *everyday knowledge*.[33] The stakes are high, since this proxemics increasingly determines, in the simplest sense of the word, the relationship to others. Whether it is the 'lived social world', the lived experience, relationism or reciprocal interrelationships, there have been many expressions, from Dilthey to Schutz by way of Mannheim, which take natural sociality and its architectonic as their *a priori* for all sociological categories.[34] Is this pre-scientific? Spontaneous sociology? Speculation? The status of such a procedure is of little importance in as much as it sketches out the plan, if only provisionally, of a configuration in progress. Stable structures were well defined by the logic of *identity* and the moral judgement that accompanied it. Undefined constellations require that we highlight successive *identifications* and the aestheticism (common emotions) which translate them. The evaluation that gradually imposed itself throughout modernity was in perfect congruence with its object: the political order. It is less certain that it can continue to apply to the throng which, from tribes to masses, will serve as the matrix for the evolving sociality. However, this throws down for us a new intellectual challenge, above and beyond political morality: what will be the socio-anthropological structures of the *passional order*?

Notes

1. Cf. F. Dumont, 'Cette culture que l'on appelle savante' in *Questions de culture*, Québec, Institut québécois sur la recherche culturelle, 1981, p. 19.
2. As applied to a specific domain. Cf. the analysis done by C.G. Dubois, *L'Imaginaire de la Renaissance*, Paris, PUF, 1986, p. 959.
3. Cf. G. Scholem, *La Mystique juive*, Paris, Cerf, 1985, p. 86.
4. On this distinction, cf. G. Scholem, *Sabbatai Tsevi*, La Grasse, Editions Verdier, 1983, pp. 25. and 29.
5. R. Mehl, *La Théologie Protestante*, Paris, PUF, 1967, p. 121.
6. R. Pipes, quoted by Venturi, *Les intellectuels, le peuple et la révolution. Histoire du populisme russe au XIXᵉ siècle*, Paris, Gallimard, 1972, p. 49.
7. On this point, I refer to my books *La Logique de la domination*, Paris, PUF, 1976, and *La Violence totalitaire*, Paris, PUF, 1979. Also cf. B. Souvarine, *Stalin, a Critical History*, London, Secker and Warburg, 1940, p. 48. One may remember that only a few anarchistic groups, such as the workers councils and the Situationists, resisted conceptual Leninism.
8. M. Gorky, *Pensées intempestives*, Lausanne, L'Age de l'homme, 1975, quoted by Souvarine, *Stalin*, p. 196; *Lettres de Sartre*, in *Temps*, 3 (1983), p. 1630; P. Valéry, *Oeuvres complètes*, Paris, La Pléiade, 1957–60, vol. 2, p. 615.
9. Cf. the preface by E. Martineau to Heidegger's text, Editions Authentica, p. 14.
10. W. Outhwaite, *Understanding Social Life: The Method Called Verstehen*, London, Allen and Unwin, 1975, p. 13. On the notion of conjunction, cf. G. Durand, 'La notion de limites' in *Eranos 1980*, Frankfurt, Insel Verlag, 1981, pp. 43 and 46.
11. T. Adorno, *Minima moralia: Reflections from a Damaged Life*, transl. E.F.N. Jephcott, London, New Left Books, 1974, p. 50 and *Notes to Literature*, transl. Sherry, Weber and Nicholson, New York, Columbia University Press, 1992, p. 244.
12. On correspondence and analogy, I refer to my book *La Connaissance ordinaire. Précis de sociologie compréhensive*, Paris, Méridiens Klincksieck, 1985. On 'mediance', cf. A. Berque, *Vivre l'espace au Japon*, Paris, PUF, 1982, p. 41, and *Le Sauvage et l'artifice*, Paris, Gallimard, 1986, pp. 162, 165.
13. E. Renan, *Marc Aurèle*, Paris, Livre de Poche, 1984, p. 314.
14. P. Brown, *Society and the Holy in Late Antiquity*, London, Faber and Faber, 1982, p. 9.
15. One may refer to G. Durand, *La Foi du cordonnier*, Paris, Denoël, 1984.
16. H. Strohl, *Luther*, Paris, PUF, 1962, p. 294; cf. also p. 308.
17. Ibid., pp. 200 and 233.
18. E. Durkheim, *The Elementary Forms of the Religious Life*, New York, Collier, 1961, p. 41, *et seq.*
19. Cf. H. Wölfflin, *Renaissance et baroque*, Brionne, Editions Monfort, 1985, and *Principes fondamentaux de l'histoire de l'art*, Paris, Gallimard, 1952.
20. Cf. E. Jünger, *Graffiti*, Paris, Editions. C. Bourgois, 1977, p. 35.

21. Maffesoli, *La Conquête du présent*, 1979.

22. J. Poirier, *Les récits de la vie*, Paris, PUF, 1984.

23. Cf. W.J. Johnston, *L'Esprit viennois. Une histoire intellectuelle et sociale*, Paris, PUF, 1985, pp. 26–28.

24. I. Pennacchioni, *De la guerre conjugale*, Paris, Mazarine, 1986, p. 79.

25. G.E. Moore, *Apologie du sens commun*, in F. Armengaud, *G.E. Moore et la genèse de la philosophie analytique*, Paris, Klincksieck, 1986, cf. p. 13, p. 135–160. The studies of the Centre d'Études sur l'Actuel et le Quotidien (Paris V) and my two books on this theme, *La Conquête du présent. Pour une sociologie de la vie quotidienne*, Paris, PUF, 1979 and *La Connaissance ordinaire*, are situated at the crossroads of this perspective and sociological phenomenology.

26. Cf. the afterword of G. Durand to his *Structures anthropologiques de l'imaginaire*, Paris, Bordas, 1969. On mythocriticism's usage of the centripetal procedure, cf. G. Durand, *Figures mythiques et visages de l'oeuvre*, Paris, Berg, 1982, p. 308.

27. Berque, *Vivre l'espace au Japon*, pp. 124 and 56.

28. Cf. Berque, *Le Sauvage et l'artifice*, p. 267.

29. Outhwaite, *Understanding Social Life*, p. 13.

30. Cf. E. Durkheim, *The Division of Labour in Society*, New York, Free Press, 1964, p. 170. Cf. also on the sterility of academic discourse, K. Mannheim, *Ideology and Utopia*, New York, Harcourt Brace, 1954. Cf. also the richly rewarding remark by E. Renan: 'it was the halting pronouncements of the people that became the second bible for the human race' in *Marc Aurèle*, p. 291.

31. Cf. Dumont, 'Cette culture que l'on appelle savante', p. 27, *et seq.*

32. Cf. Y. Lambert, *Dieu change en Bretagne*, Paris, Cerf, 1985, p. 225. In fact, Lambert's book is very interesting and one might take this statement as an analogy; unfortunately, in my opinion, it is too dependent on the 'Bourdieusian' perspective.

33. Maffesoli, *La Connaissance ordinaire*. I refer also to the research of J. Oliveira (University of Feira de Santana, Brazil) on the various forms of popular know-how: *thèse d'état* in progress.

34. Without being exhaustive, one may cite Dilthey, *Le Monde de l'esprit*, Paris, Aubier, 1947, Mannheim, *Ideology and Utopia*; A. Schutz, *Le Chercheur et le quotidien*, Paris, Méridiens Klincksieck, 1986. Cf. also a good analysis of sociality in J. F. Bernard-Bécharies, 'Meaning and sociality in marketing: guidelines for a paradigmatic research', *International Review of Marketing Research*.

INDEX

activism,
  collective bourgeois, 12
  the decline of, 35
  vs fatalism, 40
  non-, 30–33, 40, 146
  projective, 59
  the saturation of, 92
Adorno, T., 74, 156
aesthetic(s),
  aura/ambience/form/matrix/paradigm,
    9–15, 18, 76, 81, 85
  ethical, x, 20
  existential, 134
  movement, 36
  participation/attitude, 49
  and phenomenology, 86
  and the political order, 164
  of sentiment, 14, 74
  and theatricality, 77
  theory of the recital, 7
  and vitalism, 12
'affectual' nebula, 72–78,
  and humanism, 88–89
alienation, x, xii, 2
  and duplicity, 21, 50–52
  and economic-political order, 44–134
  and history, 126
  and lifestyles, 96
  and *puissance*, 72
  and secrecy, 93
  and technology, 138
  and vitalism, 32
Allais, A., 42, 96
allonomy,
  vs autonomy, 27, 93
'aloofness',
  and duplicity, 159
  and power/domination/resistance, 32, 37,
    45–53, 51
  and proxemics, 126
  and secrecy, 92
  and the 'sociology of everyday life', 114
  and the 'versatility of the masses', 62
ambience, 1
  and atmosphere/*Stimmung*, 11
  and communion, 26
  and the 'diffuse union', 73
  and 'elective sociality', 90
  and holistic climate, 14
  and identification, 75–76

  and lifestyles, 98–99
  and the multiplicity of the self, 10
  and space, 19, 129, 156
  and the 'thinking of the public square',
    162–163
  and tribes, 6
anthropology 114, 152
  and critique of individual autonomy, 27
Antiquity, 10, 33, 46, 57, 84, 94–95, 98,
    108, 114
appearance(s) (cf theatricality),
  and the logic of identity, 11
  the play of, 1, 76–77, 90, 98
  unisexualization of, 64
Aquinas, T., 20
Aragon, 114
architectonic(s),
  and architecture, 37
  of the city, 124
  and civilizations, 129
  and collective sentiment, 80, 115, 132,
    142, 162–163
  and 'conflictual harmony', 31
  and duplicity, 114
  and secrecy, 91, 95
  and the 'sect type', 85
  and sociality, 98, 148, 163
  and underground centrality, 155
architecture,
  and architectonics, 36–37
  and the everyday, 123
  and perdurability, 133
Aristotle, 20, 105, 158
art,
  and the aesthetic aura, 18
  and aesthetics, 49
  and religion, 131
  tactile vs visual, 31
  and vitalism, 158
astrology (cf occult, syncretism),
  and the aesthetic aura, 13–14
  and *puissance*, 32
  and the re-enchantment with the world,
    39
Athanasus, St., 155
atomization,
  of the individual, 13, 76, 83, 130
Augustine, St., 94, 108, 158
aura,
  aesthetic, 18–19, 23, 25, 27, 126, 135

scientific, 31
theological, political, progressive,
    aesthetic, 13

Bachelard, G., 35
Bakunin, 16
Ballanche, 41
Baltrusaitis, 128
barbarity,
    and postmodernity, 28, 109–110, 120
Baslez, M.F., 109–142
Bastide, R., 40
Bataille, G. , 2, 51, 107
Baudrillard, J, ix, 46, 76
Beckett, S., 10, 27
Beigbeder, M., 142
Benjamin, W., 18, 20, 58, 63, 66, 73, 82,
    120, 123, 126, 163
Berger, P., 82, 161
Bergson, H., x, 3, 78, 155
Berque, A., 11, 14–15, 22, 128–129, 138,
    147, 153, 156, 161
binary opposition(s),
    going beyond, 10, 11, 128
    and logic of separation, 14, 52, 147
Bismarck, 92
Bloch, E., 36, 43, 132
Bohme, J., 32, 111
Bolle de Bal, M., 3, 77
Bouglé, C., 32–33, 47, 87, 100, 110, 115,
    134, 142
Bourdieu, P., xii, 56, 163
Bourlet, M., 109
Breton, A., 85
Brown, P., 10, 21, 59, 66, 72, 108, 114,
    116, 130, 136, 157
Burckhardt, J., 158
bureaucracy,
    the relativization of, 84

Canetti, E., 58, 63, 93
capitalism,
    and the bourgeois ideal, 16
Capra, F., 36
carnival(s),
    and theatricality, 77, 117–118
caste(s),
    appraisal of, 32
    and collective sentiments, 100, 134
    and hierarchy, 115–117
causality (cf functionalism, utilitarianism),
    critique of, 7, 41, 147, 161–163
Certeau, M. de, ix
Chamoux, F., 124
charismatic,
    leaders, 84
    movements, 158
Charron, J.E., 36, 46
chiaroscuro, 159–160
Chicago School, 110, 143–144

Christianity, 22, 52, 78, 82–85, 108,
    111–112, 119, 130, 157
'church type' (cf 'sect type'), 83
Cicero, 56
civilization(s), 90
    Christian, 137
    and death/re-birth, 34, 114, 129–130
    and effervescence, 73, 81
    Hellenistic, 124
    and the monstrous mass, 65–66
    and the stranger, 107–109, 120
collective unconscious (non-conscious), 98
communion,
    with beauty and nature, 35
    with others, 10, 160
    of the saints, 40, 73, 83, 111–112, 158
    and the spectacle, 77, 98
Comte, A., 40–41, 74
'concrete universal', 19
conscience collective
    and the dionysiac, x, 76, 79
contractual,
    vs affectual, 6, 18, 72
    myth, 10–11
    perspective, 45
    rationality, 88
Coughtrie, M.E., 111
cult(s),
    of Auglaurus, 67, 109, 130
    of the body, 77
    dionysiac, 75
    of Dionysus, 10, 82
    and domination, 137
    and familialism, 129
    and re-enchantment with the world, 39
    re-resurgence of, 86, 99–100, 159
    of saints, 59, 111, 131
custom(s), 20–28
    the survival of, 47
    and the 'taken for granted', 41, 80
cybernetics,
    and mythology, 112

death,
    and alienation, 51
    desire for, 145
    and the everyday, 7
    and lifestyles, 96
    and modernity, 38
    and the nobility of the masses, 63
    and ritual, 17, 78
    and space, 67, 88
    and the 'will to live', 22–24, 31–34, 78,
    114–115
democracy,
    American, 79
    Christian, 111
    and Thomist Catholicism, 116
demotheistic (cf social divine),
    and 'immanent transcendence', 41, 43

derision,
  and domination, 48, 50–51
destiny,
  community of, 13–15, 17, 19, 123–129, 134
  and the dionysian thematic, 1
  vs individual control, 10
  and psychoanalysis, 35
  and the re-enchantment with the world,
    39
Dilthey, W., 161–163
Dionysian,
  vs 'dionysiac', 32
  thematic, x, 1, 12, 28
dionysiac,
  vs 'dionysian', 32
  and individuation, 89
  laughter of the bacchanal, 51
  logic of sociality, 104
  metaphor of confusion, 147
  and the monstrous mass, 65
  thematic, 19, 25, 42, 75, 98, 108–110,
    136, 161
  'thiases', 82
Dionysus 87,
  myth/cult of, 9–10, 32, 82
  and rootedness, 136
  and the stranger, 108–109
  and tribalism, 28
discrimination,
  the rejection of, 82
disenchantment with the world
    (Entzauberung), 72, 160
  vs re-enchantment, 28, 78, 83
disengagement (cf withdrawal), 48–49
  political, 44, 60
disindividuation,
  and Dionysian values, 12
  and identification, 73–75
  and the logic of networks, 90
  and the persona, 129
  and secrecy, 91
  and the tribe, 6
domination,
  and the libido dominandi, 36, 47–48, 62,
    116
  logic of, 21, 51
  politico-economic, 23, 137
  the reversibility of, 35
Don Juan, 10
Dorflès, G., 36, 98
drama (dramein),
  vs tragedy, 17
dream(s),
  and the everyday, 7–8
  of unity, 105
Duby, G., 131
Dumézil, G., 104, 119
Dumont, F., 26, 66, 115
Dumont, L., 163
duplicity,
  and domination, 21

and puissance, 49–50
and the sociology of everyday life, 114
and tribalism, 95
and vitalism, 160
Durand, G., 7, 10, 14, 23, 35, 72, 104, 111,
  128, 142, 153, 157, 161
Durkheim, E., x, 4, 12, 17, 21, 31, 35,
  38–42, 45, 56, 58, 64, 70, 74, 79, 82,
  87–89, 113, 124, 135, 142, 159, 162

Ebner-Eschenbach, 136
Eckhart, 111
ecstasy (ex-stasis),
  and 'being-together', 58, 111
  and everyday life, 25–26, 43, 75
  and the 'orgiastic', 19, 136
Ehrenberg, A., 77
Einstein, 114, 119
'elective sociality', 78
  and the logic of networks, 86–90
Elias, N., 65
empathetic,
  period, 11, 15, 73, 138
empathy,
  vs abstraction, 31
  and the 'affectual nebula', 73
  and formism, 3,
  and holism, 129
Engels, F., 56
Enlightenment,
  and absolutism, 52
  and collective bourgeois activism, 12
  and individualism, 10, 80, 134
  and rationalism, 144
ethic(s)/ethos, x, xii
  and the ethical (communal) experience,
    15–20, 25, 60, 126, 139
  and 'social asepsis', 50
  Protestant, 82
  of secrecy, 92
  and the 'spirit of the times', 73
  of sympathy, 75
ethnology, 114

fashion, xi, 135
  and communion, 76–77, 99
  and secrecy, 90–91
Faulkner, W., 10
Ferrarotti, F.,164
festival(s) (cf carnival),
  and communion, 77, 79, 130
  popular, 53, 63,
Feuerbach, 40
fiction, 7, 9
  and science fiction, 44
formism, 16, 162
  and empathy, 3
  and sociology, 86, 133
form(s), 6–7, 20
  archetypal/ideal-type, 10, 31, 37, 124
  artistic, 81

Christian, 111
communal, 16, 26, 61, 127
of derision, 50–51
dionysiac/tribal, 19, 32–33, 89, 109, 115–116,
ecstatic, 136
emerging, 70, 78, 81, 120, 147
empathetic, 73, 138
and lifestyles, 98
and the mass-tribe dialectic, 129
and nature, 35
religious, 87
of the secret society, 92
social, 68, 130
and the 'social given', 145
of sociality/network, 48, 84, 140
and socialization, 143
of *Verstehen*, 156
Fourier, C., 73, 116, 143
Fourierism, 16
Frankfurt School, 34
Freud, S., 34, 82, 107
Freund, J., 38, 45, 50, 104, 142
Freyre, G., 51, 110, 116, 125
functionalism (cf causality, utilitarianism), 79, 83, 114

Gemeinschaft-Gesellschaft opposition, ix, 19, 60
ghetto, 19, 42, 135
global
  perspective, 156
  village, 17, 139
glutinum mundi, 13, 126, 145, 156
Goethe, 34
Goffman, E., ix, 5, 21
Gorky, M., 154
Groddeck, 34–35, 67

Habermas, J., 153
habitus (Thomist)/*exis* (Aristotelian), xi, 20, 25, 81, 89, 130
Halbwachs, M., 13, 21, 25, 66, 68, 76, 79, 133, 136
Hannerz, U., 127, 144–145
hedonism, 32, 46, 52–53, 110, 143
Hegel, xii, 33, 88–89, 99, 154
Heidegger, M., 34
Heraclitus, 113, 115
hermeneutics, 5
Hervieu-Léger, D., 78, 131
Herzen, 16
Hillman, J.46
Hippo (Bishop of), 108
History,
  vs dynamic historical vision, 134–135
  vs everyday histories, 64, 88, 129
  and humanism, 89, 123–124
  vs masses, 58, 62–63
  and morality, 15, 17
  vs myth, 3, 161

and the relativization of experience, 163
Hocquenghem, G., 76
holism 2,
  and the communal ethic, 15, 18,
  and hierarchy, 115, 117
  and the organic community, 69, 80, 128–129, 135, 147, 161
  and religion, 131–132
  and sociology, 34
Hoffet, F., 107
Hoggart, R., 53
Hölderlin, 24, 28
hommerie, 2, 13
humanism,
  and History, 89, 123–124

idealism,
  of communicative rationality theories, xii
  and 'hommerie', 13
identity (cf logic of identity),
  and disindividuation, 65, 90, 98
  and the multiplicity of the self, 10
  and tribalism, xii, 155
identification, 164
  logic of, 72–73
  process of, 15, 136
  theory of, 75
ideology,
  abstract, 23, 41, 46–48, 51, 157, 160
  and alienation, 138
  anarchist, 16
  the blurring of, 11, 14
  and the collective sensibility, 13
  'democratic Christian', 24
  dogmatic, 68
  the dominant, 15
  individualist, 59, 80, 134
  introduction of syncretist, 128
  multiplication of, 44, 68
  Protestant, 153
  of proximity, 84
  saturation of an, 83
  theological, 130
  tribal (multiple), 90, 92, 94, 115, 145–147
  and utopia, 58
  and versatility, 63
imaginary (cf mystical/mythical),
  function of emblems, 138
  perspective, 1, 13
  the prevalence of, 74, 118
  and the return of irrationalism, 38
imagination,
  collective, 18, 22, 27, 78, 82–83, 133
  vs economics, 14
  the importance of, 137–138
  and mysticism, 59
  and myth, 148
  and non-activism, 33
  and social theory, 4
'immanent transcendence', x, 40–41, 43, 59, 67, 126, 130, 132

individualism,
  and the bourgeois order, 74, 78, 127
  and the French Revolution, 40
  going beyond, 9–10, 59, 67–68, 72,
    78–80, 86–87, 104, 129, 145
  and holism, 115
  the saturation of, 64–65, 69
  vs tribalism, 97–99
individualist,
  doxa, 15
  and economic model, 113
  ideologies, 134
  and mechanical vs organic, 79, 104
individuation (*principium individuationis*),
  156
  and the bourgeois order, 64
  critique of, 10–11
  and dionysiac thematic, 75–76, 89
  saturation of, 27, 95
intersubjectivity,
  and proximity, 132
  and relationism, 69
intuition,
  vs abstraction, 31
  and organicity, 3, 161
  and social theory, 4
irony (cf laughter, derision), 130
  and domination, 50–51, 53, 93
  and sociality, 32

Jules-Rosette, B., 42
Jung, C., 34
Junger, E., 34, 59
justice,
  abstract, 17–18

Kafka, F., 93, 107
Kierkegaard, xii
knowledge,
  accountants of, 14, 56, 107
  capital of, 1
  embodied, 25, 63
  everyday, 3, 7, 57, 148, 152–153, 155–156
  explosion of, 97
  instrumental, 4
  of the masses, 34, 68,
  of modernity, 9
  and power, 38, 56
  theological, 84

La Boétie, E. de, 45
Lacarrière, J., 34
Lambert, Y., 67, 78
Lammenais, 41
laughter (cf derision, irony),
  and domination, 50–51, 93
Le Bon, G., 17, 43, 58
leisure, 26, 129, 140
  and mass entertainment, 81
Leninism, 61, 154
Le Play, F.,79

Lefebvre, H., 52
Leroux, P., 41
Lévi-Strauss, C., 2, 104, 155
lifestyle(s), x-xi
  the *avoidance*, 92, 94
  the conformity of, 89
  and logic of identity, 11
  and the masses, x, 96–100
  and secrecy, 95
  and the 'sect type', 82, 85
  and tribalism, xi, 115, 127–128, 143
  and the 'undirected being-together', 81
local(ism),
  and Christianity, 130
  and 'elective sociality', 86
  vs global/universal, 31, 105, 141
  and the sect-type, 84
  and tribalism, 19, 137
Locke, J., 80
logic of identity, 6, 74, 163
  causalist, 163
  going beyond, 11
  refusing the, 38
  of separation, 147, 153
Loisy, 32,41
Luckmann, T., 82, 161
Lupasco, S., 112, 124, 142, 161
Luther, 158

Machiavelli, N., 1, 57–58, 148
Mafia, 15, 90, 94, 119, 141–142
Mallarmé, 21
Man, H. de, 43
Mann, T., 10
Mannheim, K., 19, 43, 58, 80, 136, 163
Martino, E. de, 99
Marx, K., 58, 61, 79
Marxism, x, 16, 61, 83
masks,
  and the persona, xii, 5, 10, 49, 90–95
Matta R. da, 66, 77, 117–118
Mauss, M., 20, 66, 68, 89
mechanical, 145
  vs organic, 3, 18, 27, 79, 104, 117, 133
Médam, A., 133
Mehl, R., 153
media (mass),
  and the global village, 17–18, 23–28, 32,
    41, 78, 138–140
  and hedonism, 52
  and the spirit of the times, 73, 106
  and syntonic relationships, 75
  and theatricality, 49
  and tribal mass rites, 98
medicine,
  New Age, 32, 99, 128–129
  traditional, 24
megalopolis,
  and appearance, 11, 76
  and effects of civilization, 129
  and the global village, 138, 140

and the stranger, 110
and 'villages within the city', 42, 47, 57,
    69, 89, 95, 97, 104, 113, 127
metaphor(s), 9, 33, 73, 110, 112, 131, 139,
    145
    of the 'black holes', 36–37, 46
    of the 'bridge and the door', 126
    of the collective body, 24
    dionysiac/orgiastic, 98, 106, 147
    and 'Einsteinized' time, 114
    of the Mafia, 90, 119, 141–142
    of the meal, 86
    and momentary truths, 5
    of passion, 88
    religious, 82
    and saturation, 61
    of sensibility, 14, 143
    and stereotype, archetype, 23, 68, 129,
        135
    of the 'thread of reciprocity', 81
    of the triad, 105
    of the tribe, 6, 19
    of underground centrality, 155
Middle Ages, 81, 100, 115, 126
Milgram, S., 146
Miller, H., 34
modernity,
    the advent of, 56
    critique of, xii, 3–4, 11, 116, 153,
        163–164
    and the dream of unity, 105
    and 'elective sociality', 86
    the end of, 38, 70
    and individualism, 64, 74, 99–100, 113
    and narcissism, 9, 15, 64
    and the political project, 83
    and politico-economic domination, 23
    and positivism, 87
    vs postmodernity, 6
Moles, A., 139
Molière, 74
monotheism, 119
    and polyphony, 111
    and syncretism, 157
monstrosity,
    and the masses, 56–57, 65–66
    vs rationality, 153–154
    and social life, 162
Montaigne, 2,13
Montesquieu, 50
Montherlant, H. de, 94
Moore, G.E., 161
moral(ity),
    and drama, 17
    vs ethic of secrecy, 37, 91–92, 94–95
    vs ethics, x, 15
    and the political, 73, 154–155, 157, 164
    and *puissance*, 46
    and religion, 131
    of responsibility, 65
Morin, E., 14, 22, 45, 49, 105, 113, 128

mystic(al),
    body, 112
    or ecological perspective, 13, 18
    and 'participation', 119
    and psychoanalytical traditions, 67
    vs rationalist, 32
    and religious images, 120
    and rootedness, 58
    sensibility, 24
    and utopian perspectives, 80
    and *Verstehen*, 156
mysticism,
    Chinese, 59
    Christian, 111
    Jewish, 4
    and psychoanalytical traditions, 67
    and secrecy, 91
mythical,
    figures, 10
    land, 135
    and the masses 49
    narrative, 7
    or postmodern era, 108, 110
    vs rational, 11
    and religion, 58
    weight of the workers' movement, 83
myth,
    and cohesion, 26
    of the commune, 61, 148
    contractual, 10–11
    dionysiac, 129
    of Dionysius, 32
    vs History, 124, 161
    of progress, 32
    la Pulcinella, 50
    restorative, 3
    the resurgence of, 140
    and Satan, 48
    solidarist, 74
mythology,
    and affective perspective, 13
    and Christianity, 157
    and cybernetics, 112
    or the everyday, 153
    and history, 159

narcissism,
    critique of, 15, 64, 72, 76, 104, 129
nationalism,
    and the 'fickleness of the crowd', 38
    tribe-like forms of, xii
Nietzsche, F., 28, 35, 49, 115, 123, 161
Nisbet, R. , 4, 56, 79
nobility of the masses, 7, 62–63
nothingness, 38, 40

obschina,
    and socialism, 16, 61, 134
occult (cf syncretism, astrology),
    and the aesthetic aura, 13

optical (cf tactile),
  vs tactile, 31–32
organic,
  balance, 114–120
  concept of the social body, 87
  context and micro-groups, 95–96
  image of a body, 107
  knowledge, 160–164
  vs mechanical, 3, 18, 27, 79, 100, 104,
    117, 133
  perspective of the group, 81
  practices of silence, 93
  vs rational, 67, 69
  solidarity, 13, 145
  system and the 'sect-type', 84
organicity,
  and the Carnival, 118
  and empathy, 31–32
  and holism, 13, 80
  and medieval society, 79
  of opposites, 105
  and religion, 40, 59
  and religiosity, 77
  and the 'social given', 145
  and unicity, 52
  and the 'will to live', 3, 24, 147
Outhwaite, W., 162

Palo Alto School, 22, 104
pantheism, 115
Pareto, V., 46, 80, 88, 111, 132, 162
passion,
  and the community ethos, 12, 60, 69, 88,
    93, 143, 164
  and conformity, 64
  and difference, 115
Pentheus, 50
Perniola, M., 12
persons/persona,
  vs the individual, 6, 10, 27, 66–67, 76,
    129
  and the role of the outsider, 120
  and secrecy, 91
phalanstery, 16, 116, 143
phenomenology,
  and a formist sociology, 86
  and pluralistic knowledge, 155
  sociological, 161
  tradition of, 73
phylum, 34, 45, 111–112, 136
Pindar, 142
Plato, 51, 56, 80
pluralism, 65, 162
  and antagonism, 99, 105, 111–112, 115
  causal, 157, 162
  and domination, 47
  and knowledge, 155
pluriculturalism (cf polyculturalism), 105,
    113, 143
Poe, E.A., 90
Poirier, J., 159

political-economic order,
  vs affinity networks, 89
  and analyses, 41
  and domination, 23, 137
  going beyond, 110
  and individuation, 64, 95, 97
  vs masses, 6
  vs passional order, 164
  and the projective, 63
  vs puissance, 4
  relativization of, 61
polyculturalism, 7, 104–120
  and extension vs 'in-tention', 124
  and the stranger, 136
polyethnism, 143
polyphony,
  and pluralism, 105, 111, 114
polytheism,
  and causal pluralism, 157
  and dionysiac ceremonies, 109
  and masses, 95–96, 110–115
  and the relativization of power, 44, 48,
    119, 125
  and tribes, 33
positivism,
  and critique of intellectualism, 2–5, 31, 56
  and dialectical traditions, 44
  Durkheimian, 4, 45, 74, 87
  and the French Positivist School, 32
  Marxist and functionalist, 83
  and mechanical or individualist
    perspectives, 79
  and relativism, 18
  reductionist, 14, 33, 159
postmodernity,
  and barbarity, 28
  and heterogeneity, 110
  vs modernity, 6
  and the withdrawal into the group, 89
Poulat, E., 24, 40–41, 48, 111–112, 116
projective,
  vs collective, 7–8, 12–13, 16, 83
  critique of, 57–59, 65, 148
  vs nature, 69
  and political saturation, 31, 89
  and the political-economic order, 63
Protagoras, 80
Proust, M., 66
proximity (cf proxemics, space),
  and the affectual, 148
  and the architectonic of the city, 124
  and the dionysiac, 147
  and familialism, 94–95, 141
  and the image, 138
  and the mass, 65
  and the neighbourhood, 12, 78, 125
  and promiscuity, 16
  vs rationalism, 136
  and religion, 35, 131–133
  and resistance, 59
  and the 'sect type', 83–85

and the social divine, 21, 25, 41
and solidarity, 63, 131
proxemics, 7, 80, 116–117, 119, 123–148,
    154
    and the aesthetic aura, 23
    and everyday life, 119
    the impersonal nature of, 12
    and lifestyles, 94
    and nature, 35, 40, 69
    and organic knowledge, 160–164
    vs the projective and universal, 57
    and saturation, 27
    and solidarity, 24
    and space, 14
    and the 'transubjective', 22
psychoanalytic tradition, 35
    and mysticism, 67–68
puissance, 1, 7, 24, 67, 81, 125
    the binding nature of, 58–59
    vs power, 4, 21, 32, 38, 63, 73, 106–107,
        133–134, 155, 158, 160
    and transcendence of the individual, 76
    the underground, 31–53

race,
    the constricting framework of, 33
racism,
    and the cult of Dionysus, 82
    and the growth of affectual networks,
        113
    and the logic of identity, 38
    and the 'non-racism' of the masses, 111
    the relativization of, 118
Raphaël, F., 134
rationalism,
    and Adorno, 74
    and the Enlightenment, 144
    and irrationalism, 38
    mono-causalist, 162
    vs proximity, 136
    Western, 105
rationalist,
    vs mystic, 32
    perspective [critique of], 39–40, 80, 137
rationality,
    affectual, 144
    communicative, xii
    contractual, 88
    instrumental, 21, 27, 69, 133
    open, 162
    and the 'sect type', 85
    Wert and *Zweck*, 23, 60
Raymond, H., 126
Raynaud, E., 69
Réau, L., 106–107
re-enchantment with the world, 34, 39
    vs disenchantment, 28, 78, 83
Reformation, 158
relationism, 86, 123, 163
    and 'elective sociality', 88–89
    and organicity, 97

and the 'spirit of the times', 68
relativism, 4
    and everyday life, xii, 32, 63
    the foundation of, 157
    and illegalities, 94
    and the institutions of power, 44, 48, 51,
        59, 61, 134
    of life, 72
    and lifestyles, 92
    and the logic of the network, 88–89
    popular, 48, 53
    and truth, 5, 65
relativization,
    of academics, 160
    of autonomy, 124
    of bureaucracy, 84
    of experience, 163
    of the future, 83
    of individualism, 80
    of power, 44, 48, 119, 125
    of racism, 118
    of values, 110
reliance, 148
    and religion (*religare*), 22–23, 82, 130
    and religiosity, 3, 77
religion,
    civic, 41
    and 'henotheism', 110
    and hierarchy, 115
    of humanity, 74
    and the logic of the network, 86
    popular, 158–159
    vs the *pro-jectum*, 57
    as *religare*, 35–36, 38, 40, 58–62, 113, 130
    and the 'religious model', 82–85
    and Satan, 48
    and space, 131–137, 140
religiosity (cf social divine),
    popular, 59
    as *reliance* or *religare*, 3, 77–78
    and tribes, x
Renaissance, 80, 158
Renan, E., 67, 83, 91, 130, 157
Renaud, G., 64
revolution(s),
    and 'aloofness', 37
    Bolshevik, 43
    Christian, 111
    Copernican, 4, 147
    French, 40, 43, 56, 79, 109, 116, 159
    and lifestyles, 96–97
    and the logic of the network, 86
    and the masses, 50–51, 58, 61
    'ouroborus', 42–43
    political or economic, 18
    vs status quo, 40
ritual(s),
    and the communal ethic, 16–17, 25, 27,
        33
    and the Dionysian thematic, 1
    and magic, 49

ritual(s) *cont.*
  and polyculturalism, 116–117
  and proxemics, 123, 129, 133, 135, 142
  and secrecy, 93
  and sociality, 20, 69
  and the 'taken for granted', 41
  tribal and mass, 98
  and the 'will to live', 21
Robespierre, 40, 58
role,
  vs function, 6, 117, 129,
  of the outsider, 120, 142
  and theatricality, 63, 137
Romanticism
  German, 129
  Hegelian, 88
  tribal, 144
rootedness ('dynamic'),
  and Hellenistic cities, 124–125
  and a mystical perspective, 33, 58,
    131–132, 136
Rousseau, J.J., 40, 45

Sade, Marquis de, 88
Saint-Just, 58
Sartre, J.P., 154,156
saturation, 61
  of activism, 92
  of the *function* of the individual, 6
  of great systems, 27, 41, 78
  of an ideology, 83
  of the mass, 112
  political, 31–33, 36, 46–47, 64, 88–89
  of the principle of individuation, 95
  Sorokin's law of, 114, 157
Savanarola, A., 1, 124
Scheler, M., 3, 75, 136
Scherer, R., 76
Schmalenbach, H., ix
Schmidt, C., 104
Schmitt, 142
Scholem, G., 4, 153
Schopenhauer, A., 78, 155
Schutz, A., 40, 73, 99, 161–163
secrecy,
  and groups, 37, 143
  the law of, 90–96
  and the 'near', 44
  and sects, 32
  and sociality, 24
sect(s) (cf 'sect type'),
  of early Christianity, 82
  and secrecy, 32
  and sectarianism, 99, 158
'sect type' (cf 'church type'), 83–85
Séguy, J., 77, 144
Sheldrake, R., 36, 68
Silesius, 160
Simmel, G., ix, 3, 20, 24, 35, 37–38, 64,
    77, 79, 81, 86, 89–90, 95
Sorokin, P., 110, 114, 157

Situationists,
  and ethics, 85
  and the 'labyrinth', 37
Situationism,
  and truth, 5
Smith, A., xi
sociability,
  and proximity, 125
  and vitalism, 158
social class,
  and the bourgeois ideal, 16
  and bourgeois philosophy, 10, 99
  and the bourgeois reign/order, 46, 74, 78
  and collective bourgeois activism, 12
  the constricting framework of, ix, 2
  and the disintegration of bourgeois
    culture, 26
  the dominant, 51
  popular vs upper, 42, 48
  the proletariat, 6, 31, 35, 38, 47, 58,
    61–62, 105
  and the bourgeoisie, 11, 64–65, 109,
    115, 127, 148, 153
social divine (cf demotheistic), 10,
  and Durkheim, 4
  and 'immanent transcendence', x, 21–22,
    41
  and massive political disengagement, 60
  and proximity, 25
'social given',
  and the 'black holes', 36
  and the *glutinum mundi*, 145
  and the 'taken for granted', 40, 162
  and the world accepted as it is, 27
socialization,
  and sociality, 81
  and tribes, 143
social movements,
  the analysis of, 40
  anarchism, 134
  charismatic, 158
  'counterculture', xi
  ecclesiastical populism, 46
  ecological, 34, 92
  feminist and homosexual, 92, 98
  mass, 18
  populism, 57, 61–62, 116, 134, 158
  Russian populism, 16, 57, 61, 153
  workers', 13, 48, 61, 83
sociality, ix, 1, 5
  and the 'affectual nebula', 88, 106
  and attraction/repulsion, 116
  baroque, 159
  black holes of, 36–37
  black-market, 21
  and custom, 25, 80
  and Dionysus, 9
  and the everyday, 119–120, 126, 152
  and familialism, 90, 94
  and 'familiarism', 65–70
  as the play-form of socialization, 81

postmodern, 147–148
and polytheism, 48
and *puissance*, 4, 7, 32
and *reliance* or *religare*, 3, 77–78
and rituals, 20
and secrecy, 24
and the 'sect type', 85
vs social, 6, 56–64, 72, 76, 86, 93, 95
and space, 126, 131, 139
and the 'spirit of the times', 57, 73
and spiritual materialism, 22, 132–133,
136
and 'the thinking of the public square',
162–164
and 'underground centrality', 92, 130, 155
and vitalism, 43–44, 160
socialism,
and the *obschina*, 16, 134
scientific, 61
sociology,
and absolutism, 52
American, 23
the birth of, 104
distrust of spontaneous, 56–57, 154
and everyday dreams, 8
of everyday life, 96, 162–163
formist, 86, 133
founding fathers of, 4
French, 74, 79, 163
German, 60, 80
modern vs postmodern, ix-xii
and an ontological vitalism, 49
and positivism, 87
of religion, 38, 82, 111
and the 'sect type', 84–85
of the senses, 76
solidarity,
and the communal form, 16, 22, 24
and the community of destiny, 13
and difference, 113–115, 119
and 'elective sociality', 86
vs individualist ideologies, 145
vs mechanical, 79, 93–94, 98
organic, 14, 81, 97, 147
and populism, 61, 116
and proximity, 63, 131
and puissance, 41, 43
and ritual, 17
and secrecy, 91
and the 'sect type', 85
and solidarist myths, 74
of tribes, x-xi
space (cf proxemics, proximity),
and an aesthetics of sentiment, 14
and ambience, 156
'areolar' vs linear, 147
and the 'black holes', 46
the desire for lost, 37
and the ethical experience, 19
and knowledge, 161
and the neighbourhood, 22

and networks, 139, 141
and the orgiastic-dionysiac tradition, 136
and rationality, 23
and spiritual materialism, 133
and time, 27, 36, 47, 65, 123–124, 126,
128–129, 134, 139–140
and vitalism, 88
Spann, O., 74
Spinoza, B., 107
spiritual materialism, 22, 132–133, 136
Stalinism, 61
state,
all-pervasive/sovereign, 18, 45
Chinese, 59
and individualism, 64
and religion, 82
stranger,
and Dionysus, 108–110
and the *glutinum mundi*, 126
and polyculturalism, 136
and polytheism, 111–112, 115–116, 118
and proxemics, 142
and triplicity, 104
and xenophilia, 106, 120
Strohl, H., 158
subjectivity (cf intersubjectivity),
and the community ethos, 60
'trans', 153
Sumner, W.G., 74
Surrealism, 85
syncretism (cf astrology, occult),
and the aesthetic aura, 13
and the Brazilian *candomblé*, 132
and monotheism, 157
synergistic relationship, 3, 81
syntonic relationship, 75

Tacitus, 56
tactile,
vs abstract, 77–78
and the dionysiac, 161
and the megalopolis, 138
vs optical, 31–32
relationship, 73
Taoism, 59, 92, 105
theatricality,
and appearances, 90
and the carnival, 77
and politics, 36, 44, 49, 63
and the 'primitive theatre', 99
and the theatre of everyday life, 5
and the *theatrum mundi*, 76
Thomas, L.-V., 17, 78
Tocqueville, A. de, 79
Tönnies, F., ix, 60, 79–80
tourism,
Club Med, 12
and festivals, 52
mass, 23
tragedy (tragic),
of the border, 107

vs drama, 17, 129
of everyday life, 127
and fatalism, 40, 51
and *puissance*, 32
and theatricality, 76
tribalism, 7, 9, 19
and the aesthetic aura, 25
vs individualism, 69, 97
mass/tribe dialectic, 95, 98–99, 127–129,
147–148, 164
and *puissance*, 41
and religiosity or *reliance* 3
and the 'social given', 27
Troeltsch, E., 83–84, 148

unicity,
of life, 3
and organicity, 52
vs unity, 105
and the 'will to live', 24
underground centrality, ix, 159
and architecture, 37
the *hypothesis* of, 92
and *puissance*, 4, 21, 58
utilitarianism (cf causality, functionalism),
79
utopia(s),
and the 'most extreme concrete', 82
and a mythical perspective, 7, 58, 83

Valéry, P., 154
Venturi, F., 16
Verdillon, C., 37
Verstehen, 156
Veyne, P., 72
vitalism,
and *avoidance* lifestyles, 92

Bergson's, x, 3
and death, 7, 67, 88
and demotheism, 43, 45
and disengagement, 60
and Durkheim, 87
and the end of modernity, 70
and individualism, 27
and *puissance*, 31–38, 51
ontological, 49, 66
and tribal religion, 19, 23
and the 'will to live', 24

Watzlawick, P, 75
Weber, M., ix, 1, 12, 19, 23, 28, 48, 60, 65,
78–79, 82, 86, 110, 112, 125, 136, 153,
156–157, 160
Willmott, P., 69, 97, 126, 141
Wirth, L., 135
Watzlawick, P, 75.
Weber, M., ix,1, 12, 19, 23, 28, 48, 60, 65,
78–79, 82, 86, 110, 112, 125, 136, 153,
156–157, 160
Willmott, P., 69, 97, 126, 141
Wirth, L., 135
withdrawal (cf disengagement, narcissism),
attitudes of, 46
from the political sphere, 48
into the self, 40, 64, 107
Wölfflin, H., 159
Worringer, W., 31, 77, 133

Young, M., 69, 97, 126, 141
Yourcenar, M., 78

Zasulíc, V., 61